39.95

DATE DUE

KNIGHTS OF THE BLACK CROSS

Hauptmann Oswald Boelcke

Knights
of the
Black Cross

GERMAN FIGHTER ACES
OF THE FIRST WORLD WAR

TERRY C TREADWELL

CERBERUS

First published in 2004

PUBLISHED BY:
Cerberus Publishing Limited
Unit 22A, Osprey Court, Hawkfield Business Park
Whitchurch, Bristol BS14 0BB, U.K.
Telephone: +44 (0)1275 545470
Facsimile: +44 (0)1275 545472
e-mail: cerberusbooks@aol.com
www.cerberus-publishing.com

British Library Cataloguing in Publication Data.
A catalogue record for this book is available from the British Library.

ISBN 1 84145 125 8

PRINTED AND BOUND IN ENGLAND

Contents

Page

INTRODUCTION

The German Army Air Service

The German Army Air Service had its beginnings in 1909 when the German Army used aircraft for the very first time. During the following years both civil and military pilots were trained and licensed by the German Aviation Association and the Inspectorate of Military Transport. The first pilot's certificate was issued to August Euler on the 1 February 1910. Euler, an engineer, went on the become and aircraft designer. During 1910 the first flying schools were set up and by the December of 1910 ten officers had completed their flying training.

The German War Department, encouraged by the results of military pilot training, allocated the sum of 110,000 marks for the purchase of military aircraft. The future German Army Air Service was slowly coming into being.

At the beginning of the First World War, the German War Ministry realised the propaganda value of casting their pilots and observers as national heroes, by awarding honours and decorations for the number of enemy aircraft shot down. At first four victories were needed to give the pilot an 'ace' status, although the Germans did not use this term, preferring to use the term '*Kanone*' – Cannon. Six kills were invariably rewarded with the award of the Knight's Cross with Swords of the Royal Hohenzollern House Order.

'Knight's of the Air' began to emerge: Oswald Boelcke, Max Immelmann and Kurt Wintgens who were among those given the ultimate award, the *Orden Pour le Mérite* or Blue Max, as it was sometimes known. A score of eight was considered to be required for nomination. The recipients of the award achieved fame and became immortalised on Sanke postcards which were collected by an increasingly admiring German public.

During the winter of 1916 the tempo of aerial conflict increased and the number of victories required for the various high honours increased. To gain nomination for the *Orden Pour le Mérite* at this stage, sixteen victories were needed, this later rose to twenty and by the end of the war – thirty were required. Strangely, there were a number of pilots who achieved high scores, among them were *Leutnant* Paul Billik who had a total of thirty-one victories and *Leutnant* Hermann Frommherz who scored twenty-nine victories, but were never awarded the honour. Thirty-five other pilots scored between fourteen and twenty-six victories but were not awarded the *Orden Pour le Mérite*. Nineteen pilots were nominated for the award but for a variety of reasons, including death, never received it. The decoration could only be awarded to a living officer and not to the family. Non-commissioned officers received their equivalent, the Golden Military Cross, of which eighty were awarded.

By the end of 1916 the German Army Air Service had twenty-four fully staffed operational *Jastas* and these began to take their toll on Allied aircraft. Many fighter pilots began to rise to prominence among them Hartmut Baldamus, Erwin Böhme, Otto Bernert, Albert Dossenbach, Wilhelm Frankl, Heinrich Gontermann, Max Müller, Werner Voss. and the legendary Manfred von Richthofen.

On 28 October fate took a hand, when Oswald Boelcke was killed when his aircraft collided with fellow pilot Erwin Böhme during a fight with DH2s of No. 24 Squadron RFC. Boelcke's death brought another name to the fore, a name that was to become synonymous with German aviation – *Rittmeister* Baron Manfred von Richthofen.[1] By the end of 1916 Richthofen had raised his score to 15 and had been given command of *Jasta* 11. Under his command and inspiring leadership it became the second highest scoring *Jasta* in the German Army Air Service. During April 1917 – known to the Allies as 'Bloody April' – Richthofen's *Jasta* 11 shot down 89 Allied aircraft with their Albatros DIIIs. Richthofen had his aircraft painted all red to distinguish himself from everyone else and from this gained the nickname 'The Red Baron'.

More and more fighter pilots started to rise to national, and international, fame, their faces appearing on Sanke cards guaranteeing their immortality. Among them were Lothar von Richthofen (brother of Manfred), Karl Schaferschleich, Adolf von Tutschek and Kurt Wolf.

In the autumn of 1917 the Fokker Dr.1 Triplane (*Dreidecker*) came into service but was withdrawn because of wing root problems. After modifications the aircraft was re-introduced into service and almost immediately Kurt Wolff was lost when his aircraft was shot down. Another 'ace' Werner Voss was killed when he was shot down by pilots from the elite No. 56 Squadron RFC. More problems with the Triplane were highlighted when Heinrich Gontermann was killed when his Triplane's top wing folded in flight.

These German 'Knight's of the Air' continued to fall in combat including Karl Schafer, Eduard *Ritter* von Dostler and Erwin Böhme. The Red Baron himself was wounded in the head and hospitalised for a number of weeks.

The German Imperial Naval Air Service, with their own seaplane fighters and land based aircraft started to come into their own as they battled with their British counterparts over the North Sea. *Oberleutnant* Friedrich Christiansen was awarded the *Orden Pour le Mérite* for his exploits, which included and air-to-surface battle with the British submarine C-25 at the mouth of the River Thames. two other naval fliers were awarded the *Orden Pour le Mérite*, *Oberleutnant* Gothard Sachsenberg and *Leutnant* Theo Osterkamp.

[1] Rittmeister was a German cavalry rank equivelant to Captain (Hauptmann). The title 'Baron' and 'Freiherr' are the sameand are often interchangeable especially when Richtofen is mentioned

The last three months of the war saw the German Army Air Service still fighting hard. On the 8 August 1918, the RAF suffered its highest casualty total of the entire war. On the ground the war was going badly for the German troops, but in the air, although outnumbered three to one, the German Army Air Service was still showing it was a force to be reckoned with. Then at 11.00 am on 11 November 1918 the last shots were fired and the war ended. The German Army Air Service was bruised, battered and bloodied, but unbowed. They had fought a hard, tenacious fight, largely with honour, but had been beaten by the overwhelming material power and resources of the Allies.

A small number of the 'Knight's of the Air' survived the war. Some were to die between the wars by murder, revolution and accident. Others were to fight again during the Second World War for the Third Reich, among them the notorious Hermann Göring.

The pilots in this book are not necessarily the most highly decorated, in fact a large number only received the barest minimum of awards and recognition, but scored amongst the highest number of victories. This becomes obvious when you see some of the pilots like *Leutnant* Paul Billik who scored thirty-one 'kills' and received just three awards, compared to *Leutnant* Rudolf Windisch who scored twenty-two 'kills' and was given ten awards.

CHAPTER ONE

Rittmeister Manfred Freiherr von Richthofen (1892 – 1918)

Manfred von Richthofen was born at Breslau on 2 May 1892, the son of *Major* Albrecht *Freiherr* von Richthofen of the 1st Regiment of Cuirassiers, and the Baroness Kunigunde von Richthofen.

The blue eyed and blond haired young man was destined to leave his mark on aviation history during his life. He entered the military school at Wahlstatt at the age of 11 and after graduating was admitted to the Royal Prussian Military Academy. At Easter 1911 he joined the famous regiment of lancers – Uhlan Regiment No 1 'Kaiser Alexander III'. In the autumn of 1912 he was commissioned as a *Leutnant* in the 1st Uhlans. At the outbreak of the First World War he went with his Uhlans into Russian Poland, but within two weeks the regiment was transferred to the Meuse in France, where his regiment was assigned to the Crown Prince's German 5th Army.

The advent of trench warfare ended Richthofen's cavalry unit. Whilst attached to 6th Army Corps he was awarded the Iron Cross 2nd Class for his active service with the Uhlans. He applied for transfer to the German Army Air Service in May 1915 and after four weeks training as an observer at *Flieger – Ersatz – Abteilung* (FEA) 7 Cologne and *Flieger – Ersatz – Abteilung* (FEA) 6 Grossenheim, he was posted to *Flieger – Abteilung* (Fl.Abt.) 69 on the Eastern Front as an observer in an Albatros BII. His pilot *Leutnant* Zeumer was dying from tuberculosis and had a death wish to die in action.

In August 1915 he was posted to the 'Mail Carrier Pigeon Unit' at Ostende, the innocuous tile being a cover name for a long range bomber unit training to bomb England.

1st September 1915 gave Richthofen his first taste of aerial combat. Flying as an observer in an AEG with *Leutnant* Zeumer – he spotted a Royal Flying Corps Farman flying nearby and ordered Zeumer to close to combat. Armed only with a rifle Richthofen opened fire on the Farman but missed with his four shots. The observer in the Farman replied and scored several hits on Richthofen's AEG. A week later Richthofen was flying as an observer in an Albatros piloted by *Leutnant*

Rittmeister *Manfred von Richthofen*

Osteroth when he sighted a solitary Farman flying over French lines. Ordering his pilot to the attack Richthofen opened fire with his machine gun and poured 100 rounds at the enemy aircraft. The stricken Farman plunged to earth and crashed nose first behind French lines. However the victory was unconfirmed and Richthofen was not credited with his first aircraft downed.

On 1 October 1915 Richthofen was posted to Metz to join another bomber unit. Whilst en route he met the already legendary Oswald

Boelcke and engaged him in conversation. Fired by Boelcke's example Richthofen decided to become a pilot and asked *Leutnant* Zeumer to teach him to fly. His first attempt to fly was an unqualified disaster when he crashed on landing. He persisted and was posted to the flight training school at Doberitz for flight training and after qualifiing on Christmas Day 1915 he became a pilot. He was immediately posted to Russia, but it was not until March 1916 that he returned to the Western Front where after receiving his pilot's badge, he was ordered to fly a two seater Albatros – not the single seat fighter he had hoped. He adapted the two seater Albatros by fitting a machine gun on the upper wing which he

Manfred von Richthofen and Kurt Wolff in the rear seat of a Rumpler flown by Leutnant *Kreft*

could fire from the pilot's seat.

His first encounter with the enemy was on 26 April 1916, when he brought his machine gun into action against a French Nieuport over French Lines. The Nieuport, riddled with bullets, crashed behind French Lines at Douaumont. Once again his victory was unconfirmed. Richthofen had not yet opened his score – officially.

Richthofen joined Oswald Boelcke's *Jasta* 2 on the 1 September 1916 flying new Albatros DIIIs. On September 17 1916, Boelcke led his eight strong *Jasta* into action and sighted eight BE2cs of 12 Squadron RFC and six FE 2bs of 11 Squadron bombing Marcoing railway station. Richthofen, flying Albatros DIII 491/16, chose an FE 2b as his target –

opened fire but missed. The enemy aircraft returned Lewis machine gun fire. Avoiding the gunfire Richthofen banked out of range then came back under and behind the FE 2b. Closing to point blank range, and unseen by the enemy aircraft's crew, he opened a burst of fire on the FE 2b's engine and cockpit which wounded both the pilot – 2nd Lieutenant LBF Morris and his observer Lieutenant T Rees. The doomed FE 2b plunged downwards with the dying pilot Morris managing to land the crippled aircraft behind German lines. Richthofen followed it down and landed nearby where he found the pilot mortally wounded and the observer dead.

Fokker E III that Manfred von Richthofen crashed on take-off.

Richthofen had scored his first officially confirmed victory and to mark the event he had a silver *Ehrenbecher* goblet made by a Berlin silversmith to commemorate the victory. It was to be the first of many such trophies.

By the end of October 1916 Richthofen had six confirmed victories to his credit. On 28 October Boelcke was killed in an aerial collision with Erwin Boehme and *Jasta* 2 was renamed *Jasta* Boelcke (Royal Prussian) with *Oberleutnant* Stephen Kirmaier in command.

Richthofen's victory score continued to increase – by 20 November 1916 he had ten confirmed kills. Two days later he shot down the Royal Flying Corps's leading ace – Major Lanoe Hawker, VC, DSO, flying a DH 2 of 24 Squadron – in an dog fight. When Richthofen learned who his opponent had been he flew over British lines and dropped a message to inform 24 Squadron of Major Hawker's death. *Jasta* Boelcke pilots arranged a military funeral for Major Hawker but Richthofen did not attend. It was not the done thing so to do.

Richthofen was promoted to flight commander with *Jasta* Boelcke and had his Albatros aircraft painted bright red. This was to let his aerial opponents know with whom they fought and led to his most famous title 'The Red Baron'. When he scored his sixteenth victory on the 4 January 1917 the Kaiser awarded him, by special citation, The *Orden Pour le Mérite*. He was just twenty-four years old and Germany's national hero.

With the decoration came promotion to *Rittmeister* (Cavalry Captain) and command of *Jasta* 11. On 11 April 1917 Richthofen had taken his score to forty confirmed kills, by the end of April it had risen to fifty-two confirmed. On April 30 he crossed swords with the Canadian ace Billy Bishop (who ended the war with seventy-two kills) over Drocourt. Try as he might Richthofen could not best Bishop who outflew him and riddled

A recovering Manfred von Richthofen visiting fellow pilots of Jasta 11

his Albatros with bullets.

Realising that discretion was the better part of valour, Richthofen broke off the duel and retreated eastward towards safe territory. On June 26 the German High Command grouped *Jastas* into JGs (*Jagdgeschwader* – hunting echelons) and Richthofen took command of JG 1 which comprised *Jastas* 4, 6, 10 and 11. These JGs were highly mobile and with their aircraft being brightly painted they were soon nicknamed 'Flying Circus'. Richthofen continued to increase his score but when flying his red Albatros with *Jasta* 11 he attacked six FE 2ds

of 20 Squadron RFC. In the ensuing dogfight the observer of one of the FEs wounded the Red Baron in the head causing him to break off combat and make a heavy landing near Wericq. After being hospitalised Richthofen returned to duty but was plagued with headaches and dizziness. Nevertheless he managed to fly and score victory after victory and by 30 November 1917 he had shot down sixty-three enemy aircraft.

The Red Baron's last year opened and during March he shot down

eleven aircraft making his total seventy-four. On 2 April he was awarded the last of his twenty-six decorations – the Order of The Red Eagle with Crowns and Swords by the Emperor. By 20 April he achieved what was to be his final score – eighty confirmed victories.

On Sunday, 21 April 1918 a concerned *Rittmeister* Manfred *Freiherr* von Richthofen, looked out at a dense, grey fog covered, airfield at Cappy. The war on the ground was not going well, but in the air the *Jastas* were holding their own against increased Allied opposition. Manfred von Richthofen and his men were buoyant as they knew as soon as the fog lifted they would be in the air hunting the enemy. As the sun started to burn off the fog a message came through that three flights of Sopwith F1 Camels – a total of fifteen aircraft – from No 209 Squadron, RAF, had been seen heading toward their sector.

At 1040 hours (German time), two flights from *Jasta* 11 took off from the airfield led by the 'Red Baron' in his all-dark red Fokker Triplane. The first flight was led by *Rittmeister* Manfred von Richthofen with his cousin *Leutnant* Wolfram *Freiherr* von Richthofen as his wingman, the second flight was led by *Leutnant* Hans Weiss. They were joined by a flight of Albatros D-5s as they neared near Cérisy. Within minutes of spotting each other the two sides were engaged over Le Hamel and the Red Baron was in the thick of it. Richthofen swung onto the tail of a 209 Squadron Camel flown by a young pilot 2nd/Lieutenant Wilfred May, and gave chase. One of May's guns had jammed and the young inexperienced pilot frantically weaved all over the sky in an attempt to shake off his pursuer. In desperation he headed for the ground, literally skimming over hedges and trees, but still the relentless pursuer would not give up. It was this fixation on his opponent that was to be Richthofen's undoing.

Captain Roy Brown, DSC, flying above, saw May's perilous position and dived to the rescue. Coming up on Richthofen's aircraft from behind Brown opened fire and scored a long burst on the all red Triplane. According to Brown the all-red Triplane went into a vertical dive and crashed into the ground.

This account was confirmed by 2nd/Lt May, who said that he remembered being chased over the German lines, then the Allied lines and hugging the ground as close as he could, then his pursuer was attacked by Captain Brown who shot his attacker down. One wonders how 2nd/Lt May could have taken all this detailed information in when he was fleeing for his life under such hostile conditions and needed all his concentration to keep his aircraft from crashing, if as he says, he was flying so close to the ground.

A report from the 53rd Australian Field Artillery Battery, 5th Division, and the 24th Australian Machine-gun Company however contradicted this. They said that they had witnessed the attack on the all-red Fokker Triplane by Captain Brown, but apparently unharmed the Fokker, flown by Richthofen as they were to find out later, continued to chase and machine-gunned 2nd/Lt May's Camel with short bursts of fire. As the all-red Fokker Triplane flew low over Morlancourt Ridge it too came under a hail of fire from Australian ground gunners beneath. Machine gun fire raked the aircraft and as the splinters of wood near the engine were seen to fly up, the gunners saw the pilot's head snap backwards in his cockpit. His aircraft sideslipped then glided into the ground nose first.

The Red Baron was dead, killed in action. There was some severe damage to Richthofen's face which had been caused by his face striking the butts of the machine-guns that were mounted in front of

The battered face on Rittmeister *Manfred von Richthofen's body after it had been removed from the wreckage of his Fokker triplane*

him, but by the time this had happened he was already dead.

Manfred von Richthofen's body was taken from the wreckage and taken Poulainville where No. 3 Squadron, AFC, were based. There his body was examined by Australian and British doctors where it was discovered that a single bullet had entered Richthofen's body between the eight and ninth rib and exited near his left nipple after passing

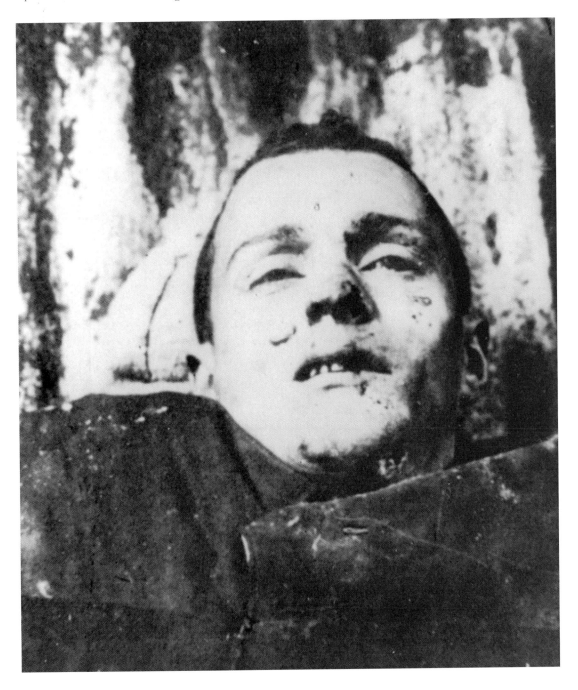

through his heart. The trajectory of the fatal bullet showed that it was likely that it had come from the ground rather that from a pursuer in the air. However others argued that because of the twisting and turning that Richthofen had carried out during his pursuit of 2nd/Lt May, it was possible that the bullet had come from Captain Brown's guns.

Once it was discovered that the body was that of Manfred von Richthofen, a guard was put on it to prevent souvenier hunters taking items of clothing and the suchlike. The wreckage of the aircraft was already under guard to prevent anymore pieces being removed from the already canablised Fokker Triplane. A large number of officers from No. 3 Squadron AFC, together with French officers from *Escadrille Spa* 93, who were stationed nearby, visited Richthofen's body on the makeshift bier where it had been placed in a hangar.

Initially it was thought that Richthofen had crashed and had been taken prisoner and because of this *Oberleutnant* Karl Bodenshatz, *Jagdgeschwader* I's adjutant, sent a telegram to *major* Albrecht von Richthofen telling him that his son was alive and in British captivity. It wasn't until the British dropped a message saying that Richthofen was dead, that their worst fears were realised.

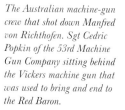

The Australian machine-gun crew that shot down Manfred von Richthofen. Sgt Cedric Popkin of the 53rd Machine Gun Company sitting behind the Vickers machine gun that was used to bring and end to the Red Baron.

The following message was dropped by a British aircraft and was addressed to the German Flying Corps.

To The German Flying Corps.

Rittmeister Baron Manfred von Richthofen was killed in aerial combat on April 21st, 1917. He was buried with full military honours.

Wreckage of Manfred von Richthofen's Fokker Triplane being examined by RFC pilots.

From British Royal Air Force.

Rittmeister Baron Manfred von Richthofen was buried with Military Honours at Bertangles with his coffin draped with the Imperial German Flag. Pilots of the German Air Service flew over his grave and dropped wreaths unhindered. His remains were returned to Berlin in 1925 and reburied at the Invaliden.

What is interesting is that the German authorities, when they found out that it was probably a bullet from a machine gun or a rifle fired from the ground that had killed Richthofen, was that they boasted that *Rittmeister Baron* Manfred *Freiherr* von Richthofen – the Red Baron, had not been bettered in combat, but had died by means of a lucky shot from the ground.

The speculation surrounding who killed Manfred von Richthofen has been going on since the day it happened, but I think it has now been accepted that it was not Captain Roy Brown who shot down the Red Baron, but was more likely to have been one of the gunners of the 24th Australian Machine-gun Company. Whoever killed the Red Baron may have killed the man, but most certainly did not kill the legend and legacy that *Rittmeister* Manfred *Freiherr* von Richthofen left behind.

Awards

Orden Pour le Mérite
Red Eagle Order 3rd Class with Crown and Swords
Knight's Cross with Swords of the Royal Hohenzollen House Order
Iron Cross 2nd Class
Iron Cross 1st Class
Bavarian Military Merit Order 3rd Class with Crown and Swords
Knight's Cross of the Saxon Military St. Henry Order
Württemberg Knight Military Merit Order
Knight 1st Class with Swords of the Saxe-Ernestine Order
Hesse General Honour Decoration 'for Bravery'
Lippe War Honour Cross for Heroic Act
Schaumburg-Lippe Cross for Faithful Service 2nd Class
Brunswick War Merit Cross 2nd Class
Saxe-Coburg-Gotha Oval Silver Duke Carl Eduard Medal with Date Clasp and Swords
Bremen Hanseatic Cross
Hamburg Hanseatic Cross
Lübeck Hanseatic Cross
Austro-Hungarian order of the Iron Crown 3rd Class with War Decoration
Bulgarian Bravery Order 4th Class, 1st Degree
Ottoman Empire Imtiaz Medal in Silver
Ottoman Empire Liakat Medal in Silver
Ottoman Empire War Medal
Pilot's Badge
Observer's Badge
Austro-Hungarian Field Pilot's Badge (Franz-Joseph Pattern)

Victory log

1916

17 Sep	FE 2b (No. 11 Sqn RFC)	Villers Plouich
23 Sep	Martinsyde G 100 (No.27 Sqn RFC)	S Beugny
30 Sep	FE 2b (No. 11 Sqn RFC)	Fremicourt
7 Oct	BE 12 (No. 21 Sqn RFC)	Equancourt
16 Oct	BE 12 (No. 19 Sqn RFC)	Ypres
25 Oct	BE 12 (No. 21 Sqn RFC)	SW Bapaume
3 Nov	FE 2b (No. 18 Sqn RFC)	NE Grevillers
9 Nov	BE 2c (No. 12 Sqn RFC)	Beugny
20 Nov	BE 2d (No. 15 Sqn RFC)	S Grandecourt
20 Nov	FE 2b (No. 18 Sqn RFC)	Geuedecourt
23 Nov	DH 2 (No. 24 Sqn RFC)	S Ligny

11 Dec	DH 2 (No. 32 Sqn RFC)	Mercatel
20 Dec	DH 2 (No. 29 Sqn RFC)	Monchy
20 Dec	FE 2b (No. 18 Sqn RFC)	Noreuil
27 Dec	FE 2b (No. 29 Sqn RFC)	Ficheux

1917

4 Jan	Sopwith Pup (No. 8 Sqn RFC)	Metz-en-Courture
23 Jan	FE 8 (No. 40 Sqn RFC)	SW Lens
24 Jan	FE 2b (No. 25 Sqn RFC)	W Vimy
1 Feb	BE 2d (No. 16 Sqn RFC)	SW Thelus
14 Feb	BE 2d (No. 2 Sqn RFC)	E Loos
14 Feb	BE 2d (No. 2 Sqn RFC)	SW Mazingarbe
4 Mar	BE 2d (No. 2 Sqn RFC)	NE Loos
4 Mar	Sopwith 1½ Strutter (No. 43 Sqn RFC)	Acheville
6 Mar	BE 2e (No. 16 Sqn RFC)	Souchez
9 Mar	DH 2 (No. 29 Sqn RFC)	SW Bailleul
11 Mar	BE 2d (No. 2 Sqn RFC)	La Folie-Fe
17 Mar	FE 2b (No. 25 Sqn RFC)	SE Oppy
17 Mar	BE 2c (No. 16 Sqn RFC)	S Givenchy
21 Mar	BE 2f (No. 16 Sqn RFC)	Neuville-St Vaast
24 Mar	SPAD VII (No. 19 Sqn RFC)	Givenchy
25 Mar	Nieuport XVII (No. 29 Sqn RFC)	Tilloy
2 Apr	BE 2d (No. 43 Sqn RFC	Farbus
2 Apr	Sopwith 1½ Strutter (No. 13 Sqn RFC)	Givenchy
3 Apr	FE 2b (No. 25 Sqn RFC)	Cite St Pierre
5 Apr	BF 2a (No. 48 Sqn RFC)	Lewarde
5 Apr	BF 2a (No. 48 Sqn RFC)	Quincy
7 Apr	Nieuport XVII (No. 60 Sqn RFC)	NE Mercatel
8 Apr	Sopwith 1½ Strutter (No. 43 Sqn RFC)	Farbus
8 Apr	BE 2d (No. 16 Sqn RFC)	W Vimy
11 Apr	BE 2d (No. 13 Sqn RFC)	Willerval
13 Apr	RE 8 (No. 59 Sqn RFC)	E Vitry
13 Apr	FE 2b (No. 11 Sqn RFC)	W Monchy
13 Apr	FE 2b (No. 25 Sqn RFC)	Noyelle-Godault
14 Apr	Nieuport XVII (No. 60 Sqn RFC)	S Bois Bernard
16 Apr	BE 2e (No. 13 Sqn RFC)	MW Gavrelle
22 Apr	FE 2b (No. 11 Sqn RFC)	Lagincourt
23 Apr	BE 2f (No. 4 Sqn RFC)	Mericourt
28 Apr	BE 2e (No. 13 Sqn RFC)	SE Pelves
29 Apr	SPAD VII (No. 19 Sqn RFC)	E Lecluse
29 Apr	FE 2b (No. 18 Sqn RFC)	SW Inchy
29 Apr	BE 2e (No. 12 Sqn RFC)	S Rouex
29 Apr	Sopwith Triplane (No. 8 Sqn RNAS)	S Henin-Lietard
18 Jun	RE 8 (No. 9 Sqn RFC)	NE Ypres
23 Jun	SPAD VII (No. 3 Sqn RFC)	N Ypres
24 Jun	DH 4 (No. 57 Sqn RFC)	Becelaere
25 Jun	RE 8 (No. 53 Sqn RFC)	Le Bizet

2 Jul	RE 8 (No. 53 Sqn RFC)	Deulemont
16 Aug	Nieuport XXIII (No. 29 Sqn RFC)	SW Houthulst
26 Aug	SPAD VII (No. 19 Sqn RFC)	Poelcapelle
1 Sep	RE 8 (No. 6 Sqn RFC)	Zonnebeke
3 Sep	Sopwith Pup (No. 46 Sqn RFC)	S Bousbecque
23 Nov	DH 5 (No. 64 Sqn RFC)	Bourlon
30 Nov	SE 5a (No. 41 Sqn RFC)	Moeuvres

1918

12 Mar	BF 2b (No. 62 Sqn RFC)	NE Nauroy
13 Mar	Sopwith Camel (*Compaigne Aerostieres* 61)	Banteux
18 Mar	Sopwith Camel (No. 54 Sqn RFC)	Aubigny
24 Mar	SE 5a (No. 41 Sqn RFC)	Combles
25 Mar	Sopwith Camel (No. 3 Sqn RFC)	Bapaume
26 Mar	Sopwith Camel (No. 1 Sqn RFC)	Contalmaison
26 Mar	RE 8 (No. 15 Sqn RFC)	NE Albert
27 Mar	Sopwith Camel (No. 73 Sqn RFC)	NE Aveleux
27 Mar	BF 2b (No. 2 Sqn RFC)	Foucaucourt
27 Mar	BF 2b (No. 79 Sqn RFC)	NE Guignolles
28 Mar	AWFK 8 (No. 52 Sqn RFC)	E Mancourt
2 Apr	RE 8 (No. 52 Sqn RAF)	NE Moreuil
6 Apr	Sopwith Camel (No. 46 Sqn RAF)	Bois de Hamel
7 Apr	SE 5a (No. 73 Sqn RAF)	Villers Brettoneux
7 Apr	SPAD VII (No. 73 Sqn RAF)	N Villers Brettoneux
20 Apr	Sopwith Camel (No. 3 Sqn RAF)	SW Bois de Hamel
20 Apr	Sopwith Camel (No. 53 Sqn RAF)	Villers Brettoneux

Total victories claimed: 80

CHAPTER TWO

Oberleutnant Ernst Udet
(1896 – 1941)

Born in Frankfurt-am-Main on the 26 April 1896 Ernst Udet was probably one of the most charismatic German pilots of WWI. Unlike most of his contemporaries, Ernst Udet was the son of a wealthy landowner and had an intense keeness for anything mechanical owning his own motor cycle. At the age of seventeen, he applied to join the Army, but was turned down on a number of occasions before he was finally able to persuade the authorities to accept him as a courier. When on the 7 August, 1914, German troops occupied Liège, Ernst Udet was assigned to the German Automobile Club with his motor cycle as a dispatch rider. On the 21 August, 1914, he joined the Army and was posted to the 26th Württemburg Reserve Division as a motor cycle messenger.

During the following months, Eernst Udet rode his motor cycle backwards and forwards behind enemy lines delivering messages. Then on one particularly bad night, when the sound of guns appeared to be encircling him, he swerved to miss a shell-hole in the road and crashed. After spending ten days in hospital he was sent to Belgium to catch up with his division, but could not find them because of the chaos in the area at the time. In Liège he was given the job of delivering messages and it was there that he met *Leutnant* von Waxheim, a pilot, who was to become a major influence Udet's life.

When orders came for Udet to be sent home he immediately volunteered for the Pilot's Reserve Detachment in Schleissheim. His meeting with von Waxheim had convinced him that this was where his future lay. Whilst waiting for a response to his request, he trained as a pilot at his own expense, sending further applications to Darmstadt and Döberitz. A few weeks later orders came through for him to go to Darmstadt for pilot training. After completion of his training, Udet was posted to *Flieger-Abteilung* (Fl.Abt (A)) 206 as a *Gefreiter*. He was assigned *Leutnant* Bruno Justinus as his observer and three weeks later, after a spell of patrols in which they never saw an Allied aircraft, spotted a French monoplane attacking a railway station. As they approached they realised that the Frenchman was in trouble and was gliding toward the ground. Udet tucked in behind and noticed that the aircraft had a gun

mounted behind the propeller. The French aircraft, encouraged by Udet, made a forced landing and before the pilot could set fire to the aircraft captured by German soldiers. The pilot, it was discovered later, was Roland Garros and the capture of his aircraft together with the gun and its interruptor gear intact, was to alter the course of air-to-air fighting dramatically. In recognition of the incident Udet received the Iron Cross 2nd Class.

On the 18 March 1916, Udet was posted to *Flieger-Abteilung* (Fl.Abt.) 68, which later became *Kek Habsheim*, and during a raid by French aircraft, scored his first victory when he shot down a Farman F40 whilst defending Mulhausen. It is claimed that he attacked 22 hostile aircraft flying on his own in his Fokker DIII 356/16, how true this is no one knows, but it came at a time when the German public needed heroes.

On September 28 he was posted to *Jasta* 15, where by the end of the year he had raised his tally to two. This was a very ignominious start to someone who was to become one of Germany's highest scoring fighter aces. At the beginning of January of 1917, he was awarded the Iron Cross 1st Class and at the end of the month his commission to *Leutnant*.

A young Ernst Udet and Leutnant *Weingärtner* *with their Fokker EIII*

Udet recorded his sixth victory in the May of 1917 and requested a transfer to *Jasta* 37. This was agreed and he was transferred on the 19 June, 1917. In November Udet received a telegram saying that his friend *Leutnant* Gontermann had been killed and that he was to take command of *Jasta* 37. Two weeks later he was awarded the Knight's Cross with Swords of the Royal Hohenzollern House Order, by this time he had raised his tally to fifteen confirmed victories.

On the 23 March, 1918 Udet was posted to *Jasta* 11 as commanding officer until the 8 April. Three days before his 22nd birthday a telegram arrived, it read:

Ernst Udet getting ready to fly his Fokker DVII. Note flying clothes on the wing

'His Majesty the Emperor has been gracious enough to bestow upon you the *Orden Pour le Mérite* in recognition of the twenty planes shot down by you.'

The very next day he was given command of *Jasta* 4.

Like most of the top German fighter pilots Udet's Fokker DVII aircraft was very distinctive. The fuselage was painted red and the upper surfaces of the top wing had red and white candy stripes. Written on the upper tail surface for any attacker from the rear to read, was the inscription *'Du noch Nich!'* (Not you yet). Most of his aircraft also carried the christian name of his fiancee – 'Lo'. During a dogfight with a Breguet bomber, with his tally of victories standing at forty, he was shot down during a dogfight and escaped with only slight injuries. As his aircraft spun earthwards, Udet scrambled out of the cockpit only to find that his parachute harness had caught on the control column. Frantically struggling for what seemed an eternity, he managed to extricate himself and hurled himself out of the cockpit, his parachute opening just 300 feet from the ground. He landed heavily in a shell hole and was rescued by German infantry.

Ernst Udet dressed as a cowboy and carrying the Mexican Colt revolver with which he was later to commit suicide

By the beginning of September he had raised his tally to sixty confirmed victories and was awarded the Lubeck Hanseatic Cross and the Hamburg Hanseatic Cross. Then on the 26 September, 1918, with his tally raised to sixty-two, he was badly wounded in the thigh putting to an end his combat flying days.

Udet became a test pilot and a movie stunt pilot after the war flying all over the world. At the beginning of WWII he was persuaded to join the Luftwaffe and attained the rank of *Generaloberst* (Colonel-General). Given the post of GOC Aircraft Production, Udet immediately set about developing a new fighter bomber. In his rapid rise up the ladder of promotion, he had made a number of enemies and none more deadly that *Generaloberst* Ehard Milch. Milch set about undermining Udet's authority and causing him many problems.

Then on the 17 September, 1941, word came out that Ernst Udet had died while testing a new aircraft. The story had been put out by the German propaganda machine after it had been discovered that Udet had committed suicide by shooting himself with a Mexican Colt revolver he had brought back from America during his stunt pilot days there. It was because of the political infighting within the Luftwaffe and the fact that his position was being completely undermined, that caused him to take his own life.

Hitler announced that he would be given a state funeral and his coffin was placed on the catafalque in the Air Ministry's Hall of Honour in the Wilhelmstrasse and then taken by gun carriage via the Louisenstrasse to the Invaliden Cemetery. There he was buried with full military honours.

Awards

Orden Pour le Mérite
Knight's Cross with Swords of the Royal Hohenzollern House Order
Württemburg Merit Cross with Swords
Hamburg Hanseatic Cross
Lübeck Hanseatic Cross
Wound Badge in Silver
Iron Cross 2nd Class
Iron Cross 1st Class
Pilot's Badge – German Army

Victory log

1916

18 Mar	Farman F 40 (*Escadrille* MF 29)	Mulhausen
12 Oct	Breguet-Michelin (*Escadrille* N 81)	Rustenhart
24 Dec	Caudron G IV (*Escadrille* C 34)	Oberaspach

1917

20 Feb	Nieuport Scout (No. 25 Sqn RFC)	Aspach
24 Apr	Nieuport (No. 1 Sqn RFC)	Chavignon

5 May	SPAD VII (No. 23 Sqn RFC)	Bois de Ville
14 Aug.	DH 4 (No. 25 Sqn RFC)	Pont-a-Vendin
15 Aug	Sopwith 1 Strutter (No. 43 Sqn RFC)	Pont-a-Vendin
21 Aug	DH 4 (No. 27 Sqn RFC)	Ascq
17 Sep	DH 5 (No. 41 Sqn RFC)	S Izel
24 Sep	Sopwith Camel (No. 43 Sqn RFC)	E Loos
28 Sep	Sopwith Camel (No. 43 Sqn RFC)	W Wingles
28 Sep	Sopwith Camel (No. 43 Sqn RFC)	Vermelles
18 Oct	SE 5a (No. 84 Sqn RFC)	Deulemont
28 Nov	DH 5 (No. 32 Sqn RFC)	Poelcapelle
5 Dec	SE 5a (No. 56 Sqn RFC)	Westroosbeke

1918

6 Jan	Nieuport XXIV (*Escadrille N* 89)	Bixschoote
28 Jan	Sopwith Camel (No. 54 Sqn RFC)	SE Bixschoot
29 Jan	BF 2b (No. 22 Sqn RFC)	Zillebeke
18 Feb	Sopwith Camel (No. 10 Sqn RNAS)	Zandvoorde
27 Mar	RE 8 (No. 16 Sqn RFC)	Albert
28 Mar	Sopwith Camel (No. 43 Sqn RFC)	Albert-Bapaume
6 Apr	Sopwith Camel (No. 43 Sqn RAF)	Hamel
31 May	Breguet XIV (*Escadrille Br* 29)	SW Soissons
2 Jun	Breguet XIV (*Escadrille Br* 108)	NW Neuilly
5 Jun	SPAD VII (*Escadrille Spa* 157)	S Buzancy
6 Jun	SPAD XII (No. 27 Sqn RAF)	S Faverolles
7 Jun	SPAD XIII (*Escadrille Spa* 78)	E Villers Cotterets
13 Jun	SPAD (*Escadrille Spa* 37)	NW Faverolles
14 Jun	SPAD (*Escadrille Spa* 153)	N Pierre-Aigle
23 Jun	Breguet XIV (*Escadrille Spa* 216)	La Ferte Milon
23 Jun	Breguet XIV (*Escadrille Spa* 96)	Crouy
24 Jun	Breguet XIV (*Escadrille Br* 107)	Montigny
25 Jun	SPAD XIII (*Escadrille Spa* 96)	Longpont Woods
25 Jun	SPAD XIII (*Escadrille Spa* 96)	Chavigny Ferme
30 Jun	SPAD XIII (*Escadrille Spa* 87)	Faverolles
1 Jul	Breguet XIV (*Escadrille Br* 219)	Pierrefont-Morte
1 Jul	SPAD VII (*Escadrille Spa* 57)	Faverolles
2 Jul	Nieuport 28 (27th Aero Sqn USAS)	Bezu-St Germaine
3 Jul	SPAD XIII (*Escadrille Spa* 65)	Laveraine
1 Aug	Nieuport 28 (27th Aero Sqn USAS)	N Cramaille
1 Aug	Breguet XIV (*Escadrille Spa* 62)	Muret-Crouettes
1 Aug	SPAD XIII (*Escadrille Spa* 84)	N Bagneux
4 Aug	SPAD XI (*Escadrille Spa* 63)	N Braisne
8 Aug	SE 5a (No. 41 Sqn RAF)	Fontaine-le-Cappy
8 Aug	SE 5a	SE Barleux
8 Aug	Sopwith Camel (No. 54 Sqn RFC)	SE Foucaucour
9 Aug	Sopwith Camel (No. 201 Sqn RAF)	S Vauvillers
9 Aug	Sopwith Camel (No. 65 Sqn RAF)	SE Herleville
10 Aug	Sopwith Camel (No. 3 Sqn RAF)	S Morocourt

10 Aug	Sopwith Camel (No. 43 Sqn RAF)	E Fay
11 Aug	DH 9 (No. 98 Sqn RAF)	Chaulnes
12 Aug	SE 5a (No. 40 Sqn RAF)	Peronne
14 Aug	BF 2b (No. 88 Sqn RAF)	Vermandouvillers
15 Aug	Sopwith Camel (No. 204 Sqn RAF)	Herleville
16 Aug	SPAD VII (*Escadrille Spa* 3)	S Foucaucourt
21 Aug	SE 5a (No. 56 Sqn RAF)	S Hebuterne
21 Aug	Sopwith Camel (148th Aero Sqn USAS)	Courcelles
22 Aug	Sopwith Camel (No. 80 Sqn RAF)	N Bray
22 Aug	SE 5a	Maurepas
26 Sep	DH 9 (No. 99 Sqn RAF)	Buch
26 Sep	DH 9 (No. 99 Sqn RAF)	S Metz

Total victories claimed: 62

CHAPTER THREE

Oberleutnant Erich Löwenhardt
(1897 – 1918)

Erich Löwenhardt was born in Breslau on the 7 April, 1897 the son of a local doctor. He was sent to the military cadet school at Lichterfelde to complete his education and on the outset of war was posted to Infantry Regiment Nr. 141. His regiment was moved almost immediately to the Eastern Front, where on the 2 October, 1914, he was commissioned in the rank of *Leutnant*. During a bitter groundfight at the end of October, he was wounded quite badly and was awarded the Iron Cross 2nd Class for his part in the battle. At the beginning of January, after being discharged from hospital, Löwenhardt returned to his unit and was assigned to duties in the Carpathian Mountains. It was whilst in action in these mountains, that he saved the lives of five wounded soldiers for which he was awarded the Iron Cross 1st Class and then transferred to the Alpine Corps at his own request.

In the October of 1915, Löwenhardt requested a transfer to the German Army Air Service as an observer which was granted. After completing his training at the beginning of 1916, he spent the remainder of the year as an observer flying missions over various Fronts. Löwenhardt then requested pilot training and after graduating was posted to *Feldflieger-Abteilung* (FFl.Abt.) 265 early in 1916. After nearly a year as a reconnaissance pilot, he undertook fighter training early in 1917 and on completion was posted to *Jasta* 10 in March, 1917.

Within a week of arriving at *Jasta* 10, Löwenhardt scored his first victory when, on 24 March, he shot down a French observation balloon belonging to 58 *Cie* over Recicourt. His second victory wasn't until 14 August when he shot down an RE 8 belonging to No. 9 Squadron RFC. By the end of September he had raised his tally to five and almost got himself killed, when he was slightly wounded in a dogfight with a British fighter and managed to force land his aircraft near Roulers. Then on the 6 November, 1917, with his tally raised to eight, his lower starboard wing broke whilst engaged in a dogfight and again he had to make a forced landing, this time near Winkel St Eloi.

At the beginning of the new year Löwenhardt increased his tally, when on the 5 January he destroyed another observation balloon, bringing the number of balloons he had destroyed to five. Another two balloons followed on the 12 and 15 March together with a BF 2b on the 18 January. By the end of March he had raised his tally to fifteen. One week short of his twenty-first birthday his skill as a fighter pilot and his ability to command the respect of the men he flew with, was rewarded when he was appointed commander of *Jasta* 10 – one of the youngest commanders in the German Army Air Service. With his tally at thirty, he was awarded the Knight's Cross with Swords of the Royal Hohenzollern House Order on 11 May, 1918. On patrol with *Leutnant* Franz Hemer on 28 May, Löwenhardt, who was also acting commander of the Geschwader, added to his score by shooting down a two-seater SPAD.

Then on the 31 May Erich Löwenhardt was awarded Germany's most prestigious honour, the *Orden Pour le Mérite*. Löwenhardt continued his unerring destruction of the Allied aircraft and by the

Staffel-Führers *of JG 1.*
L-R: Wüsthoff, Reinhard,
Manfred von Richthofen,
Erich Löwenhardt, Lothar
von Richthofen

end of July 1918, his tally had risen to forty-seven. During the months of June and July, he had been acting commander of the *Jagdgeschwader* an incredible responsibility for a man who was still only twenty-one.

On the 8 August, 1918, one day after he had been promoted to *Oberleutnant*, a patrol led by Löwenhardt encountered a patrol of Sopwith Camels. Löwenhardt himself accounted for three whilst the rest scattered, this brought his tally to fifty, the third of only three German pilot to reach this figure.

Then tragedy struck on the 10 August whilst engaged in a dogfight with a SE5as from 56 Squadron RAF. Löwenhardt had just shot down an SE5a, when he collided in mid-air with *Leutnant* Alfred Wenz a member of *Jasta* 11, whose patrol had joined up with that of *Jasta* 10. Both pilots had been after the same aircraft, but Löwenhardt had come into attack from above and to the right of Wenz. Unable to see the aircraft below him Löwenhardt continued on down after his victim, it was then that a startled Wenz looked up and saw the yellow

Fokker DVII so close to him that he could almost touch it. Löwenhardt's undercarriage ripped in to the upper wing of Wenz's aircraft tearing a large section of the fabric away. Almost immediately Wenz lost control of the aircraft and bailed out. It is not certain what happened to Löwenhardt's Fokker, but one would have thought that the damage would not have been that severe and he possibly could have made a forced landing if the undercarriage had been damaged. Both pilots took to their parachutes. Wenz's parachute opened and he inside German lines, but Löwenhardt's failed to open and he plunged

Oberleutnant *Erich Löwenhardt (left) with* Leutnant *Fritz Freidrichs.*

to his death.

Awards

Orden Pour le Mérite
Knight's Cross with Swords of the Royal Hohenzollern House Order
Austrian Military Merit Cross 3rd Class War Decoration
Iron Cross 2nd Class
Iron Cross 1st Class

Pilot's Badge
Victory log

1917

24 Mar	Balloon (*Compagnie d'Aerostierer*s 58)	Recicourt
14 Aug	RE 8 (No. 9 Sqn RFC)	Zillebeke
5 Sep	Sopwith Pup (No. 46 Sqn RFC)	St Julien
9 Sep	Balloon (*Compagnie d'Aerostieres* 93)	Alveringhen
21 Sep	Balloon (Balloon Company 47-11-2)	Vlammertinghe
14 Oct	Balloon (Balloon Company 34-20-5)	NE Ypres
18 Oct	BF 2b (No. 22 Sqn RFC)	Schloss Ardoie
30 Nov	Sopwith Camel (No. 3 Sqn RFC)	Moeuvres-Bourlon

1918

5 Jan	Balloon (*Compagnie Aerostieres* 82)	W St Quentin
18 Jan	BF 2b	Le Catelet
12 Mar	Balloon (Balloon Company 37-3-1)	Lacouture
15 Mar	Balloon (Balloon Company 19-4-5)	Villers Faucon
18 Mar	Breguet XIV (*Escadrille Br* 131)	S Le Cateau
21 Mar	Balloon (Balloon Company 31-8-3)	Fins
27 Mar	DH 4 (No. 25 Sqn RFC)	W Miraumont
12 Apr	Sopwith Camel (No. 43 Sqn RFC)	NW Peronne
23 Apr	BF 2b (No. 57 Sqn RFC)	W Morisel
2 May	SE 5a (No. 56 Sqn RFC)	N Montauban
9 May	SE5a (No. 29 Sqn RFC)	Hamel
10 May	DH 9 (No. 27 Sqn RFC)	Chaulnes
15 May	DH 9 (No. 57 Sqn RFC)	Mametz
16 May	SPAD XIII (*Escadrille Spa* 3)	Maricourt
18 May	Sopwith Camel (No. 210 Sqn RFC)	Beaucourt
20 May	Balloon (Balloon Company 41-15-5)	SW Arras
2 Jun	SPAD XIII (*Escadrille Spa* 112)	La Croix
3 Jun	SPAD XIII (*Escadrille Spa* 93)	Dammard
5 Jun	SPAD (*Escadrille Spa* 163)	Chateau Thierry
22 Jun	Breguet XIV (*Escadrille Br* 11)	Beauvardes
27 Jun	SPAD XIII (*Escadrille Spa* 99)	Dommieres
28 Jun	SPAD VII (*Escadrille Spa* 88)	Billy
28 Jun	SPAD XI (*Escadrille Spa* 20)	Dampleux
30 Jun	SPAD XI (*Escadrille Spa* 87)	La Ferte Milon
2 Jul	Nieuport 28 (27th Aero Sqn USAS)	Bennes
2 Jul	Nieuport 28 (27th Aero Sqn USAS)	Courchamps
14 Jul	Breguet XIV (*Escadrille Br* 23)	Verdilly
15 Jul	Sopwith Camel (No. 54 Sqn RFC)	N Dormans
16 Jul	SPAD XI (*Escadrille Spa* 212)	Igny la Jard
18 Jul	SPAD XIII (*Escadrille Spa* 77)	Chouy
18 Jul	SPAD XIII (*Escadrille Spa* 266)	Grisolles
19 Jul	SPAD XIII (*Escadrille Spa* 85)	Courchamps

19 Jul	SPAD XIII (*Escadrille Spa* 85)	Dormans
21 Jul	Sopwith Camel(No. 54 Sqn RFC)	Fere-en-Tardenois
22 Jul	Sopwith Camel (No. 73 Sqn RFC)	Longpont
25 Jul	SPAD XII (*Escadrille Spa* 62)	Villers-Helon
28 Jul	SPAD VI (*Escadrille Spa* 15)	Fere-en Tardenois
29 Jul	SPAD XII (*Escadrille Spa* 78)	Coincy
30 Jul	Sopwith Camel (No. 73 Sqn RFC)	Arcy
30 Jul	Sopwith Camel (No. 43 Sqn RFC)	Saponay
8 Aug	Sopwith Camel (No. 201 Sqn RFC)	Proyart
8 Aug	Sopwith Camel (No. 80 Sqn RFC)	E Bray
8 Aug	Sopwith Camel (No. 209 Sqn RFC)	Estrees
9 Aug	Sopwith Camel (No. 54 Sqn RFC)	Estrees
9 Aug	Sopwith Camel (No. 201 Sqn RFC)	S Cerisy
10 Aug	SE 5a (No. 56 Sqn RFC)	Chaulnes

Total victories claimed: 54

CHAPTER FOUR

Leutnant Werner Voss
(1897 – 1917)

Werner Voss was born in Krefeld on the 13 April, 1897 the eldest son of an industrial dyer. As was the tradition in those days it was expected that Werner would follow in his fathers footsteps and enter the trade of dyeing that had been the tradition of the Voss family for generations. But Werner Voss had other ideas, he was to enter another trade concerned with another kind of dying and one that was to see him meet his demise at the early age of twenty.

As soon as he became old enough Werner Voss became a member of the Krefeld Militia, and liked nothing better than to wear the uniform of the Krefeld Hussars two evening a week and for two months during the summer. With the outbreak of war he was assigned to the 11th Westphalian Hussar Regiment and sent to the French border of Lorraine. Within days of reaching the border, France declared war on Germany and Voss found himself in the last battle in which the cavalry was to play a vital role. Elsewhere in Germany the cavalry units were being disbanded, as it became more and more apparent that they did not belong in this kind of war and the Hussars were being turned into infantrymen. Voss's world was turned upside down with this decision and the thought of tramping across fields of mud during the winter horrified him. He immediately put forward a request for transfer to the German Army Air Service and after being accepted applied for pilot training. By this time Voss was considered to be a veteran, promoted to Unteroffizier and awarded the Iron Cross 2nd Class – he was just eighteen years old.

Voss was sent to pilot school at Crefeld where it was soon discovered that he was a natural pilot. Voss completed the course on 12 February, 1916 and was immediately posted to *Flieger-Ersatz-Abteilung* (FEA) 7 as an instructor. At the end of March he was promoted to *Vizefeldwebel* and posted to *Kampgeschwader* 4 initially as an observer, but on receipt of his pilot's badge flew the Aviatak two-seater fighter/bomber on numerous photo-reconnaissance missions. In September he was promoted to *Leutnant* and posted to *Jasta* 2 in the November, where he joined the legendary Baron Manfred von Richthofen. On 27 November he scored

his first two victories, a Nieuport Scout of No. 60 Squadron RFC and a DH 2 from No. 9 Squadron RFC for which he was awarded the Iron Cross First Class. By the end of February 1917 his tally of victims had risen to twelve and in the March was awarded the Knight's Cross with Swords of the Royal Hohenzollern House Order. Werner Voss was becoming a household name in Germany and on the 8 April, 1917, with his tally now at twenty-four, was awarded the *Orden Pour le Mérite*, Germany's highest award.

Werner Voss in the cockpit of his Triplane with its padded headrest.

Leutnant Werner Voss was posted to *Jasta* 5 in May 1917, where, by the end of June he had taken his tally to thirty-four. He was given command of *Jasta* 29 for the month of July and then on to *Jasta* 14 as acting commander – he was just twenty years old. At the end of July he was appointed *Staffelführer* of *Jasta* 10 with his tally standing at thirty-four. Voss was flying the Fokker Dr I with the distinctive chrome yellow cowling of *Jasta* 10, only his had a face painted on it. During the August and September, Voss, who had become known as the 'Hussar of Krefeld', increased his tally to forty-eight, but then on the 23 September, 1917, he became engaged in what was to later become known as one of the most famous dog-fights of the war.

Werner Voss standing in front of his Fokker Dr I Triplane.

Whilst on patrol with members of his *Jasta*, Voss came across a flight of British SE5s from 56 Squadron, but unknown and also unfortunately for him, the flight consisted of a number of Allied top 'Aces', including

McCudden, Rhys-Davids, Barlow, Muspratt, Cronyn, Childlaw-Roberts and Bowman. For over ten minutes, Werner Voss almost single-handed, fought the flight inflicting damage, some serious, on all the aircraft. It was Lieutenant Arthur Rhys-Davids who finally managed to get on the tail of the elusive Voss and a burst from his machine guns sent Voss's Fokker Triplane 103/17 plummeting to the ground. He was buried by British soldiers on the spot where he crashed. Major James McCudden said of Voss afterwards,

Oberleutnant *Werner Voss taxiing out his Fokker Dr I Triplane.*

> 'His flying was wonderful, his courage magnificent and in my opinion he is the bravest German airman whom it has been my privilege to see fight.'

Rhys-Davids, on being conratulated when he returned to his airfield, commented, 'I only wish I could have brought him down alive.'

Leutnant Werner Voss was just twenty years old.

It is ineresting to note that Werner Voss was the fourth highest scoring fighter ace of the German Army Air Service and yet received just four awards for his achievement.

Awards

Orden Pour le Mérite
Knight's Cross with Swords of the Royal Hohenzollern House Order
Iron Cross 2nd Class
Iron Cross 1st Class
Pilot's Badge

Victory log

1916

27 Nov	Nieuport Scout (No. 60 Sqn RFC)	Miraumont
27 Nov	DH 2 (No. 18 Sqn RFC)	S Bapaume
21 Dec	BE 2d (No. 7 Sqn RFC)	Miraumont

1917

1 Feb	DH 2 (No. 29 Sqn RFC)	Essarts
4 Feb	BE 2d (No. 16 Sqn RFC)	Givenchy
10 Feb	DH 2 (No. 32 Sqn RFC)	SW Serre
25 Feb	DH 2 (No. 29 Sqn RFC)	St Sauveur
25 Feb	DH 2 (No. 29 Sqn RFC)	Arras
26 Feb	BE 2c (No. 16 Sqn RFC)	Ecurie
27 Feb	BE 2c (No. 8 Sqn RFC)	Blaireville
27 Feb	BE 2c (No. 12 Sqn RFC)	St Catherine
4 Mar	BE 2d (No. 8 Sqn RFC)	S Berneville
6 Mar	DH 2 (No. 32 Sqn RFC)	Favreuil
11 Mar	FE 2b (No. 22 Sqn RFC)	Combles
11 Mar	Nieuport Scout (No. 60 Sqn RFC)	Bailleul
17 Mar	FE 2b (No. 11 Sqn RFC)	NE Warlemont
17 Mar	DH 2 (No. 32 Sqn RFC)	SW Bapaume
18 Mar	BE 2d (No. 8 Sqn RFC)	Neuville
18 Mar	BE 2d (No. 4 Sqn RFC)	Boyelles
19 Mar	RE 8 (No. 59 Sqn RFC)	St Leger
24 Mar	FE 2b (No. 11 Sqn RFC)	SE St Leger
24 Mar	BE 2d (No. 16 Sqn RFC)	SE Mercatel
1 Apr	BE 2c (No. 15 Sqn RFC)	E St Leger
6 Apr	BE 2e (No. 15 Sqn RFC)	S Lagincourt
7 May	SE 5 (No. 56 Sqn RFC)	Etaing
9 May	BE 2c (No. 52 Sqn RFC)	Havrincourt
9 May	Sopwith Pup (No. 54 Sqn RFC)	Lesdain
9 May	FE 2b (No. 22 Sqn RFC)	Le Bosquet
23 May	FE 2b (No. 18 Sqn RFC)	N Havrincourt
26 May	Sopwith Pup (No. 54 Sqn RFC)	SW Gouzeaucourt
28 May	FE 2d (No. 25 Sqn RFC)	SE Douai
4 Jun	Sopwith Pup (No. 54 Sqn RFC)	Aubenscheul-aux-Bois
5 Jun	FE 2b (No. 22 Sqn RFC)	N Vaucelles
6 Jun	Nieuport Scout (No. 6 Sqn RNAS)	W Graincourt

10 Aug	SPAD XIII (*Escadrille Spa* 31)	S Dixmude
15 Aug	FE 2d (No. 20 Sqn RFC)	Zillebeke Lake
16 Aug	Sopwith Camel (No. 70 Sqn RFC)	St Julien
23 Aug	SPAD XIII (No. 19 Sqn RFC)	SW Dixmude
3 Sep	Sopwith Camel (No. 45 Sqn RFC)	N Houthen
5 Sep	DH 5 (No. 32 Sqn RFC)	St. Julien
5 Sep	Caudron G 6 (*Escadrille C* 53)	Bixschoote
6 Sep	FE 2d (No. 20 Sqn RFC)	SE Boesinghe
10 Sep	Sopwith Camel (No. 70 Sqn RFC)	Langemarck
10 Sep	Sopwith Camel (No. 70 Sqn RFC)	SW Poelcapelle
10 Sep	SPAD VII (*Escadrille Spa* 37)	E Langemarck
11 Sep	BF 2b (No. 22 Sqn RFC)	Langemarck
11 Sep	Sopwith Camel (No. 45 Sqn RFC)	E St Julien
23 Sep	DH 4 (No. 57 Sqn RFC)	S Roulers

Total victories claimed: 48

CHAPTER FIVE

Leutnant Fritz Rumey
(1891 – 1918)

Fritz Rumey was born in Konigsberg, Bavaria on the 3 March, 1891. In 1911, at the age of twenty, he joined the 45th Infantry Regiment as an infantryman. With the outbreak of the First World War, his regiment was mobilised and sent to the Russian Front. Rumey was detached to the 3rd Grenadier Regiment and found himself immediately in the action. In the following twelve months the regiment found itself fighting almost continuously and Rumey distinguished himself to the extent that he was awarded the Iron Cross 2nd Class. After months of fighting in harsh winter of Russia and the sea of mud that followed, Fritz Rumey looked to find another way to fight the war and it wasn't long before he realised that there was another kind of war going on, the war in the air.

At the beginning of 1915, Fritz Rumey applied to be transferred to the

Vzfw Fritz Rumey (second from right) with members of Jasta 5.

German Army Air Service and on August 5, he was posted to flying school. After training and gaining his observers badge, he was posted to *Flieger-Abteilung* (A) (Fl.Abt.(A)).219 as an observer.

Vzfw *Fritz Rumey saluting Manfred von Richthofen whilst the latter was on a visit to* Jasta 5

After just over a year of flying as an observer on photo-reconnaissance missions, Fritz Rumey applied for training as a pilot and was posted to *Jastaschule* on the Western Front at the beginning of 1917. On completion of his training, Rumey was posted to *Jasta* 2 in the May of 1917 and then to *Jasta* 5 on the 10 June with the rank of *Vizefeldwebel*. At the end of June he was promoted again and commissioned to the rank of *Leutnant* and celebrated this promotion by shooting down an observation balloon over Boursies on 6 July. For this he received the Bavarian Military Merit Cross

Vzfw *Rumey (extreme right) with members of* Jasta 5 *entertaining two British airmen.*

2nd Class with Swords on the 7 July. This was followed by his first aerial combat 'kill', an RE 8 from No. 59 Squadron, RFC on 19 August. During one combat mission on the 25 August, 1917, he was badly wounded and only just managed to get himself and his aircraft back to the field. After two weeks he was back in the air adding to his tally and by the end of the year had raised it to five.

Three more victories were added to his tally during January 1918, then one more in February followed five in March. By the end of May 1918, Rumey's tally had risen to twenty-one and had been awarded the Golden Military Merit Cross of Prussia. June brought another six victories with a further two in July. The British ace Lt E C Eaton of No. 65 Squadron fell to his guns on 26 June 1918 taking his tally to twenty-five.

His efforts had not gone unnoticed and with his tally at twenty-nine, was awarded Germany's most prestigious award the *Orden Pour Le Mérite*. Fritz Rumey continued to wreak havoc amongst the British squadrons until the 27 September, 1918, when in the midst of a dogfight over Neuville-St Remy, the top wing of his Fokker DVII collided with the wing of an SE5a flown by Captain G E B Lawson of No. 32 Squadron RAF. With his aircraft spinning towards the ground, Fritz Rumey took to his parachute, but it failed to deploy and he was killed. Captain Lawson on the other hand managed to guide his badly damaged SE5a to the ground and survived.

Fritz Rumey was twenty-seven years old.

Awards

Orden Pour le Mérite
Prussian Golden Military Merit Cross
Iron Cross 2nd Class
Iron Cross 1st Class
Bavarian Military Merit Cross 2nd Class
Pilot's Badge

Victory log
1917

6 Jul	Balloon (British Balloon 41-15-4)	Boursies
19 Aug	RE 8 (No. 59 Sqn RFC)	Epehy
22 Nov	Sopwith Camel (No. 43 Sqn RFC)	Marcoing
23 Nov	Sopwith Camel (No. 3 Sqn RFC)	Bourlon Wood
23 Nov	AWFK 8 (No. 8 Sqn RFC)	SW Marcoing

1918

13 Jan	BF 2b (No. 11 Sqn RFC)	S Beaumont
28 Jan	BF 2b (No. 11 Sqn RFC)	Graincourt
29 Jan	DH 4 (No. 25 Sqn RFC)	St Quentin

26 Feb	DH 4 (No. 25 Sqn RFC)	N Bussigny
17 Mar	SE 5a (No. 64 Sqn RFC)	Marcoing
23 Mar	Sopwith Dolphin (No. 79 Sqn RFC)	Cartigny
24 Mar	RE 8 (No. 53 Sqn RFC)	
28 Mar	Sopwith Camel (No. 43 Sqn RFC)	Bray-sur-Somme
12 Apr	Sopwith Dolphin	NW Albert
2 May	Sopwith Camel (No. 65 Sqn RAF)	Villers Brettoneux
9 May	Breguet XIV (*Escadrille Br* 107)	N Villequier
10 May	SE 5a (No. 56 Sqn RAF)	E Hamel
16 May	SE 5a (No. 84 Sqn RAF)	SW Courcelette
17 May	SE 5a (No. 74 Sqn RAF)	Puzieux
18 May	SPAD XIII (*Escadrille Spa* 153)	Moreuil
20 May	Sopwith Camel (No. 65 Sqn RAF)	S Morlancourt
2 Jun	Sopwith Camel (No. 65 Sqn RAF)	Hangard
7 Jun	SE 5a (No. 24 Sqn RAF)	Rosieres
25 Jun	SE 5a (No. 24 Sqn RAF)	W Albert
26 Jun	Sopwith Camel (No. 65 Sqn RAF)	E Bouzincourt
27 Jun	Sopwith Dolphin (No. 23 Sqn RAF)	Somme
27 Jun	Sopwith Camel (No. 70 Sqn RAF)	Bray-sur-Somme
1 Jul	Sopwith Camel (No. 23 Sqn RAF)	Somme
3 Jul	Sopwith Camel (No. 54 Sqn RAF)	Estrees
3 Sep	DH 9 (No. 98 Sqn RAF)	N Bertincourt
4 Sep	Sopwith Camel (No. 70 Sqn RAF)	Queant
5 Sep	SE 5a (No. 64 Sqn RAF)	N Bouchain
7 Sep	DH 4 (No. 205 Sqn RAF)	St Quentin
14 Sep	SE 5a (No. 84 Sqn RAF)	S Le Catelet
16 Sep	DH 9 (No. 57 Sqn RAF)	Villers-Guislain
16 Sep	SE 5a (No. 57 Sqn RAF)	Marquion
16 Sep	Sopwith Camel (No. 3 Sqn RAF)	Marquion
17 Sep	SE 5a (No. 84 Sqn RAF)	Rumilly
17 Sep	Sopwith Camel (17th Aero Sqn USAS)	NW Cambrai
17 Sep	Sopwith Camel (No. 46 Sqn RAF)	SW Cambrai
23 Sep	Sopwith Dolphin (No. 87 Sqn RAF)	SW Queant
24 Sep	SE 5a (No. 32 Sqn RAF)	S Buissy
26 Sep	DH 4 (*Compagnie Aerostieres* 39)	Gouzeaucourt
26 Sep	BF 2b (No. 87 Sqn RAF)	Cambrai
27 Sep	Sopwith Camel (No. 54 Sqn RAF)	E Marquion

Total victories claimed: 45

CHAPTER SIX

Hauptmann Rudolf Berthold
(1891 – 1920)

Rudolf Berthold was born at Ditterswind, Near Bamberg, northern Bavaria on the 24 March, 1891. His early childhood was uneventful and in 1910 at the age of twenty-one, he joined the army and was assigned to the 3rd Brandenburg Infantry Regiment Nr. 20. But the humdrum life of a soldier at that time was not for Berthold, so he decided to learn to fly at one of the private flying clubs that were starting to spring up. After gaining his licence No. 538 on the 26 September, 1913, he asked for a transfer to the newly formed German Army Air Service. At the outbreak of war in 1914, Berthold was posted for flying training as an observer on Halberstadt two-seaters with *Feldflieger-Abteilung* (FFl.Abt.) 23. By the end of the year he had been awarded the Iron Cross 1st and 2nd Class and promoted to *Feldwebel* for the valuable information he had acquired during flights during the Battle of Marne.

In November 1914 Berthold started pilot training and completed it by the end of January 1915. He returned to FFl.Abt. 23 this time as a pilot and was immediately transferred to the large AEG. ' Battle Planes' and carried out a large number of reconnaissance flights during the following year. On 15 September, 1915 on returning from one long reconnaissance mission, the aircraft suffered engine failure as it approached to land and crashed. Fortunately Berthold and the three other members of the crew suffered only minor injuries. He was not so lucky on 2 October when his aircraft was attacked by a British fighter and two of his crew were mortally wounded.

Berthold asked for a transfer to fighters and was sent to *Jastaschule* in the December of 1915 and on graduating was posted back to FFl.Abt. 23 replacing Hans-Joachim Buddecke who had been assigned to Turkey. Berthold took over Buddecke's single-seater Fokker E.III, flying as cover for the AEGs. The beginning of January saw the number of Fokker E IIIs increased to five, so the fighter unit was redesignated *Kampfeinsitzer-Kommando-Vaux* (KeK Vaux).

On the 2 February, 1916, Rudolf Berthold opened his tally by shooting down a Voisin whilst on patrol over Chaulnes. By the end of April his

tally stood at five and he had been awarded the *Bayerisch Kriegsverdeinst-Orden* IV Class, the *Ritterkreuz* of the St Heinrichs Order and the Saxon Knight's Cross of the Military St. Henry Order. He also suffered severe injuries from crash landing a Pfalz E IV after a serious misjudgment. Berthold returned to his unit before his wounds had properly healed, (demonstrating an impatience he was later to repeat) and was commissioned to *Leutnant*.

In the August of 1916, Berthold was given command of *Jasta* 4 after forming this from Kek Vaux. Then on the 27 August came another award, the prestigious Knight's Cross with Swords of the Royal Hohenzollern House Order. On the 14 October he handed the reins of *Jasta* 4 over to Hans Buddecke before taking command of *Jasta* 14. Berthold then started to mould his pilots into a team, and it wasn't until 24 March, 1917 that he was to increase his personal tally by shooting

Leutnant *Rudolf Berthold (left) with his mechanics and his Fokker Scout.*

down a Farman from *Escadrille* F 7. Then in the May his patrol was attacked by an Allied patrol and he was shot down by a British fighter. His aircraft crashed within his own lines and he was pulled from the wreckage, sustaining a fractured skull, a broken nose, pelvis and thigh. After two months in hospital, Berthold again discharged himself and returned to *Jasta* 14. On the 12 August he was given command of *Jasta* 18 and promotion to *Oberleutnant*. He celebrated this by shooting down a SPAD on the 21 August and raising his tally to thirteen. In the month of September he scored fourteen victories bringing his tally to twenty-seven. On the 2 October he scored his twenty-eighth victory by shooting down a DH 4 from 57 Squadron RFC, but on the 10 October, 1917, during a dogfight with a British patrol, his right upper arm was smashed by a bullet. Whilst in hospital he received Germany's highest award, the *Orden Pour le Mérite* and ten days later promotion to *Hauptmann*.

Once again he discharged himself early and returned to his *Jasta*. Berthold was given command of *Jagdgeschwader* (JG) Nr. II in March 1918, but he took with him nearly all the best pilots of *Jasta* 14,

Pilots of Jasta *18 with Berthold and Buddecke in front and to the right of the picture.*

exchanging them with the pilots of *Jasta* 15. Not exactly an exercise in morale boosting for the men of *Jasta* 15! His aircraft with his distinctive livery of a red and blue fuselage (red from the nose to the cockpit, then blue to the tail) and its winged sword painted on the fuselage, was an aircraft to be wary of from the Allied standpoint. The injuries he had sustained in the October continued to cause him great discomfort, so much so, that he had his aircraft modified so that he could fly it with his left hand giving his right hand very limited use. He quickly earned himself the nickname the 'Iron Knight'.

Rudolf Berthold with his Fokker D VII.

Then in May 1918 his *Jasta* was given the new Siemens-Schuckert SSW DIII and it fell to berthold to give the aircraft a thorough testing. His report to *Idflieg* was not very encouraging.

'Basically the new Siemens-Halske S III engine is sound and the pilots have faith in it. One particular advantage is that the engine power remains constant even at high altitude. After rectifying the defects reported to the Commander General of the Air Service by *Jagdgeschwader* 2 on 17 April, 1918, and particularly after reducing the control forces and the excessive left-hand torque suffer by the aircraft, the SSW DIII can be considered a perfectly acceptable front-line machine, but the aircraft cannot be used at the present time as, after seven to ten hours of continuous running of the Sh.III engines the pistons sieze, the crowns being torn off and the pieces dropping into the crankcase.'

The result of the test led to thirty-five SSW DIIIs being withdrawn from the front-line *Jastas* and returned to the factory for major modifications to be made. By the time they were ready for service the war was coming to an end and they were relegated to home defence duties. The *Jasta* in the meantine reverted back to the tried and tested Fokker DVII.

On the 10 August Berthold's patrol became involved with a patrol of DH 4s and during the ensuing dogfight, during which Berthold shot down two of the Allied aircraft, he collided with the last one. His Fokker DVII was badly damaged and Berthold struggled to keep it in the air but in vain. It smashed into a house and although he survived the horrendous crash, it effectively ended his combat career.

On release from hospital, he found that the war was over, so in 1919 he joined the *Freikorps* and fought during the post-war revolution. On the 15 March, 1920, Berthold was in Harburg on the Elbe when he was attacked by rioters and it is said that he was beaten then strangled with the ribbon of his *Orden Pour le Mérite*,

An ignominious end to such a respected Knight of the air and one that was echoed by the inscription on his gravestone:

'Honoured by his enemies – slain by his German brethren'.

Awards

Orden Pour le Mérite
Knight's Cross with Swords of the Royal Hohenzollern House Order
Iron Cross 2nd Class
Iron Cross 1st Class
Bavarian Military Merit Order 4th Class with Swords
Knight's Cross of the Saxon Military St Henry Order
Pilot's Badge
Observer's Badge

Victory log

1916

2 Feb	Voisin (*Escadrille* VB 108)	Chaulnes
5 Feb	BE 2c	Irles
13 Mar	BE 2c (No. 8 Sqn RFC)	Cambrai
1 Apr	Maurice Farman (*Escadrille* MF 54)	Lihons
16 Apr	BE 2c (No. 9 Sqn RFC)	Maurepas
24 Aug	Nieuport (*Escadrille* N 48)	Peronne
17 Sep	Martinsyde G100 (No. 27 Sqn RFC)	Cambrai
26 Sep	BE 12 (No. 19 Sqn RFC)	Bertincourt

1917

24 Mar	Farman (*Escadrille* F 7)	Aizy-Vailly
6 Apr	Caudron (*Escadrille* F 35)	Malval-Ferme
11 Apr	SPAD VII (*Escadrille* N 73)	Corbeny
14 Apr	SPAD VII (*Escadrille* N 73)	Bois de Beau Mavais
21 Aug	Martinsyde G100 (No. 27 Sqn RFC)	Dixmuiden
4 Sep	RE 8 (No. 9 Sqn RFC)	N. Ypres

4 Sep	RE 8 (N. 7 Sqn RFC)	St. Jean
5 Sep	DH 4 (No. 55 Sqn RFC)	Thielt
15 Sep	DH 4 (No. 55 Sqn RFC)	Zillebeke Lake
16 Sep	RE 8 (No. 6 Sqn RFC)	W. Becelaere
16 Sep	RE 8 (No. 4 Sqn RFC)	Zonnebeke
19 Sep	RE 8 (No. 6 Sqn RFC)	Becelaere
20 Sep	SPAD VII	E. Zillebecke Lake
21 Sep	SPAD VII (No. 19 Sqn RFC)	W. Menin
22 Sep	BF 2b (No. 22 Sqn RFC)	Zillebeke Lake
25 Sep	SPAD VII (No. 19 Sqn RFC)	Gheluvelt
26 Sep	Sopwith Camel (No. 70 Sqn RFC)	Beceleare
28 Sep	DH 5 (No. 32 Sqn RFC)	Hollebeke
30 Sep	Sopwith Pup (No. 66 Sqn RFC)	Deulmont
2 Oct	DH 4 (No. 57 Sqn RFC	Roulers

1918

28 May	Nieuport XXVII	Soissons
29 May	SPAD XIII (*Escadrille Spa* 77)	Soissons
29 May	Breguet XIV (*Escadrille Br* 237)	Soissons
5 Jun	DH 9 (No. 205 Sqn RAF)	N. St. Juste
11 Jun	Breguet XIV (*Escadrille Br* 282)	
12 Jun	Spad 2 (*Escadrille Spa* 266)	
18 Jun	SE 5a (No. 84 Sqn RAF)	Villers Bretonneux
18 Jun	SE 5a (No. 84 Sqn RAF)	Villers Bretonneux
27 Jun	BF 2b (No. 48 Sqn RAF)	Villers Bretonneux
19 Jul	SPAD XIII (*Escadrille Spa* 152)	Soissons
20 Jul	SPAD 2 (*Escadrille Spa* 62)	SE. Dormans
1 Aug	Salmson 2A2 (1st Aero Sqn USAS)	Fére-en-Tardenois
9 Aug	Sopwith 1 Strutter	Tricot
9 Aug	Sopwith 1 Strutter	Beaucourt
10 Aug	DH 4 (No. 49 Sqn RAF)	Licourt
10 Aug	DH 4 (No. 49 Sqn RAF)	Ablaincourt

Total victories claimed: 44

CHAPTER SEVEN

Leutnant Paul Baümer
(1896 – 1927)

Paul Baümer was born on the 11 May, 1896 at Duisberg and spent most of his childhood fascinated by the giant Zeppelins that operated from Friedrichshafen near his home spending every second he could watching them. On leaving school he found himself a job as a dental assistant and among the dentist's patients was a pilot who persuaded him that he ought to take up flying. He joined the local flying club, paying for his own lessons. His first flight had a rather ignominious end to it as he landed in a tree whilst trying to land. However he persevered, finally obtaining his licence. When the war broke out, Paul Baümer tried to enlist as a naval airman, but was turned down. The reason is not known. He then volunteered for the 70th Infantry Regiment at Saarbrucken and after training saw combat at St Quentin in France. In the early part of 1915 he was posted to the XXI Army Corps on the Russian Front where he was badly wounded in the left arm.

Whilst recovering in hospital he applied for transfer to the German Air Service, but again was refused. He then saw vacancies in the German Air Service for technicians and using his experience as a dental assistant, persuaded the authorities to accept his transfer. At the beginning of 1916, he was accepted for 'General Duties' in the German Air Service and posted to Doberitz. Within a few months he had persuaded the Commanding Officer to look at his previous flying experience and put his name forward for flying training. The spring of 1916 saw Paul Baümer at flying school and such was the ease with which he qualified, that he was posted in October to *Armee Flugpark* No. 1 as a ferry pilot and flight instructor. It was recognised that Baümer had a great deal to offer and he was promoted on the 19 February, 1917 to the rank of Grefreiter and posted to *Flieger-Abteilung* (Fl.Abt.) 7 on the 26 March. Three days later he was promoted again to *Unteroffizier*.

On the 15 May, Paul Baümer was awarded the Iron Cross 2nd Class and within two days was sent for fighter training. On completion of his training he was posted to *Jasta* 2 (*Jasta* Boelcke) on the 28 June for just two days, then on to *Jasta* 5. On the 12, 13 and 15 of July he scored his first three

Portrait shot of Paul Baumer

victories when he shot down three reconnaissance balloons, and for this he was awarded the Iron Cross 1st Class. Baümer was posted back to *Jasta* 2 in the August of 1917 and by the end of the year his tally had risen to eighteen.

On the 12, February 1918, in recognition of his bravery, he was awarded the Gold Military Merit Cross. His nineteenth victory, a Sopwith Camel shot down whilst on patrol over N Zonnebecke on the 9 March, was recognised by granting him a commission to the rank of *Leutnant* on the 10 April. The 200th victory of *Jasta* 2 on the 23 March, was Baümers' twentieth and was made even more remarkable by him shooting down two RE 8 aircraft and one Camel in under three hours. Nine days later however, whilst trying to land a badly shot-up Pfalz D VIII, Paul Baümer was injured in the crash landing, breaking his jaw amongst other injuries.

He returned to *Jasta* 2. in the September and was immediately given the nickname of '*Der Eiserne Adler*' (The Iron Eagle). By the end of September he had increased his tally to thirty-eight, including shooting down eight Allied aircraft in less than a week during one period. Luck was on his side at this time, when he became one of the few pilots of the First World War to escape from his burning aircraft by using a parachute. His thirtieth victory brought the nations highest award, a recommendation for the *Orden Pour le Mérite* which was awarded to him on the 2 November, 1918.

Paul Baümer having his parachute harness tightened just prior to a mission

When the war ended, Paul Baümer had taken his tally to forty-three victories. He went to work for Blohm and Voss, the ship and aeroplane builders, at their factory in Hamburg, but he could not settle and returned to his studies to become a professional dentist. Baümer continued his interest in flying by taking part in aerobatic competitions, before starting his own aircraft company – Baümer Aero GmbH – in Hamburg. His designers were the Guether Brothers who later became famous working with the Ernst Heinkel design team. During an aerobatic display in Copenhagen, whilst he was testing the Rohrbach Rofix fighter, an all metal cantilever

Paul Baümer about to fly a Fokker DV at Boistrancourt on a winters day

monoplane, the aircraft stalled at 2000 feet and spun into the waters of the Oere Sound. His body was later recovered and interred at Ohesdorf, near Hamburg.

Awards

Orden Pour le Mérite
Golden Military Merit Cross
Iron Cross 2nd Class

Iron Cross 1st Class
Wound Badge in Black
Pilot's Badge – German Army
1917

12 Jul	Balloon	Nurlu
13 Jul	Balloon (French *Compagnie* 41)	St Quentin
15 Jul	Balloon (French *Compagnie* 45)	St Quentin
9 Sep	RE 8 (No. 52 Sqn RFC)	Mannessvaere
20 Sep	Sopwith Camel (No.9 Sqn RNAS)	Ramskapelle
21 Sep	Sopwith Camel	Boesinghen
5 Nov	Sopwith Camel	St Julien
6 Nov	Sopwith Camel (No. 65 Sqn RFC)	Vierlavenhoek
6 Nov	SPAD (No. 19 Sqn RFC)	E.Zonnebeke
7 Nov	RE 8 (No. 4 Sqn RFC)	Moorslede
8 Nov	SE 5a (No. 84 Sqn RFC)	Zillebeke
8 Nov	SE 5a (No. 60 Sqn RFC)	Zonnebeke
18 Nov	RE 8	Zillebeke

1918

9 Mar	Sopwith Camel	Zonnebek
23 Mar	Sopwith Camel (No. 46 Sqn RFC) St Léger	
23 Mar	RE 8 (No. 5 Sqn RFC)	Tilloy
23 Mar	RE 8 (No. 59 Sqn)	Beugnâtre
5 Sep	DH 4 (No. 57 Sqn RAF)	Douai
6 Sep	BF 2b (No. 11 Sqn RAF)	Cantaing
14 Sep	RE 8	Cantaing
16 Sep	Bf 2b	Henin-Lietard
20 Sep	Sopwith Camel (No. 203 Sqn RAF)	E. Rumancourt
21 Sep	DH 9 (No. 57 Sqn RAF)	Bourlon Wood
21 Sep	DH 9 (No. 205 Sqn RAF)	Lagnicourt
21 Sep	DH 9 (No. 205 Sqn RAF)	Morchies
24 Sep	Sopwith Camel (No. 4 Sqn AFC)	Sailly
24 Sep	DH 9 (No. 49 Sqn RAF)	SW Clairy
27 Sep	Sopwith Snipe	S. Oisy
27 Sep	DH 4 (No. 25 Sqn RAF)	Cambrai
27 Sep	SE 5a (No. 56 Sqn RAF)	Cambrai
29 Sep	Bf 2b (No. 22 Sqn RAF)	Marcoing
29 Sep	Sopwith Camel (No. 46 Sqn RAF)	Bourlan Wood
29 Sep	Sopwith Camel (No. 46 Sqn RAF)	S. Sailly
3 Oct	Bf 2b	Rumilly
4 Oct	SE 5a	Montbréhain
4 Oct	Bf 2b	Cambrai
8 Oct	Sopwith Camel	Bautigny
9 Oct	Bf 2b (No. 62 Sqn RAF)	Presau

Total victories claimed: 43

CHAPTER EIGHT

Leutnant Josef Carl Peter Jacobs (1894 – 1978)

Josef Jacobs was born in Kreuzkapelle, Rhineland on the 15 May. 1894, the son of a middle class businessman. Whilst still at school he watched mounted troops carrying out their drills and flimsy aircraft flying about. This increased his interest in all things mechanical and showed itself in 1912, when at the age of eighteen he learned to fly under the tutelage of Bruno Werntgen at the *Jastaschule* at nearby Hangelar. Unfortunately Werntgen was killed in a crash before Jacobs had finished his course. In 1914, at the outbreak of the First World War, Josef Jacobs enlisted in the German Army Air Service and was posted to *Flieger-Ersatz-Abteilung* (FEA).9 to be trained as a military pilot. On graduating he was posted to *Flieger-Abteilung* (Fl.Abt.) Nr. 11 as a reconnaissance pilot and for over a year was engaged in missions over the lines flying LVGs. On two different occasions Jacobs, flying an unarmed reconnaissance LVG came

Leutnant Josef Jacobs with his ground crew in front of his Fokker Eindecker

under attack and only just managed to fend the attacked off with small arms fire. He was awarded the Iron Cross 2nd Class at this time.

Early in 1916, he was posted to *Fokkerstaffel-West*, flying Fokker E.IIIs. He opened his tally unofficially on the 12 May when he claimed a Caudron, but although it was initially unconfirmed, subsequent enquiries did confirm the victory. The end of March brought a successful claim for a balloon, for which he was awarded the Iron Cross 1st Class, but it wasn't the victory Jacobs wanted for his Ehrenbecher (Honour Cup), he wanted a definitive 'kill' in combat not for the shooting down of a stationery object in the sky.

Jacob's vocal dissatisfaction with the Fokker E III's performance finally paid off when he took possession of a Fokker E IV. On its first mission the engine failed, causing Jacobs to struggle to get the aircraft back to his field. The aircraft was returned to Germany to be repaired and Jacobs was back flying his old Fokker E III. Then in September 1916, after a couple of near disasters which Jacobs put down to the underpowered Fokker E III, he took possession of the latest Fokker D-Type.

On the 25 October, 1916, Jacobs long-time friend *Oberleutnant* Erich

Josef Jacobs at Jastaschule *Valenciennes: L-RL:* Ltn *Gromer,* Ltn *Stock,* Oblt *Hans Berr,* Ltn *von Schell,* Ltn *Breitbach,* Ltn *Walter Krause,* Ltn *Spitzhoff and* Ltn *Josef Jacobs.*

Leutnant Josef Jacobs in his Fokker Eindecker with a victoy laurel leaf.

Honemanns, Commander of *Jasta* 22, requested the posting of his friend to his *Jasta*. Within weeks of his arriving at *Jasta* 22, Jacobs was posted temporarily to *Jastaschule* 1 as an instructor where he stayed throughout the winter. Returning to *Jasta* 22 at the end of January 1917 he found that the *Jasta* had been equipped with Halberstadt and Albatros DII fighters and he celebrated by opening his tally with the squadron by shooting down a Caudron R.4 whilst on patrol over Terny Sorny on the 23 January. By the end of August, his tally had risen to five and he was appointed commander of *Jasta* 7. With the appointment came the award of the Knight's Cross with Swords of the Royal Hohenzollern House Order. By the end of 1917 Jacobs tally had risen to twelve and his *Jasta* was re-equipped with Fokker Triplanes. Jacobs had his aircraft painted all black and it was soon to become instantly recognisable by Allied airmen.

The beginning of the 1918 with *Jasta* 7 was quiet, there was a lull in the hostilities and the Jacobs used the time to work his *Jasta* into a fighting unit. The lull didn't last long and in April Jacobs claimed his latest victim, an RE 8 of 7 Squadron RFC, over W. Stende. The fighting became intense and by the end of July, after surviving a mid-air collision with another Fokker Triplane, Jacobs tally had risen to twenty-four and he was awarded Germany's most prestigious award, the *Orden Pour le Mérite*. The award came on 18 July, 1918 and Jacobs was notified by means of a meassage that read:

18.7.18

Lt d. Res. Jacobs
Commanding Officer Fighter Section 7

His majesty has in recognition of your excellent accomplishment as a fighter pilot bestwoed upon you the Order of Merit.
It gives me great pleasure to inform you of this fact and to congratulate you on this, the supreme token of distinction from your highest War Lord.

The Commanding Officer General von Hoeppner.

Josef Jacobs with his mechanics collecting his new Fokker D II

Jacobs gradually became Germany's greatest exponent of the Fokker Triplane and by the end of 1918 had disposed of fortu-one confirmed of the Allies aircraft. Even after the Armistice, he, along with Osterkamp and Sachsenberg, fought against the communists in the Baltic.

In the early 1920's Jacobs became a flight instructor with the Turkish Army, helping them develop quite a formidable air force. In 1931 he became a director of the Adler Works still maintaining his interest in aviation. Two years later he set up his own aircraft manufacturing plant at Erfurt although this was not a great success. Speed was still a passion and he became involved in the world of car and powerboat racing and bob-sledding. Prior to the start of the Second World War, Jacobs did not volunteer for the newly formed Luftwaffe but at the onset was commissioned a Major in the reserves. He was a reluctant officer in the Luftwaffe and his views on the National Socialist Party were well known and documented. At one point he even moved his company away from Germany to Holland in order to prevent Göring becoming a major shareholder. Göring was incensed and regarded it as an insult and when Holland was invaded, gave orders that Jacobs be arrested and interned in

Josef Jacob's Ehrenbecher
(Honour Goblet)

a concentration camp. Fortunately for Jacobs the military governor at the time was Friedrich Christiansen, who himself had been awarded the *Orden Pour le Mérite* as an ace in the First World War and no great admirer of Hermann Göring. He respected Josef Jacobs and made him aware of what Göring had ordered. Jacobs went into hiding for the rest of the war.

At the end of the war, Josef Jacobs moved away from aviation and started a crane operating company, but such was his love of aviation that he became one of the greatest sources of information on World War One aircraft and personnel for historians. He died at the age of eighty-four in Munich on 29 July, 1978.

Awards

Orden Pour le Mérite
Knight's Cross with Swords of the Royal Hohenzollern House Order
Iron Cross 2nd Class
Iron Cross 1st Class
Knight 2nd Class with Swords of the Saxe-Ernestine House Order
Knight 2nd Class with Swords of the Saxe-Weimar Order of the White Falcon
Reuss Honour Cross 3rd Class with Swords
Oldenburg Friedrich – August Cross 2nd Class
Saxe-Weimar General Honour Decoration in Silver with Swords
Hamburg Hanseatic Cross
Wound Badge in Silver
Pilot's Badge – German Army
Field Pilot's Badge – Austro-Hungarian Empire (Karl pattern)
Pilot's Badge – Ottoman Empire

Postwar awards

Baltic Cross – Germany
St George's Bravery Medal – Russian
Russian Order of St Stanislaus 2nd Class with Swords
Russian Order of St Anna 2nd Class with Swords
Turkish Red Crescent Medal
Saxon War Merit Cross
Austrian Malta Merit Cross (Breast)

Victory log

There were said to be some forty-eight 'kills' attributed to Jacobs but seven of these were unsubstantiated.

1916

22 Mar   Balloon (*Cie Aérostieres* 66)

1917

23 Jan	Caudron R 4 (*Escadrille C 46*)	Terny Sorny
9 Feb	Caudron R 4	Cerny
6 Apr	Balloon (*Cie 21*)	Blanzy-Vailly
13 Apr	Farman 40 (*Escadrille F 41*)	Barisis
16 Apr	Balloon (*Cie 21*)	Laffaux
20 Aug	Sopwith Triplane (No. 10 Sqn RNAS)	Langemarck
10 Sep	SPAD (*Escadrille Spa 48*)	Keyem
11 Sep	Sopwith Camel (No. 70 Sqn RFC)	Koekost
18 Oct	DH 4	Zillebeke Lake
9 Nov	SPAD (Escadrille No. 102)	Woumen
6 Dec	SPAD (No. 23 Sqn RFC)	Passchendaele
18 Dec	Sopwith Camel (No. 65 Sqn RFC)	Dixmude

1918

11 Apr	RE 8 (No. 7 Sqn RAF)	W Ostende
21 Apr	Sopwith Camel (No. 54 Sqn RAF)	S Armentieres
14 May	Balloon (*Compagne d'Aerostieres* 27)	N Ypres
14 May	Balloon (*Comapgne d'Aerostieres* 50)	NW Ypres
23 May	SE 5a	Kruisstraet
1 Jun	BF 2b (No. 20 Sqn RAF)	NW Dickebusch
5 Jun	Sopwith Camel (No. 203 Sqn RAF)	W Bailleul
10 Jun	Sopwith Camel (No. 73 Sqn RAF)	S Poperinghe
19 Jun	RE 8 (No. 21 Sqn RAF)	E Zwartelen
26 Jun	Sopwith Camel (No. 210 Sqn RAF)	Menin
17 Jul	Sopwith Camel (No. 80 Sqn RAF)	SW Nieuport
19 Jul	SE 5a (No. 74 Sqn RAF)	Moorslede
13 Sep	RE 8 (No. 52 Sqn RAF)	Kemmel-Bailleul
15 Sep	AWFK 8 (No. 82 Sqn RAF)	Passechendale
16 Sep	SE 5a (No. 29 Sqn RAF)	W Menin
16 Sep	Balloon (Balloon Company 5-5-2)	Poperighe
19 Sep	Sopwith Camel (No. 204 Sqn RAF)	Dixmude
21 Sep	DH 9 (No. 107 Sqn RAF)	Dixmude
24 Sep	Sopwith Camel (No. 204 Sqn RAF)	Dixmude
28 Sep	SE 5a (No. 41 Sqn RAF)	Moorslede
28 Sep	SE 5a (No. 41 Sqn RAF)	Moorslede
1 Oct	DH 9 (No. 107 Sqn RAF)	
2 Oct	DH 9 (No. 108 Sqn RAF)	Stadenberghe
2 Oct	SPAD VII (*Escadrille Spa* 165)	Houthulst Forest
3 Oct	Sopwith Camel (No. 201 Sqn RAF)	Rumbeke
3 Oct	Sopwith Camel (No. 204 Sqn RAF)	Rumbeke
4 Oct	SPAD XIII (*Escadrille Spa* 93)	Rumbeke
7 Oct	Sopwith Camel No. 70 Sqn RAF)	
8 Oct	Balloon (*Cie Aérostieres* 26)	SW Dixmude
9 Oct	Balloon (*Cie Aérostieres* 26)	SW Dixmude

14 Oct	Sopwith Camel	
15 Oct	Breguet XIV	Wervicq
19 Oct	SPAD (*Escadrille Spa* 82)	Wyndendale
19 Oct	SPAD (*Escadrille Spa* 82)	Wyndendale
27 Oct	BF 2b (No. 48 Sqn RAF)	

Total victories claimed: 41

CHAPTER NINE

Hauptmann Bruno Loerzer
(1891 – 1960)

Bruno Loerzer was born in Berlin on the 22 January, 1891. On leaving school at the age of seventeen, he became a cadet with the Badisches Infanterie-Regiment Prinz Willhelm Nr. 112. Later he was awarded a place at Military school and after graduating, rejoined his old regiment in January 1913 with the rank of *Leutnant*. It was in the regiment that *Leutnant* Bruno Loerzer met Hermann Göring, the two of them were to become almost inseparable throughout there military careers. Bruno Loerzer soon tired of the infantry and applied for flying school where he was accepted. In July 1914, he started flying training at the flying school at Habsheim, near Mühlhausen and on graduating on the 11 October, was sent to *Flieger-Ersatz-Abteilung* (FEA)3 at Darmstadt for a couple of weeks and then on 3 November to *Flieger-Abteilung* (Fl.Abt.) 25 as a reconnaissance pilot. In the meantime, his close friend Hermann Göring was having problems with the authorities back at the regiment and was on the point of being court-martialled, and on the 13 October he took it in to his head to join his friend Loerzer as his observer. It appears that the regiment was glad to see the back of him and approved his transfer unofficially. It was only out of respect for Göring's father, the former Governor of German South West Africa and the influence of his godfather *Ritter* von Epstein, that they did not pursue the matter. Göring spent two weeks at FEA 3 before being posted to Fl.Abt.25 to join up with his friend Bruno Loerzer. For the next seven months they flew mission after mission, and were awarded the Iron Cross 2nd Class.

Then in April, *General* Erich von Falkenhayn, whose armies were being held back because of the chain of forts in the Verdun area, demanded some good clear photographs of the fortresses. All missions to accomplish this were fruitless, the Loerzer and Göring volunteered for the mission. For the next three days, Loerzer cruised low over the forts sideslipping and weaving, whilst Göring hung over the side of the aircraft taking photographs. Falkenhayn was delighted with the result, so much so in fact that Crown Prince Wilhelm invested Loerzer and Göring with the Iron Cross 1st Class in the field.

Studio portrait of
Oberleutnant *Bruno*
Loerzer

During the next few months the pair of them carried out numerous reconnaissance flights over the enemy lines resulting on 27 April the award of the Knight's Cross with Swords of the Baden Zähringen Lion to Loerzer. It appears that Göring received nothing.

But by the end of June 1915, Bruno Loerzer was getting tired of just carrying out observation and photographic flights and asked to be transferred to a fighter squadron. He was transferred to Fl.Abt. 60 for a couple of weeks and then to FFl.Abt. 203 with its *Eindecker* attachment. (A number of the reconnaissance units had small fighter units attached for escort duties). At the same time his friend Hermann Göring applied to become a pilot and was posted to the flying training school at Freiburg.

On completion of his fighter training he was posted to *Kampfeinsitzer-*

Kommando Jametz (KEK Jametz), where on the 21 March, 1916, he recorded his first victory. It was around this time that Bruno Loerzer was joined by his brother Fritz who had been a pastor before the war. Ten days later he had raised his tally to two, but on 3 April he was badly wounded during a fight with Allied fighters. The wounds kept in hospital for a number of months and it was January 1917 before he was fit to fly again. He briefly returned to his old unit before being given command of *Jasta* 26 and by the end of 1917 his personal tally had risen to twenty. Honours were to bestowed upon him before the year was out, among them the Knight's Cross with Swords of the Hohenzollern House Order. Then on the 12 March he was awarded the *Orden Pour le Mérite* and nine days later given command of *Jagdgeschwader* Nr.III and with it came the Fokker DVII's powered by the BMW engine. This aircraft was inflict heavy casualties on the Allied fighters right up to the end of the war.

Bruno Loerzer with Ernst Udet

Bruno Loerzer still continued to fly with *Jasta* 26, alongside his younger brother Fritz, who had now joined the unit. In the October of 1918, Bruno Loerzer was promoted to *Hauptmann* and by the end of the war had raised his tally of victories to forty-four.

During the second World War, Loerzer rose rapidly through the ranks to *GeneralLeutnant* of the Luftwaffe and awarded the Iron Cross 1st Class and later the Knight's Cross of the Iron Cross. When he was promoted to *Generaloberst*, it was quite obvious to all that his long-term friendship with *Reichsmarschall* Hermann Göring had had a great influence on the appointment. Bruno Loerzer died on the 23 August 1960.

From R-L:Unknown, Loerzer, Noak, Schubert, Crown Prinz, von Zobelitz, von Schaesbieg, Hübner, Unknown

Bruno Loerzer (centre) with fellow pilots from Jasta *26*

Awards

Orden Pour le Mérite
Knight's Cross with Swords of the Royal Hohenzollern House Order
Iron Cross 2nd Class
Iron Cross 1st Class
Knight's Cross Military Karl-Friedrich Merit Order
Knight 2nd Class with Swords Order of the Zähringen Lion
Pilot's Badge – German Army

Victory Log

1916

21 Mar	Farman	Fosse Wood
31 Mar	Aircraft not known	

1917

6 Mar	Nieuport 16 (No. 60 Sqn RFC)	Dannekirch
10 Mar	SPAD VII (*Escadrille Spa* 81)	Altkirch-Carpasch
30 Apr	Aircraft not known	
16 Aug	SPAD (*Escadrille Spa* 3)	Langemarck
15 Sep	Nieuport (No. 1 Sqn RFC)	Bousbecque
20 Sep	SE 5a (No. 60 Sqn RFC)	Gravenstafel
22 Sep	SE 5a (No. 60 Sqn RFC)	Westroosebeke
24 Sep	Sopwith Camel (No. 66 Sqn RFC)	NW Dixmude
26 Sep	Sopwith Camel (No. 70 Sqn RFC)	Gravenstafel
30 Sep	Sopwith Camel (No. 70 Sqn RFC)	Koekuit
5 Oct	SE 5a (No. 56 Sqn RFC)	E Menin
9 Oct	RE 8 (No. 9 Sqn RFC)	Langemarck
12 Oct	DH 4 (No. 57 Sqn RFC)	SE Thielt
15 Oct	BF 2b (No. 22 Sqn RFC)	Aerseele
17 Oct	Sopwith Pup (No. 54 Sqn RFC)	S Nieuport
21 Oct	Sopwith Camel (No. 4 Sqn RNAS)	Wynedaele
27 Oct	Sopwith Camel (No. 70 Sqn RFC)	W Dixmude
30 Oct	Nieuport Scout (No. 1 Sqn RFC)	Westroosebeke

1918

3 Jan	DH 4 (No. 57 Sqn RFC)	SE Gheluvelt
19 Jan	BF 2b (No. 20 Sqn RFC)	S Houthulst Forest
18 Feb	Sopwith Camel (No. 70 Sqn RFC)	Houthulst Forest
23 Mar	Sopwith Camel (No. 70 Sqn RFC)	Beugny
30 May	SPAD VII (*Escadrille Spa* 84)	
13 Jun	SPAD (*Escadrille Spa* 37)	Dommiers
16 Jul	Nieuport 28 (27 Aero Sqn USAS)	Putnay
19 Jul	SPAD XIII (*Escadrille Spa* 156)	Couevres
20 Jul	SPAD XIII (*Escadrille Spa* 62)	Couevres
13 Aug	SE 5a (No. 60 Sqn RFC)	Chaulnes

14 Aug	SE 5a (No. 92 Sqn RFC)	Chaulnes
26 Aug	Sopwith Camel (No. 62 Sqn RFC)	Beugny
29 Aug	Sopwith Camel (No. 43 Sqn RFC)	Cherisy
29 Aug	Sopwith Camel (No. 43 Sqn RFC)	Cherisy
1 Sep	BF 2b (No. 62 Sqn RFC)	Dury
2 Sep	Sopwith Camel (No. 54 Sqn RFC)	Dury
3 Sep	SE 5a (No. 32 Sqn RFC)	Doua
4 Sep	Sopwith Camel (No. 70 Sqn RFC)	Monchecourt
5 Sep	SE 5a (No. 92 Sqn RFC)	Inchy
16 Sep	BF 2b (No. 11 Sqn RFC)	Dourges
16 Sep	SE 5a (No. 84 Sqn RFC)	
22 Sep	Sopwith Camel (17th Aero Sqn USAS)	
26 Sep	Sopwith Camel (No. 203 Sqn RFC)	Cambrai
26 Sep	Sopwith Camel (No. 208 Sqn RFC)	St Quentin

Victories Claimed: 41

CHAPTER TEN

Hauptmann Oswald Boelke
(1891 – 1916)

The son of a schoolteacher, Oswald Boelke was born in Giebichenstein, near Halle in Saxony on the 19 May, 1891, one of six children. Their father ensured that all the children in the family were educated to their full extent which gave them all enquiring minds. This was to become obvious in later years, when Oswald Boelke wrote his famous report on air fighting and tactics. On completing his educaiton, Oswald Boelke decided on a military career, much against the wishes of his family and joined the Prussian Cadet Corps in March 1911 and posted to No. 3 Telegrapher's Battalion at Koblenz. On completion of his initial training, he was posted to the War School at Metz to complete his officer training.

Almost immediately on graduating, Boelke applied for transfer to the German Army Air Service for training as a pilot. In October 1914 he was posted to the flying school in Halberstadt, completing his flying training. His first posting on graduating was to the *Fleugpark* at Trier and two weeks later was posted to his first combat unit – *Flieger-Abteilung* (Fl.Abt.) 13 – near Montmédy to join his older brother Wilhelm who stationed there as an observer. The two brothers joined up and flew reconnaissance missions together over the Argonne region. At the end of October 1914, Boelke received the Iron Cross 2nd Class for his work flying reconnaissance missions.

For the next three months Oswald Boelke continued flying reconnaissance missions and during this time he received the Iron Cross 1st Class. At the beginning of May, Boelke was transferred to *Flieger-Abteilung* (Fl.Abt.) 62 who had recently been equipped with LVG C.1s. Oswald Boelke opened his tally on the 4 July, 1915, when, together with his observer *Leutnant* Heinz von Wühlisch, Boelke was on patrol over Valenciennes and encountered a Morane Parasol. After a short skirmish the Morane Parasol was shot down.

The fearless way that he engaged the enemy aircraft whenever possible, prompted the squadron commander to transfer Boelke on to single-seater fighters. The single-seat Fokker Eindeckers had recently

A youthful looking
Oberleutnant *Oswald*
Boelke in a portrait shot

been assigned to the squadron for the purpose of scouting and protection of the reconnaissance aircraft.

At the beginning of July 1915, Boelcke saved the life of a fourteen year old French boy by diving into a fast flowing river and pulling the young lad to safety, for which he was awarded a Life Saving Medal.

Boelcke claimed his second victim on the 19 August, when, whilst flying in a Fokker Eindecker from Douai, he shot down a Bristol biplane over the Front lines. It was whilst at Douai that he came into contact with Max Immelmann and became good friends. By the end of the year, Boelcke's tally had risen to six for which he was awarded the Knight's

Cross with Swords of the Hohenzollern House Order.

Boelcke shot down three more Allied aircraft in the first two weeks of January 1916, bringing his total to nine and with it came Germany's highest award, the *Orden Pour le Mérite*. and Boelcke was the first fighter pilot to receive it.

As the months went by almost all the communiques to the German High Command contained the name of Boelcke, as he steadily increased his tally. Boelcke became a household name in Germany and was revered by many and by the end of June 1916 he had increased his score to nineteen.

Hauptmann *Oswald Boelke when leader of* Jagdstaffel *2 showing the strains of war and leadership.*

The death of Max Immelmann in June 1916, caused the German High
Command to send Boelcke on an inspection/public relations tour of
Vienna, Budapest, Belgrade and Turkey. They could not afford the loss
of another of their famous fighter pilots and during the long journeys, it
gave Boelcke the chance to think of the German air was progressing. The
result was that Boelcke wrote a paper entitled, 'Air Fighting Tactics' a
collection of his thoughts and ideas and submitted it to the German High
Command. It was to become the 'bible' amongst the German fighter
pilots in the following years.

Oberleutnant *Alfred Keller
(left) talking with*
Hauptmann *Oswald
Boelke*

Boelcke was recalled from his tour at the end of July, promoted to
Hauptmann and given command of *Jasta* 2. This gave Boelcke the
opportunity to choose his own pilots and among them were, Manfred
von Richthofen, Max Muller and Erwin Böhme. Böhme was to play a
significant part in Boelcke's demise later that year. On the 2 September,
Boelcke scored his twentieth victory when he shot down a DH 2 from 37
Squadron, RFC. By the end of the month he had shot down nine more
aircraft and brought his total of claimed vitories to twenty-nine.

Jasta 2 was creating a reputation for itself amongst the Allied pilots, as being one of the most feared in the German Army Air Service. Boelcke continued to wreak havoc amongst the Allies and by the end of October he had shot down a further eleven, bringing his total to forty.

Then on the 28 October whilst on patrol with Manfred von Richthofen and Erwin Böhme, they dived to attack seven enemy aircraft. Boelcke and Böhme flying in tandem chased a British fighter, then just as they closed on it, another British fighter, chased by von Richthofen cut across in front of them. Erwin Böhme immediately reacted and rolled out of the way, at the same time Boelcke rolled across his path and the two aircraft collided. Böhme maintained control of his aircraft, but the damage to Boelcke's Albatros D.II was severe and the aircraft spun out of control toward the ground. The stricken aircraft crashed behind a German gun emplacement where the crew pulled Boelcke from the wreckage. He had died almost immediately, no doubt helped along by the fact that he never wore a helmet or a seat belt.

The body of Oswald Boelke lying beside the wreckage of his aircraft

Awards

Orden Pour le Mérite
Iron Cross 2nd Class
Iron Cross 1st Class
Knight's Cross with Swords of the Royal Hohenzollern House Order
Prussian Life Saving Medal
Knight 1st Class with Swords of the Ducal House Order of Albert the Bear
Knight 2nd Class with Swords of the Ducal House order of Albert the Bear

Anhalt Friedrich Cross 2nd Class
Bavarian Military Merit Order 4th Class with Swords
Bulgarian Bravery Order 4th Class, 2nd Degree
Knight's Cross of the Württemberg Military Merit Order Ottoman Emnpire War Medal
Turkish Imtiaz Medal in Silver with Sabres
Knight's 1st Class with Swords of the Ducal Saxe-Ernestine House Order
Mecklenburg-Strelitz Cross for Distinction in War 2nd Class
Pilot's Badge – German Army
Pilot's Badge – Ottoman Empire

Victory log

1915

4 Jul	Morane Parasol (*Escadrille* MS 15)	Valenciennes
19 Aug	Bristol Biplane	British Front Line
9 Sep	Morane two-seater	French Front Line
25 Sep	Voisin	Pont-a-Mousoo
16 Oct	Voisin B1 (*Escadrille* VB 13)	St. Souplet
30 Oct	Morane two-seater	Tahure

1916

5 Jan	BE 2c (No. 2 Sqn RFC)	Harnes
12 Jan	RE 7 (No. 12 Sqn RFC)	NE Tourcoing
14 Jan	BE 2c (No. 8 Sqn RFC)	Flers
12 Mar	Maurice Farman (*Escadrille* MF 63)	E. Mare
13 Mar	Voisin (*Escadrille* VB 107)	Malincourt
19 Mar	Farman (*Escadrille* MF 19)	Cuissy
21 Mar	Caudron (*Escadrille* C 42)	Fossers Wood
28 Apr	Caudron (*Escadrille* C 53)	Nr. Vaux
1 May	Caudron (Paris Defence Group)	French Front Line
18 May	Caudron (*Escadrille* C 56)	Ripont
21 May	Nieuport (*Escadrille* N 65)	Morte Homme
21 May	Nieuport (*Escadrille* N 65)	Boisse-de-Hesse
27 Jun	Nieuport XI	Douamont
2 Sep	DH 2 (No. 32 Sqn RFC)	NE Thiepval
8 Sep	FE 2b (No. 22 Sqn RFC)	Flers
9 Sep	DH 2 (No. 24 Sqn RFC)	Bapaume
14 Sep	Sopwith 1½ Strutter (No. 70 Sqn RFC)	Hesbecourt
14 Sep	DH 2 (No. 4 Sqn RFC)	Driencourt
15 Sep	Sopwith 1½ Strutter (No. 70 Sqn RFC)	Ypres
15 Sep	Sopwith 1½ Strutter (No. 70 Sqn RFC)	Eterpigny
17 Sep	FE 2b (No. 11 Sqn RFC)	Equancourt
19 Sep	Morane Bullet (No. 60 Sqn RFC)	Grevillers Wood
27 Sep	Martinsyde G 100 (No. 27 Sqn RFC)	Ervillers
1 Oct	DH 2 (No. 32 Sqn RFC)	Flers
7 Oct	Nieuport XII (*Escadrille* F 24)	Amiens

10 Oct	FE 2b (No. 11 Sqn RFC)	Morval
16 Oct	BE 2d (No. 15 Sqn RFC)	Hebuterne
16 Oct	DH 2 (No. 24 Sqn RFC)	N.Beaulencourt
17 Oct	FE 2b (No. 11 Sqn RFC)	W.Beaulencourt
20 Oct	FE 2b (No. 11 Sqn RFC)	W. Agny
22 Oct	Sopwith 1½ Strutter (No. 45 Sqn RFC)	Grevillers Wood
22 Oct	BE 12 (No. 21 Sqn RFC)	SW Bapaume
25 Oct	BE 2c (No. 4 Sqn RFC)	Puisieux-au-Mont
26 Oct	BE 2c (No. 15 Sqn RFC)	SW Serre

Total victories claimed: 40

CHAPTER ELEVEN

Leutnant Franz Büchner
(1898 – 1920)

Franz Büchner was born on the 2 January, 1898, in Leipzig the son of a wealthy businessman. At the onset of war in 1914, Büchner was only sixteen but he joined up immediately with the Royal Saxon Infantry Regiment Nr. 106. The regiment was soon in action in Ypres and Büchner was already showing his leadership qualities even at that early age. In November 1914, he contracted typhoid fever and it wasn't until the February of 1915, that he was able to rejoin his regiment. The regiment moved to the Russian Front in the March and in the August Büchner was commissioned. Moving back to France in the September with his regiment, he was awarded the Iron Cross 2nd Class after being involved in a number of actions. On the 3 April, 1916, he was wounded during a battle on the Western Front and it was while in hospital recuperating, that he decided to ask for a transfer to the German Army Air Service. Büchner was accepted and posted to *Flieger-Abteilung* (A) (Fl.Abt.) 270 for training as a pilot. On graduating in the July of 1916, he was posted to *Jasta* 9 flying single-seater aircraft, but had very little success. In fact he had only one success in the period from July 1916 to August 1917, and that was a Nieuport fighter on the 17 August whilst on patrol over Chappy. *Jasta* 9 at the time was under the command of *Oberleutnant* Kurt Student who, during the Second World War, was to become the General in charge of the German Paratroopers.

In the October, Büchner was posted to *Jasta* 13, one of the *Jastas* under the control of *Jagdgeschwader* 2 which was under the command of *Hauptmann* Rudolf Berthold, and although he still was experiencing difficulties in scoring, his leadership qualities were showing through. Then on the 10 and 11 June he increased his score by shooting down two SPADs whilst on patrol over Vauxaillion. Büchner was appointed Staffelführer of *Jasta* 13 on the 15 June, despite only having scored four victories such was the high regard in which he was held. His scoring rate started to improve rapidly in July and by the end of the month it had risen to twelve. Büchner was awarded the Iron Cross 1st Class in August, followed by the Knight's Cross with Swords of the Hohenzollern House Order and the Saxon Merit Order 2nd Class with Swords. He celebrated these awards shooting down

another eight Allied aircraft, bringing his tally to twenty by the end of August.

On the 12 September, 1918, Büchner shot down a DH 4 from the 8th Aero Squadron, USAS, whilst on patrol over Hattonville. This was one of the first contacts the Germans had had with the Americans and it wasn't going to be the last. Also on that day he shot down another DH 4 and a Breguet XIV bomber. By the end of September Büchner had become the scourge of the US Aero Squadrons and had shot down eighteen of their aircraft, bringing his personal tally to thirteen. For this achievement he was awarded the Military St Heinrich's Order (Saxony's highest award) and the Saxon Albert Order 2nd Class with Swords. But still the coveted award of the *Orden Pour le Mérite* eluded him and Büchner felt a certain amount of resentment considering other recipients had scored no where

Leutnant *Franz Büchner* with his ground crew.

Leutnant *Franz Büchner* with a victors laurel wreath celebrating his 20th victory with fellow pilots.

near the number of 'kills' he had achieved.

October started well for Büchner with the shooting down of a Salmson 2A2 bomber, but on the 10 October a collision with one of his fellow pilots nearly ended his life. Both aircraft had attacked an Allied bomber, when they collided in mid-air. The pilots took to their parachutes and fortunately for them both, the parachutes opened (a rarity in those early days) taking them safely to the ground. Büchner managed to add another two 'kills' to his score before the war ended. At the age of twenty he was awarded Germany's highest award the *Orden Pour le Mérite* on the 25 October, 1918, just days before the Kaiser went into exile. He had finally achieved the ultimate accolade to a top fighter pilot whose tally of

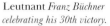

victories at the end of the war numbered forty.

The war may have ended in Europe for the Allies, but it still continued within Germany as the post-war revolutionaries attempted to take over. Büchner continued to fight on with the *Reichwehr*, but on the 18 March 1920 he was shot down by ground fire and killed whilst on a reconnaissance flight near his hometown of Leipzig. Like Rudolf Berthold he was killed by his own countrymen, something the British, French and Americans had failed to do in four years of intensive fighting.

Awards

Orden Pour le Mérite
Knight's Cross of the Saxon Military St Henry Order
Knight 2nd Class with Swords of the Saxon Merit Order
Knight 2nd Class with Swords of the Saxon Albert Order
Knight's Cross with Swords of the Royal Hohenzollern House Order
Iron Cross 2nd Class
Iron Cross 1st Class
Pilot's badge
Wound Badge in Black

Victory log

1917

17 Aug	Nieuport XXIV (*Escadrille* N 92)	SE Chappy
15 Oct	SPAD 7 (No. 9 Sqn RFC)	Margivil

1918

10 Jun	SPAD (*Escadrill Spa* 69)	S Vauxaillion
11 Jun	SPAD VII (*Escadrille Spa* 159)	Méry
28 Jun	SE 5a (No. 56 Sqn RAF)	Fricourt
1 Jul	Sopwith Camel (No. 65 Sqn RAF)	Morlancourt
2 Jul	Sopwith Dolphin (No. 87 sqn RAF)	Contay
7 Jul	Sopwith Camel (No. 209 Sqn RAF) Nr Hamel	
16 Jul	Breguet XIV (*Escadrille Br* 132)	
16 Jul	Breguet XIV (*Escadrille Br* 132)	
19 Jul	SPAD XI (*Escadrille Spa* 53)	
29 Jul	Sopwith Camel (No. 73 Sqn RAF)	Venizel
9 Aug	SPAD 2 (*Escadrille Spa* 289)	Lignieres
10 Aug	BF 2b (No. 11 Sqn RAF)	Laon
11 Aug	Sopwith Camel (No. 54 Sqn RAF)	Roye
11 Aug	SPAD XIII (*Escadrille Spa* 163)	Estrees
14 Aug	Sopwith Camel (No. 46 Sqn RAF)	Chaulnes
19 Aug	DH 9 (No.104 Sqn RAF)	Pertain
20 Aug	SPAD (*Escadrill Spa* 155)	
20 Aug	Breguet XIV (*Escadrille Br* 108)	
12 Sep	DH 4 (50th Aero Sqn, USAS)	N Hattonville
12 Sep	DH 4 (8th Aero Squadron, USAS)	Vieville-en-Haye
12 Sep	Breguet XIV (*Escadrille Br* 132)	Thiacourt
13 Sep	SPAD XIII (*Escadrille Spa* 85)	Allamount
13 Sep	SPAD VII (*Escadrille Spa* 102)	
14 Sep	Breguet (*Escadrille Br* 132)	Mars la Tour
14 Sep	Breguet (*Escadrille Br* 132)	Latour
14 Sep	Breguet (*Escadrille C* 46)	Conflans
15 Sep	SPAD XIII (*Escadrille Spa* 92)	Thiaucourt
15 Sep	SPAD XIII (*Escadrille Br* 132)	Lachausse

17 Sep	Salmson 2A2 (24th Aero Sqn, USAS)	Dampvitoux
18 Sep	SPAD XIII (27th Aero Sqn, USAS)	W. Chambley
18 Sep	SPAD XIII (95th Aero Sqn, USAS)	Dampvitoux
18 Sep	SPAD XIII (11th Aero Sqn, USAS)	Chambley
26 Sep	SPAD XIII (27th Aero Sqn, USAS)	Consenvoye
26 Sep	SPAD XIII (94th Aero Sqn, USAS)	Charpentrie
26 Sep	SPAD XIII (94th Aero Sqn, USAS)	Etreillers
26 Sep	SPAD XIII (1st Aero Sqn USAS)	Gercourt
28 Sep	Salmson 2A2 (88th Aero Sqn USAS)	Nantillois
1 Oct	Salmson 2A2 (1st Aero Sqn USAS)	
21 Oct	Aircraft Unknown.	Argonne
22 Oct	DH 9 (No. 108 Sqn RAF)	Ghent

Total victories claimed: 40

CHAPTER TWELVE

Oberleutnant Lothar Freiherr von Richthofen (1894 – 1922)

Lothar von Richthofen the younger brother of the famous Red Baron – Manfred von Richthofen, was born on 27 September, 1894 on the Richthofen family estate at Breslau. In 1913, just prior to the outbreak of the First World War Lothar von Richthofen was sent for his compulsory military training at *Kriegsschule* in Danzig (Gdansk) Dragoon Regiment. At the outbreak of war he returned he returned to his parent unit the Dragoner-Reg 'von Bredow Nr. 4 at Lüben and was immediately involved in the attack on Belgium. Later his unit was dispatched to the Russian Front to counteract the threat to Eastern Germany from the Russian Army. In the meantime his brother Manfred had transferred to the *Fliegertruppe* (Air Service) and had trained first as an observer then as a fighter pilot.

Determined to follow the example of his elder brother Lothar von Richthofen transferred to the German Air Service in the autumn of 1915. Serving first as an observer with *Kampfgeschwader* (KG)4 he was determined to be a fighter pilot, and after training, gained his pilot's badge in 1916.

On the 10 March, 1917, he had his first operational posting as a pilot to *Jasta* 11 now commanded by his brother Manfred. Flying with *Jasta* 11 he scored his first victory on the 28 March, 1917, when he shot down FE 2b, 7715, of No. 25 Squadron, Royal Flying Corps. Remarkably, his victory total began to increase almost daily. On the 11 April he shot down two aircraft: another two on the 13 April and two more on the 14 April, 1917. By the 30 April he had downed another nine aircraft making his tally for April 1917 fifteen confirmed kills. He was awarded the Iron Cross 1st Class to add to his Iron Cross 2nd Class which he had been awarded when with the cavalry.

The command of *Jasta* 11 was handed over to Lothar von Richthofen by his brother Manfred with a simple handshake. As if to celebrate, Lothar continued his relentless pursuit of Germany's enemies and that same morning an FE 2d of 25 Squadron went down beneath his guns bringing his total to seventeen confirmed victories. On the dark, rainy evening of 7

Studio portrait of Lothar von Richthofen.

May one of the fiercest battles took place between arguably the two top opposing squadrons – *Jasta* 11 and No. 56 Squadron, RFC. During the encounter Lothar von Richthofen's all-red Albatros was attacked by Captain Albert Ball in his SE 5. How the aircraft never collided in the rapidly decreasing light is a mystery, but none did. The battle between Richthofen and Ball was witnessed by Wilhelm Allmenröder, brother of fighter ace Karl Allmenröder and in his report said:

> I thought that they wanted to stop the fight because of the darkness, but then both turned and rushed at each other as if they intended to collide. Lothar dipped under the other aircraft and then both turned and rushed at each other firing all the time. At the third frontal attack, both of them firing their guns, both appeared to dive toward the ground and disappeared.

It turned out later that Lothar von Richthofen's Albatros had been damaged forcing him to land. He himself was uninjured and was back flying the next day. Albert Ball on the other hand, according to eyewitness's, came out of the very low cloud in an inverted position and crashed into the ground and was killed. Richthofen claimed the victory, but experts maintained that there were no injuries to Albert Ball and what damage had been inflicted on his aircraft would not have been enough to cause it to crash. One theory is that Ball, because of the dark, became disoriented after coming out of the clouds in an upside down position and in a shallow dive, and was unable to right the aircraft before hitting the ground. No doubt the debate will go on.

Lothar von Richthofen with his famous brother Manfred von Richthofen.

*Relaxed shot of Lothar von
Richthofen wearing his
leather flying coat.*

On the 10 May Lothar von Richthofen was awarded the Knight's Cross
with Swords of the Hohenzollern House Order. By the 13 May another
seven aircraft were shot down to bring his score of kills to twenty four.
But the 13th proved unlucky for Lothar as he was badly wounded in
combat and hospitalised. The 14 May proved better. Lying in hospital he
was awarded Germany's highest honour for bravery in combat – the
Orden Pour le Mérite. A short five months after the same award to his
brother Manfred – the Red Baron.

On 24 September 1917, Lothar returned to flying duty and took
command of *Jasta* 11. Six weeks later on the 9 November he was back in
combat and shot down a BF 2b of 8 Squadron near Zonnebeke. On the
23 November he added his twenty sixth kill to his score by bringing
down another BF 2b. It was three months into 1918 before he scored
again. On the 11 March he shot down a BF 2b of 62 Squadron followed
the next day by two more BF 2bs.

The next day was the 13 March and again the number proved unlucky for Lothar when he was again severely wounded in combat and had to be sent back to German for medical treatment. Whilst in hospital he was promoted to *Oberleutnant*, he was also awarded the Bavarian Military Merit Order 4th Class with Swords. Returning to *Jasta* 11 on the 19 July be shot down his thirtieth aircraft – a Camel of 73 Squadron on the 25 July. Ten more enemy aircraft went to his credit during August – three of them in one day – the 8th. His final victories came on the 12 August

Lothar von Richthofen sitting on the wing of a Bristol F2 A of No. 48 Squadron, RAF after forcing it down.

when he brought down two Sopwith Camels of 98 and 209 Squadrons,bringing his total to forty confirmed victories. Again he was badly wounded and did not return to combat, but he survived the war only to die in a flying accident on the 4 July 1922.

Awards

Orden Pour le Mérite
Knight's Cross with Swords of the Royal Hohenzollern House Order
Iron Cross 2nd Class
Iron Cross 1st Class
Bavarian Military Merit Order 4th Class with Swords
Hamburg Hanseatic Cross
Ottoman Empire Liakat Medal in Silver
Wound Badge in Silver
Pilot's Badge
Observer's badge

Victory log

1917

28 Mar	FE 2b (No. 25 Sqn RFC)	E Vimy
11 Apr	BF 2a (No. 48 Sqn RFC)	N Fresnes
11 Apr	BE 2e (No. 8 Sqn RFC)	NE Fampoux
13 Apr	RE 8 (No. 59 Sqn RFC)	NE Biache
13 Apr	RE 8 (No. 59 Sqn RFC)	Pelves
14 Apr	Nieuport XXIII (No. 60 Sqn RFC)	E Fouquieres
14 Apr	SPAD VII (No. 19 sqn RFC)	SE Vimy
16 Apr	Nieuport XVII (No. 60 Sqn RFC)	S Rouex
21 Apr	Nieuport XVII (No. 29 Sqn RFC)	SE Vimy
23 Apr	BE 2g (No. 16 Sqn RFC)	N Vimy
26 Apr	BE 2g (No. 16 Sqn RFC)	SE Vimy Ridge
27 Apr	FE 2b (No. 11 Sqn RFC)	Fresnes
29 Apr	SPAD VII (No. 19 Sqn)	Izel
29 Apr	BE 2e (No. 12 Sqn RFC)	NE Monchy
30 Apr	BE 2g (No. 16 Sqn RFC)	SE Vimy
30 Apr	FE 2d (No. 57 Sqn RFC)	Izel
1 May	FE 2d (No. 25 Sqn RFC)	W Acheville
6 May	AWFK 8 No. 2 Sqn RFC)	SE Givenchy
7 May	Nieuport XVII (No. 40 Sqn RFC)	W Biache
7 May	SE 5 (No. 56 Sqn RFC)	Annoeulin
9 May	BF 2b (No. 48 Sqn RFC)	NE Fampoux
10 May	Sopwith Pup (No. 66 Sqn RFC)	S Vitry
11 May	BF 2b (No. 48 Sqn RFC)	Izel
13 May	BF 2e (No. 5 Sqn RFC)	W Fresnoy
9 Nov	BF 2b (No. 8 Sqn RFC)	NW Zonnebeke
23 Nov	BF 2b (No. 56 Sqn RFC)	W Seranvillers

1918

11 Mar	BF 2b (No. 62 Sqn RAF)	N Fresnoy-le-Petit
12 Mar	BF 2b (No. 62 Sqn RAF)	Maretz
12 Mar	BF 2b (No. 62 Sqn RAF)	Clary
25 Jul	Sopwith Camel (No. 73 Sqn RAF)	Fismes
1 Aug	SPAD XIII (*Escadrille Spa* 73)	
1 Aug	SPAD XIII (*Escadrille Spa* 84)	
8 Aug	Sopwith Camel (No. 43 Sqn RAF)	W Peronne
8 Aug	SE 5a (No. 60 Sqn RAF)	
8 Aug	SE 5a (No. 84 Sqn RAF)	Estrees
9 Aug	DH 9 (No. 107 Sqn RAF)	Villers-Carbonnel
9 Aug	DH 9 (No. 107 Sqn RAF)	Foucaucourt
11 Aug	DH 9 (No. 98 Sqn RAF)	
12 Aug	Sopwith Camel (No. 98 Sqn RAF)	NW Peronne
12 Aug	Sopwith Camel (No. 209 Sqn RAF)	NW Misery

Total victories claimed: 40

CHAPTER THIRTEEN

Hauptmann Karl Menckhoff
(1883 – 1948)

Born on 4 April, 1883, at Herford, Westphalia, Karl Menckhoff joined the German Army at the age of twenty in 1903. His time in the army was short lived, within six weeks he was taken ill with acute appendicitis and invalided out. He returned to Herford where he stayed for the next eleven years, then war broke out in 1914. He immediately volunteered and joined the Infantry Regiment No.106 at Leipzig. Such was the demand for men at the time, that his training was a matter of collecting his uniform, cleaning his rifle and heading for the front line at Alsace Lorraine and ultimately the Battle of the Marne. Menckhoff was an aggressive soldier and rapidly made his mark. Toward the end of his first year as a soldier, he was selected for a mission behind the lines dressed in a French uniform, for which he was awarded the Iron Cross 2nd Class. Within months he was seriously wounded during a battle and returned to Herford to recuperate and whilst there was awarded the Iron Cross 1st Class.

His recovery was extremely slow and when finally recovered, was deemed to be unacceptable for infantry duties. Karl Menckhoff immediately applied for flying duties and was accepted. During his training it was discovered that his aggression on the ground was matched by his aggression in the air. He took to flying naturally and was a good pilot, but on the ground his maverick and cavalier attitude toward army discipline and etiquette caused problems. He may have been a good fighter, but he was not a good soldier and it was only the fact that his instructors maintained that his exceptional flying ability outweighed his indifference toward the drillbook and army etiquette, that kept him in the German Air Service. The fact that Germany was in desperate need of pilots also may have had something to do with it.

His first posting was to the Eastern Front where he gained a great deal of flying knowledge but very little combat experience. Early in 1916, he was recalled for duty as an instructor in Russia, but his aggressive nature soon made it clear that he would be far better employed with a fighting squadron. He was posted to Flamars for a

Leutnant *Karl Menckhoff
wearing his* Pour le
Mérite.

special short course in air combat, then early in April 1917, posted to
Jasta 3 in Flanders with a promotion to *Vizefeldwebel*. Within days he
had scored his first victory, a Nieuport XXIII of 29 Squadron, RFC.
Two more had followed by the end of the month and by September he
had raised his tally to twelve.

On 28 September he was shot down and wounded by aircraft from 56
Squadron, RFC. After recovering from his wounds he returned to *Jasta*
3 and threw himself back into the war and by the end of 1917 had raised
his tally to eighteen. In February 1918, after recovering from his
wounds, he was awarded a commission and given command of *Jasta* 72.
He was also awarded the Knight's Cross with Swords of the Royal
Hohenzollern House Order. This was followed on 23 April, 1918, by the
award of the *Orden Pour le Mérite*.

The following four months saw Karl Menckhoff's tally rise to thirty-nine, then three days after his twelfth victory he met his equal when he encountered Lt William Avery of the 95th Aero Squadron, USAS. After a short fight, Menckhoff was forced down behind Allied lines near Chateau Thierry and taken prisoner. After interrogation, he was transferred to Camp Montoire near Orleans where he joined an ever-growing number of pilots from the German Air Service. His impatience was fuelled by his aggression and tired of waiting for repatriation, he escaped on August 23 and headed for Switzerland. One week later he crossed the border into Switzerland and remained there until the end of the war. Seeing the state of Germany after the war, Karl Menckhoff decided to stay in Switzerland and set up in business there. There he remained until his death in 1948.

Leutnant *Karl Menckhoff* *with pilots of* Jasta 72.

Awards

Orden Pour le Mérite
Knight's Cross with Swords of the Royal Hohenzollern House Order
Iron Cross 2nd Class
Iron Cross 1st Class
Pilot's Badge

Victory log

1917

5 Apr	Nieuport XXII (No. 29 Sqn RFC)	Athies
6 Apr	RE 8 (No. 59 Sqn RFC)	Thelus-Rouvroy
30 Apr	Nieuport XVII (No. 209 Sqn RFC)	Cantin

7 May	RE 8	Tilloy
9 May	Sopwith Triplane (No. 8 Sqn RNAS)	Farbus
28 Jul	Sopwith Camel (No. 70 Sqn RFC)	Gravenstafel
26 Aug	SPAD (No. 19 Sqn RFC)	Zonnebeke
26 Aug	RE 8 (No. 9 Sqn RFC)	Langemarck
11 Sep	Sopwith Camel (No. 45 Sqn RFC)	Moorslede
13 Sep	SPAD VII	Zillebeke
14 Sep	SE 5a (No. 56 Sqn RFC)	De Ruiter
25 Sep	SPAD VII (*Escadrille N 85*)	Noordschoote
12 Oct	Sopwith Triplane (No.4 Sqn RFC)	Zonnebeke
12 Oct	RE 8 (No. 1 Sqn RNAS)	Broodseinde
27 Oct	SE 5a (No. 60 sqn RFC)	Belleward
28 Nov	BF 2b	Pilckem
5 Dec	SE 5a (No. 56 Sqn RFC)	Passchendale
29 Dec	SPAD (No. 19 Sqn RFC)	Draaibank

1918

22 Jan	AWFK 8 (No. 35 Sqn RFC)	Draaibank
4 Feb	SE 5a (No. 20 Sqn RFC)	Poelcapelle
1 Apr	Breguet XIV (*Escadrille Br 120*)	Mesnil
6 Apr	Letord L 2 (*Escadrille Sal 10*)	
7 Apr	SPAD XI (*Escadrille Spa 228*)	Montdidier
11 Apr	Nieuport	Belle Assise
22 Apr	SPAD VII (*Gourp Divisions d'Entrainment*)	Montdidier
19 May	SPAD VII (*Escadrille Spa 31*)	
21 May	Breguet XIV (*Escadrille Br 123*)	
31 May	SPAD VII (*Escadrille Spa 57*)	Soissons
1 Jun	Breguet XIV (*Escadrille Br 237*)	
2 Jun	SPAD VII (*Escadrille Spa 112*)	
2 Jun	Sopwith Camel	Foret de Laigue
5 Jun	Breguet XIV (*Escadrille Br 129*)	St Leger
11 Jun	Sopwith Camel (No. 73 Sqn RAF)	Faverolles
15 Jun	SPAD (Escadrille Spa 94)	Rethondes
4 Jul	Sopwith Camel (No. 54 Sqn RAF)	Estrees
15 Jul	SPAD VII (*Escadrille Spa 154*)	Bony
15 Jul	SPAD VII (*Escadrille Spa 154*)	Bony
16 Jul	SPAD VII (*Escadrille Spa 161*)	Reims
19 Jul	SPAD XIII (*Escadrille Spa 84*)	S Mont Voisin

Total victories claimed: 39

CHAPTER FOURTEEN

Leutnant Heinrich Gontermann (1896 – 1917)

Heinrich Gontermann, the son of a cavalry officer, was born on the 25 February, 1896, in Siegen, southern Westphalia. After leaving school Gontermann's future seemed to be destined for the army, then in August 1914 his future was decided for him. He joined the 6th Uhlan Cavalry Regiment in Hanau and after initial training was sent to the front. Within days of arriving his regiment was in action. The following months were hard, but Heinrich Gontermann's leadership qualities started to show themselves. He was wounded in the September, but not seriously and was promoted to *Feldwebel*. Early in the spring of 1915, because of his leadership qualities he was given a field commission to *Leutnant* and was awarded the Iron Cross 2nd Class. He continued to lead his men throughout 1915, then in October he was transferred to the 80th Fusilier Regiment.

This transfer was not exactly what Heinrich Gontermann wanted. For some months previously he had been looking at the newly formed German Army Air Service and applied for a transfer to the service. He was accepted and sent for pilot and observer training. On graduation early in 1916, he was posted to *Kampfstaffel* Tergnier as a reconnaissance pilot flying the Roland C.II. In the spring he was posted again, this time to *Feldflieger-Abteilung* (FFl.Abt.). 25 where he flew both as a pilot and as an observer on AGO C.Is. After nearly a year of flying reconnaissance missions, Gontermann applied for *Jastaschule* and the transfer to a fighter unit. He was accepted and after graduating on the 11 November, 1916, was posted to *Jasta* 5. Within three days he had opened his tally, by shooting down an FE 2b whilst on patrol over Morval.

It wasn't until the March of 1917 that Gontermann scored another victory, although not for the want of trying. On the 5 March he was awarded the Iron Cross 1st Class. Starting on the 6 March he shot down an FE 2b of 57 Squadron, RFC, and by the end of the month had raised his tally to five. During the month of April Gontermann shot down five aircraft and seven balloons, all confirmed and had

Leutnant *Heinrich Gontermann*

raised his total to seventeen and was promoted becoming the *Staffelführer* of *Jasta* 15. Gontermann celebrated his promotion by shooting down a SPAD whilst on patrol over SE Caronne on the 4 May. There was more to celebrate on the 6 May, when he was awarded the Knight's Cross with Swords of the Hohenzollern House Order. Gontermann celebrated this on the 10 May by shooting down another

(Above) Heinrich Gontermann's Fokker Triplane. (Below) The wreckage of Heinrich Gontermann's Fokker Triplane in which he died.

SPAD and a Caudron R4. The following day he shot down another SPAD, then on the 14 May, he was awarded Germany's highest accolade, the *Orden Pour le Mérite* with his score standing at twenty-one. he celebrated the honour by shooting down a balloon on 24 May.

From June until the end of September, Gontermann added seventeen more victories bringing his total to thirty-eight. Eleven of the seventeen victories were observation balloons, four of which were

shot down on the evening of the 19 August within a space of three minutes of each other. On the 2 October, 1917, he shot down a SPAD whilst on patrol over Laon. Then on the 29 October, Gontermann took one of the latest Fokker Triplanes that had just been delivered to the *Jasta* up for a flight test. Minutes later whilst flying above La Neuville airfield, the upper wing of the Fokker Triplane suffered structural failure of the upper wing and the aircraft spun out of control into the ground. Heinrich Gontermann was pulled from the wreckage still alive, but died from his injuries the following day. He was just twenty-one years old.

Leutnant *Heinrich Gontermann in the cockpit of a British FE after he had forced it to land*

Awards

Orden Pour le Mérite
Knight's Cross with Swords of the Royal Hohenzollern House Order
Iron Cross 2nd Class
Iron Cross 1st Class
Pilot's Badge – German Army

Victory log

1916

14 Nov	FE 2b	Morval

1917

6 Mar	FE 2b (No. 57 Sqn RFC)	S Mory
11 Mar	FE 2b (No. 18 Sqn RFC)	S Bapaume
17 Mar	FE 2b (No. 22 Sqn RFC)	St Pierre
24 Mar	Sopwith 1½ Strutter (No. 70 Sqn RFC)	Oisy-le-Verge
25 Mar	Sopwith 1½ Strutter (No. 70 Sqn RFC)	Haplincourt
6 Apr	FE 2b (No. 57 Sqn RFC)	Neuville
8 Apr	Balloon (41 *Cie d'Aerostieres*)	W. St Quentin
13 Apr	FE 2d (No. 57 Sqn RFC)	Vitry
13 Apr	Balloon (55 *Cie d'Aerostieres*)	SE St Quentin
14 Apr	BE 2c (No. 52 Sqn RFC)	Metz-en-Couture
16 Apr	Balloon (Balloon Company 14-14-4)	Manancourt
16 Apr	Balloon (Balloon Company 6-15-4)	Manancourt
22 Apr	Balloon (Balloon Comapny 33-11-3)	Arras
22 Apr	Balloon (Balloon Company 3-13-5)	Arras
23 Apr	RE 8 (No. 12 Sqn RFC)	SE Arras
24 Apr	Sopwith Triplane (No. 8 Sqn RNAS)	Bailleul
26 Apr	Balloon (Balloon Company 8-1-1)	Arras
4 May	SPAD VII (*Escadrille* N 102)	SE Caronne
10 May	SPAD VII (*Escadrille* N 7)	Berry-au-Bac
10 May	Caudron R.4 (*Escadrille* C 46)	Berry-au-Bac
11 May	SPAD 7 (N0. 23 Sqn RFC)	Berry-au-Bac
24 Jun	Balloon (*Cie d'Aerostieres* 65)	Pontavert
27 Jun	Balloon (*Cie d'Aerostieres* 51)	SE Reims
16 Jul	Balloon (*Cie d'Aerostieres* 53)	S Reims
24 Jul	SPAD VII (*Escadrille* N 3)	Staudecken
5 Aug	Nieuport (No. 29 Sqn RFC)	SW Staudecken
9 Aug	Balloon (*Cie d'Aerostieres* 46)	Foret de Hesse
9 Aug	Balloon (*Cie d'Aerostieres* 51)	Foret de Hess
17 Aug	Balloon (*Cie d'Aerostieres* 28)	Aisne
17 Aug	Balloon (*Cie d'Aerostieres* 39)	Aisne
19 Aug	SPAD VII (*Escadrille* N 67)	SW Jouy
19 Aug	Balloon (*Cie Aérostieres* 28)	S Aisne-Tal
19 Aug	Balloon (*Cie Aérostieres* 28)	S Aisne-Tal

19 Aug	Balloon (*Cie Aérostieres* 39)	S Aisne-Tal
19 Aug	Balloon (*Cie Aérostieres* 39)	S Aisne-Tal
15 Sep	Caudron R.4 (*Escadrille* C 46)	Cerny
30 Sep	SPAD VII (*Escadrille* R 46)	Staudecken
30 Sep	Caudron R.11 (*Escadrille* C 46)	NE La Fere
2 Oct	SPAD VII (*Escadrille Spa* 62)	Laon

Total victories claimed: 39

CHAPTER FIFTEEN

Oberleutnant zur See Theodor Osterkamp (1892 – 1975)

Theodor Osterkamp was born in Duren in the Rhineland on 15 April, 1892, the son of a forestry worker. When war was declared Theodor was studying forestry at college and suddenly all around him young men were being conscripted into the army. Rather than wait for his turn to come he chose to enlist in the Imperial German Navy Flying Corps, which he did in August 1914. Initialy he requested to be trained as a pilot, but the need for observers was greater and so he was turned down and assigned to observer school. On the 24 March, 1915, he completed his training and was was posted to the II *Marine Feldflieger-Abteilung*, where for the next two years he flew operational missions along the Belgian coast. It was during this period that his promotion to *Vizeflugmeister* was approved and he was transferred to I. *Marine Feldflieger-Abteilung*. His success was rewarded with the Iron Cross 2nd Class and his being commissioned on 13 July, 1916, to the rank of *Leutnant der Reserves der Matrosenartillerie* (Lieutenant of Reserves of Naval Artillery).

Theo Osterkamp, leaning on his cane, entertaining a British pilot after the latter had been shot down by him.

Osterkamp began to tire of the reconnaissance missions so he decided to look toward becoming a single-seat fighter pilots, who appeared to have excitement surrounding them all the time. He applied for fighter pilot training in February of 1917 and in March he was accepted and began his training, graduating on 14 April. Within days he was posted to *Marine Feldjasta* I and on 30 April opened his score when he shot down a Sopwith Camel whilst on patrol over Oostkerke. A second victim, another Sopwith Triplane from No.10 Squadron RNAS, fell to his guns on 12 May, followed a third on 5

(Above) Osterkamp sitting on the wheel of his Fokker D VIII. (Below) Osterkamp in front of his Fokker D II

June when he shot down a Sopwith Camel from No. 4 Squadron, RNS, over Nieuport. By the end of July 1917, Osterkamp had raised his tally to five and was rewarded with The Iron Cross 1st Class and the Knight's Cross of The Hohenzollern House Order on 20 August. On 24 September whilst on patrol over Westroosbeke he encountered a Spad from *Escadrille Spa* 31 and shot it down bringing his tally to six.

These victories resulted in his promotion to *Oberleutnant* and command of II *Marine Feldjasta* (MFJ.II).

At the end of September 1917 Osterkamp was on a familiarisation flight in one of the new Fokker E.V monoplane when he was jumped by three SPAD VIIs. After a twisting, diving attempt to escape, his aircraft was hit several times forcing him to bale out. Fortunately he landed unhurt behind his own Lines. At the beginning of 1918, Osterkamp spent time reorganising the unit, making it more efficient and this was reflected in the way the victories started to come their way. By the end of July 1918, Osterkamp's personal tally had risen from six to nineteen and by the end of August was standing at twenty-three. For this and other acts of bravery, he received Prussia's highest award, the *Orden Pour le Mérite* on 2 September 1918. His war against the Allies ended in 1918, but he continued to fight in the Baltic area until 1920.

In 1935, Theodor Osterkamp joined the Luftwaffe as it started to rebuild. He was given command of *Jagdfliegerschule* Nr. 1 in 1939, a post he held until the following year when he took over command of *Jagdgeschwader* 51 (JG.51). Almost immediately he was in action against the French and in the months of May and July shot down a total of six Allied fighters, which included three Hurricanes and a Spitfire. For this he was awarded *Ritterkreuz* (the Knight's Cross of The Iron Cross) on the 22 August 1940. He became commander of fighters in Northern France and later in Sicily holding the rank of *GeneralLeutnant*. He also became very critical about the High Command and the way they were operating the war in the air and because of his outspokenness was retired in 1944. It was probably the tremendous respect that the Luftwaffe pilots and ground crews felt for him, that prevented an alternative fate befalling him.

He died in Baden-Baden on 2nd january 1975

Awards

Orden Pour le Mérite
Knight's Cross with Swords of the Royal Hohenzollern House Order
Knight 1st Class with Swords of the Anhalt House Order of Albert the Bear
Iron Cross 2nd Class
Iron Cross 1st Class
Anhalt Friedrich Cross 1st Class
Anhalt Friedrich Cross 2nd Class
Oldenburg Friedrich-August Cross 1st Class
Oldendurg Friedrich-August Cross 2nd Class
Hamburg Hanseatic Cross
Ottoman Empire War Medal
Pilot's Badge (Navy)
Observer's Badge (Navy)
Austro-Hungarian Pilot's badge (Karl Pattern)

Victory log
1917

30 Apr	Nieuport (Belgian *Escadrille* 5me)	Oostkerke
12 May	Sopwith Triplane (No. 10 Sqn RNAS)	Ostende
5 Jun	Sopwith Camel (No. 4 Sqn RNAS)	Nieuport
11 Jul	Sopwith 1 Strutter	N Furnes
12 Jul	SE 5 (No 56 Sqn RFC)	Zandvoorde
24 Sep	SPAD VII (*Escadrille Spa* 31)	W Westroosebeke

1918

16 Mar	Sopwith Camel (No. 3 Sqn RFC)	S.Pervyse

26 Mar	Sopwith Camel (No. 54 Sqn RFC)	Avekapelle
23 Apr	Sopwith Camel (No. 70 Sqn RFC)	Ostende
25 Apr	SPAD VII (*Escadrille Spa* 49)	Pervyse
11 May	Sopwith Camel (No. 213 Sqn RAF)	Breedene
7 Jun	Sopwith Camel (No. 56 Sqn RAF)	Rampskapelle
12 Jun	DH 4 (No.202 Sqn RAF)	SW Pervyse
27 Jun	Sopwith Camel (No. 213 Sqn RAF)	Wenduyne
28 Jun	Sopwith Camel (No. 56 Sqn RAF)	SW Blankartsee
29 Jun	BF2b (No. 213 Sqn RAF)	SE Pervyse
20 Jul	Sopwith Camel (17th Aero Sqn USAS)	E. Nieuport
25 Jul	Sopwith Camel (Belgian *Escadrille* 11)	S. Nieuport
29 Jul	DH 4 (No. 202 Sqn RAF)	S Gudekapelle
12 Aug	Sopwith Camel (17th Aero Sqn USAS)	Ramskapelle
16 Aug	DH 9 (No. 218 Sqn RAF)	Blankenberghe
21 Aug	DH 9 (No. 202 Sqn RAF)	Breedene
23 Aug	Sopwith Camel (17th Aero Sqn USAS)	Pervyse
16 Sep	Sopwith Camel (No. 210 Sqn RAF)	Coxyde
16 Sep	Sopwith Camel (No. 210 Sqn RAF)	Coxyde
20 Sep	Sopwith Camel (No. 204 Sqn RAF)	Praet Bosch
28 Sep	Sopwith Camel (No. 204 Sqn RAF)	Woumen
28 Sep	Breguet XIV (Belgian *Escadrille* 6)	Pierkenshock
29 Sep	Breguet XIV (*Escadrille Spa* 34)	W Zarren

Total victories claimed: 38

CHAPTER SIXTEEN

Leutnant Max Ritter von Müller (1887 – 1918)

*L*eutnant Max Ritter von Müller was an enigma. He was the first man in the German military to be promoted from the ranks and given a Regular Army Commission instead of the usual Reserve Commission. He was also raised to the nobility by his home state, albeit posthumously.

Born on the 1 January, 1887, in Rottenburg, Lower Bavaria, of a ordinary workng class family, Max Müller rose from obscurity to become one of Germany's top fighter aces of the First World War.

On leaving school Müller became an apprentice to a locksmith, but his thoughts and dreams were elswhere, so in 1912 he joined the army as driver where it was discovered that he had a natural mechanical aptitude. His skill as a mechanic and a driver soon came to the notice of his superiors and he was assigned as chauffeur to the Bavarian War Minister. It was while driving the War Minister around the various aviaiton extablishments that Max Müller had acquired an interest in aviation. It is said that every time he opened the door for the minister, he asked to be transferred to the small Bavarian Air Service. His persistence was rewarded, more one feels out of a need to get rid of him, than one of a desire to help him.

He was posted to the Army flying school at Schleissheim on 1 December, 1913. After four months of training, he qualified as a pilot and received his certificate but it wasn't until the 4 April, 1914, that he received his Bavarian Pilot's Badge. This was the practice at the time, that after a pilot or observer had completed their training, they were assigned to a unit and, after proving themselves under combat conditions, only then were they awarded their aviators badge. With the situation worsening by the day, the German Army was mobilised and this included the air service. Müller was posted to *Flieger-Abteilung* (Fl.Abt.) 1b as a reconnaissance pilot and carried out several missions. Müller was only one of a handful of non-commissioned officers who were awarded their pilot's badge at the beginning of the war.

On 18 August, 1914, just two weeks after the start of the war, Müller, together with his observer Peter Müller (no relation), was flying an Otto

aircraft on a dangerous reconnaissance mission over enemy lines when they were attacked by a French Farman and shot down. Fortunately Max Müller managed to get the crippled aircraft down on German held territory. Ground troops rushed to extricate them both from the wreckage and it was discovered the Max Müller had broke both his legs in the impact. Peter Müller escaped with just minor injuries. After eight weeks in hospital Max Müller made a full recovery and was soon back in the air, this time with the rank of *Offizier-Stellvertreter*. Then for flying an extremely dangerous photographic mission on the 13 December, 1915, he was awarded the Bavarian Bravery Medal in Silver.

By May the following year he had made over 160 missions as a reconnaissance pilot and had been awarded the Iron Cross 1st and 2nd Class and the Bavarian Military Merit Cross 3rd Class with Crown and Swords. He was now one of the most experienced reconnaissance pilots in the German Army Air Service, but he wanted more, so he applied for a transfer to a fighter squadron. He was transferred to single-seater training at Mannheim, where on the 18 May, 1916, after graduating, was posted to *Kampfeinsitzer-Kommando* B (KeK B), which was attached to *Flieger-Abteilung* (Fl.Abt.) 32.

Just a few weeks later Kek B was redesignated *Abwehrkommando Nord* and equipped with the new Fokker Eindecker Scout. One of Müller first assignments was to fly protection for the two-seater reconnaissance aircraft when they undertook their photo-reconnaissance missions. Max Müller remained at *Abwehrkommando Nord* until the end of August 1916, when he was posted to *Jasta* 2 which was under the command of the legendary Oswald Boelcke. His experience soon helped him settle into the squadron and on the 10 October he scored his first victory, when he shot down a DH 2 of 24 Squadron RFC. A second followed ten days later and by the end of the year his tally had risen to five. The formation of the new *Jasta* 28, under

Leutnant *Max Müller standing in front of his Albatros.*

the command of *Oberleutnant* Rudolf Lang, prompted the move of a   Leutnant *Max Müller*
number of experienced pilots including Max Müller and *Leutnant* Ray, to   *talking with his mechanic.*
form the backbone of the *Jasta.*

When Lang was eventually replaced his place was taken by *Leutnant* Karl-
Emil Schäfer from *Jasta* 11, even though Müller would have been the
obvious choice. The problem was that Max Müller was not an officer and
only officers could command. By the end of May, Müller's tally had risen to
thirteen making him the top scoring fighter pilot in the *Jasta*, in fact he was
the top scoring non-commissioned officer in the *Luftstreitkräfte* (Air Service).

Karl-Emil Schäfer was shot down and killed on 5 June, 1917, and was
replaced five days later by *Oberleutnant* Otto Hartmann from *Schusta* 3.
During the five-day transition period Müller shot down a further three
aircraft taking his total to eighteen. For his exploits Max Müller was
awarded the Gold Military Merit Medal by the King of Württemberg.

On the 26 August the unprecedented step of promoting Max Müller
to a *Leutnant* in the regular army was taken. Usually these promotions
were in the reserve but this was the first time promotion into the regular
army had ever occurred.

Müller grew from strength to strength and by the end of September
1917 had raised his tally to twenty-seven and with it came the *Orden
Pour le Mérite* making him the most decorated pilot, next to Manfred
von Richthofen, in the German Army Air Service. A well earned leave
resulted in him asking to rejoin his old squadron *Jasta* 2, also known
as *Jasta* Boelcke, to assist his old friend Erwin Böhme in bringing it
into shape. His request was granted and he was posted to *Jasta* 2 on
the 3 November, 1917. On the 6 January, 1918, following the death of
the commanding officer *Leutnant* Walter von Bülow and with his own

tally standing at thirty-six, he took over command of *Jasta* 2. Three days later whilst on patrol over Moorslede, he and his patrol attacked an RE 8 of 21 Squadron, RFC. As he did so, two SE 5as, flown by two very experienced fighter pilots, Captains F O Soden and R L Childlaw-Roberts, jumped him at the same time from above and behind. Müller's aircraft reeled from the assault and spiralling towards the ground, burst into flames. As the flames reached the cockpit, Müller, who was not wearing a parachute, jumped to his death rather than be burnt alive.

After the war a posthumously awarded Knight's Cross of the Military Max-Joseph Order, conferred a knighthood (*Ritter*) on *Leutnant* Max Müller, the man from humble beginnings, the award being backdated to the 11 November, 1917.

Leutnant Max Ritter von Müller was 31 years old.

Awards

Orden Pour le Mérite
Member's Cross with Swords of the Royal Hohenzollern House Order
Knight's Cross of the Military Max-Joseph Order
Bavarian Military Merit Order 4th Class with Swords
Bavarian Bravery Medal in Gold
Bavarian Bravery Medal in Silver
Bavarian Military Merit Cross 3rd Class with Crown and Swords
Iron Cross 2nd Class
Iron Cross 1st Class
Württemberg Military Merit Medal in Gold
Bavarian Prinzregent Luitpold Medal in Bronze
Bavarian Long Service Distinction 3rd Class
Pilot's Badge – Bavaria

(Max von Müller was the only aviator in World War One to hold both the Bavarian Bravery Medal in Gold and Silver).

Victory log

1916

10 Oct	DH 2 (No. 24 Sqn RFC)	Mory-Vraucourt
20 Oct	BE12 (No. 21 Sqn RFC)	SW Grevillers Wood
3 Nov	FE 2b (No. 22 Sqn RFC)	Haplincourt
16 Nov	BE 2c (No. 7 Sqn RFC)	NE Fleurs
27 Nov	Nieuport XVII (No. 60 Sqn RFC)	Hebuterne

1917

7 Apr	FE 2d (No. 20 Sqn RFC)	Ploegsteert Wood
30 Apr	Sopwith 1½ Strutter (No. 45 Sqn RFC)	E Armentieres
2 May	BE 2e (No. 12 Sqn RFC)	Ploegstreert Wood
7 May	FE 2d (No. 20 Sqn RFC)	Boesinghe

12 May	RE 8 (No. 53 Sqn RFC)	Hollebeke
23 May	FE 2d (No. 20 Sqn RFC)	Houthem-Warneton
24 May	Nieuport XXIII (*Escadrille* N 92)	St Eloi
27 May	Sopwith 1½ Strutter (No. 45 Sqn RFC)	NE Ypres
3 Jun	Sopwith 1½ Strutter (No. 45 Sqn RFC)	Quesnoy
7 Jun	SPAD (No. 23 Sqn RFC)	Comines-Warneton
7 Jun	Sopwith Pup (No. 46 Sqn RFC)	SE Roulers
8 Jun	Sopwith Triplane (No. 1 Sqn RNAS)	Quesnoy
20 Jun	RE 8	Armentieres
28 Jul	Sopwith 1½ Strutter (No. 45 Sqn RFC)	NE Ploegsteert
10 Aug	SPAD (No. 23 Sqn RFC)	Godshuis
10 Aug	DH 4 (No. 57 Sqn RFC)	Inglemunster
17 Aug	SE 5 (No. 56 Sqn RFC)	NE Quesnoy
19 Aug	SPAD VII (*Escadrille* N. 15)	Zillebeke Lake
19 Aug	Nieuport XIV No. 1 Sqn RFC)	Menin
21 Aug	Martinsyde G.100 (No. 27 Sqn RFC)	Douvrin
21 Aug	DH 4 (No. 57 Sqn RFC)	Ledeghem
11 Sep	Sopwith Camel (No. 70 Sqn RFC)	W Houthulst Forest
22 Oct	Sopwith Pup (No. 54 Sqn RFC)	W Beerst
22 Oct	Sopwith Pup (No. 54 Sqn RFC)	W Beerst
7 Nov	SPAD VII (*Escadrille* N 31	SW St Julien
11 Nov	DH 5 (No. 32 Sqn RFC)	Wieltje
29 Nov	DH 5 (No. 68 Sqn AFC)	Schap Baillie
2 Dec	DH 4 (No. 57 Sqn RFC)	NW Menin
5 Dec	SE 5a (No. 56 Sqn RFC)	SW Poelcapelle
7 Dec	SPAD (No. 19 Sqn RFC)	Moorslede
16 Dec	Sopwith Camel	W Passchendale

Total victories claimed: 38

CHAPTER SEVENTEEN

Leutnant Julius Buckler
(1894 – 1960)

Born in Mainz on 28 March, 1894, Julius Buckler, was an exceptionally bright schoolboy with aspirations of being an architect. At the age of fifteen he went to work for a short time in the design office of Anthony Fokker, the Dutch aircraft builder and designer, but events at home resulted in him joining the army. Buckler joined the Infantrie-Liebregiment Grossherzogin (3.Ilessisches) Nr. 117 (Infantry Life Regiment Nr.117) in 1913, just as the war clouds were starting to gather. Julius Buckler and his regiment were in action on the Western Front within days of the outbreak of war and in less than three weeks, for meritorious service, he had received the Iron Cross 2nd Class. In August 1914 during one particularly fierce battle he was badly wounded, and after being released from hospital in October 1914, was deemed to be unfit for army service. But Buckler, despite having been involved in some of the heaviest fighting and suffered some terrible injuries, wanted to get back to the heart of the fighting.

Realising that he would be unable to get back into the army, Buckler applied in November 1914, for flying duties and was accepted for training as an observer. He joined *Flieger-Ersatz-Abteilung* (FEA).6 in Grossenhain two weeks later and after only four weeks instruction, passed his flight exams and was granted his certificate. His natural aptitude and ability made him the perfect candidate to teach others, so Buckler was ordered to remain at FEA.6 as an instructor. After spending just over six months teaching at FEA.6, he was posted to *Flieger-Abteilung* (A) (Fl.Abt.(A)). 209 as an observer. Buckler spent nearly a year with Fl.Abt (A).209, in which he was awarded the Iron Cross 1st Class, flying missions as a spotter for the artillery.

Buckler soon became dissatisfied with his role as an observer and applied for pilot training. He was accepted as sent to *Jastaschule* 1 for training and on graduating Buckler received a telegram asking him if he would like to join the newly formed *Jasta* 17. Realising that this was his opportunity to fly the single-seater fighters he had always wanted to, he accepted and was posted to *Jasta* 17 with the rank of *Vizefeldwebel* and

almost immediately was in action over Verdun. The pilots of the newly formed *Jasta*, among them were Hermann Göring, Stephen Kirmaier and Bruno and Fritz Loerzer, spent the first few weeks familiarising themselves with their Fokker D-Type aircraft. Initially there were three to four pilots to each aircraft, such was the shortage of fighter aircraft at the time, but gradually the strength of the *Jasta's* aircraft was increased.

On the 17 December Buckler opened his tally by shooting down a twin-engined Caudron whilst on patrol over the Verdun battlefield. He had espied a German two-seater aircraft circling the ruins of Fort Douaumont, which the French had recently re-taken, and instantly thought that it might have come from his old *Abteilung* – Fl.Abt.(A) 209. As he started to descend to confirm this he spotted a twin-engined Caudron stalking it. On his first pass he missed the French aircraft completely, resulting in the French pilot engaging him and ignoring the two-seat reconnaissance aircraft. After a short skirmish Buckler shot the Caudron down and watched it plunge into the ground. On his return he reported to his commanding officer *Rittmeister* Anton von Brederlow, claiming the victory. Word came back from the reconnaissance aircraft of confirmation and the *Jasta* 17's first victory was notched up.

On Christmas Day, Buckler was sent on a mission to attack a French observation balloon seen floating over Pont-a-Mousson. Taking off in his Albatros D.II he had made sure that his guns had been armed with incendiary ammunition and making sure that he had a permit saying that he was on a mission to attack a balloon (it was a general acceptance that any flier caught by the enemy with incendiary bullets without such a permit would be shot). As he approached the balloon he opened fire, but although he seemed to be striking the balloon it did not explode.

Leutnant *Julius Buckler* *after having been awarded his* Pour le Mérite.

Suddenly he came under attack from three French fighters and Buckler decided that discretion was the better part of valour, and raced back toward his own lines. Just as approached the German lines a bullet from one of his pursuers hit his engine causing it to seize up. Buckler managed to glide over the lines and crash landed close to an army camp. He was given a Christmas breakfast and then a lift back to his *Jasta*.

He added two more French Caudrons on the 14 and 15 February to his tally and brought his score to three. By the end of April he had raised his score to six. Then, whilst on flight back to *Jastaschule* 1 in May 1917, he was attacked by three French fighters and shot down. Buckler himself remembered nothing about the incident save for coming round briefly lying beside the wreckage of his aircraft, then coming round in hospital. He returned to his *Jasta* seven days later and one week after that was back flying.

Vzfw. *Julius Buckler (second from right) with pilots from* Jasta *1 in Palestine.*

Then on 17 July, 1917, his luck ran out whilst on patrol over Keyem. Buckler had continued to score steadily up to this point, but then his flight ran into a patrol of Sopwith Camels and Pups. After shooting down one Sopwith Pup, Buckler was wounded in a fight with another, but he managed to break away and return to his field. Then on the 12 August, 1917, he was again shot and wounded in a tussle with a Sopwith Camel but again managed to break away and return to his field.

On the 18 November after his twenty-fifth victory, he was promoted to *Leutnant* and awarded the Golden Military Merit Cross. He celebrated this by shooting down an RE 8 from No. 21 Squadron, RFC, on the 15 November, followed by two balloons and an RE 8 on the 18 November. Then on the 30 November, 1917, after being attacked by Allied fighters, he was shot down, and survived a terrifying plummet to the ground from almost 800 metres. His injuries, considering the fall, were extremely light, two broken arms and numerous bruises. His score at this time stood at thirty and whilst he was in hospital he was visited by *General der Kavallerie* Georg von der Marwitz, *Oberbefehlschaber* of the German Second Army who awarded him Germany's highest award on the 4 December, 1917 – the *Orden Pour le Mérite*.

At the beginning of April 1918, Buckler returned to *Jasta* 17 and was soon back in action. His thirty-first victim fell to his guns on 16 April when shot down a Breguet XIV whilst on patrol over Vaux and on the another Breguet XIV five days later whilst over Mareuil. Buckler was wounded again on the 6 May, this time in the ankle. It was a wound that was to put him in hospital for nearly eight weeks and was to win him the award of a Golden Wound Badge – it was his fifth wound. At the beginning of July he returned to *Jasta* 17 and fortunately the air war settled down to a period of inactivity. Then on 22 September, 1918, he was made *Staffelführer* a post he held until the end of the war. His tally at the end of hostilities stood at thirty-six.

During the Second World War, Julius Buckler served with training squadrons of the Luftwaffe. He died in Berlin on the 23 May, 1960, one of the few World War One pilots to make it through two world wars.

Awards

Orden Pour le Mérite
Golden Military Merit Cross
Silver Military Merit Cross
Saxon Friedrich August Medal in Silver
Iron Cross 1st Class
Iron Cross 2nd Class
Hesse General Honour Decoration
Hamburg Hanseatic Cross
Wound Badge in Gold
Pilot's Badge – German Army

Victory log

1916

17 Dec	Caudron G4 (C 74)	Bras

1917

14 Feb	Caudron G4 (GDE)	W. Facq Wood
15 Feb	Caudron G4 (GDE)	Pont-a-Masson
15 Apr	SPAD VII (Escadrille N. 3)	Prouvais
16 Apr	Nieuport XXIII (Escadrille N. 83)	Barry-au-Bac
26 Apr	Balloon (No. 36 Cie)	Boise de Genicourt
6 May	SPAD VII (Escadrille N. 69)	Pont-a-Vert
12 May	Nieuport XXIV (Escadrille N. 75)	La Malmaison

11 Jul	Sopwith Triplane (No. 10 Sqn RNAS)	SE Zillebeke
13 Jul	FE 2d (No. 11 Sqn RFC)	Stuivekenskerke
14 Jul	BE 2f (No. 9 Sqn RNAS)	Leffinghe
17 Jul	Sopwith Pup (No. 54 Sqn RFC)	Keyem
9 Aug	Sopwith Camel (No. 9 Sqn RNAS)	SE Nieuport
11 Aug	RE 8 (No. 52 Sqn RFC)	W Spermalie
29 Sep	DH 5 (No. 41 Sqn RFC)	Fleubair
30 Sep	Sopwith Camel (F 55)	Lens-Arras
11 Oct	RE 8 (No. 5 Sqn RFC)	Rodincourt
11 Oct	Sopwith Camel (No. 9 Sqn RNAS)	Armentieres
17 Oct	BF 2b (No. 20 Sqn.RFC)	Rocourt
24 Oct	RE 8 (No. 16 Sqn.RFC)	Mericourt
28 Oct	RE 8 (No. 16 Sqn.RFC)	Mont St.Eloi
29 Oct	Balloon (Balloon Company 20-1-1)	Neuville
29 Oct	Nieuport Scout (No. 1 Sqn RFC)	E Houthen
31 Oct	AWFK 8 (No. 10 Sqn RFC)	La Basse
31 Oct	Balloon(Balloon Company 42-4-1)	Laventie
12 Nov	RE 8 (No. 6 Sqn. RFC)	Oostkerke
15 Nov	RE 8 (No. 21 Sqn.RFC)	Ypres
18 Nov	Balloon(Balloon Company 36-17-2)	Ypres
18 Nov	Balloon	Dickebusch
18 Nov	RE 8 (No. 9 Sqn RFC)	Bixschoote
29 Nov	Balloon (Balloon Company 31-18-3)	Bapaume

1918

16 Apr	Breguet XIV(Sal 225)	Vaux
21 Apr	Breguet XIV(Br 220)	Mareuil
3 May	Balloon	Tricot
5 Oct	Salmson 2A2 (Sal 27)	
24 Oct	Breguet XIV (Br 257)	Mery
30 Oct	EA Claimed	
8 Nov	RE 8 (No. 53 Sqn RFC)	

Total victories claimed: 38

CHAPTER EIGHTEEN

Leutnant Gustav Dörr
(1887 – 1928)

Born on 5 October, 1887, Gustav Dörr was one of a number of high scoring fighter pilots who was never awarded the prestigious Prussian *Orden Pour le Mérite*. His victories totalled thirty-five and he had been nominated for the prestigious order but the Kaiser abdicated and the war had ended before it could be awarded.

Gustav Dörr joined the 176th Infantry Regiment in September 1908 and was with the regiment with the rank of *Unteroffizier* when the war started. The war was only a couple of months old when, on the 20 August, 1914, he was wounded during a battle against the French. On returning to the regiment in November he was once again in the thick of the fighting and on 17 February, 1915, was wounded again. It was to be May before he was fit enough to return to the Front and it was whilst in hospital that he saw a notice asking for volunteers to join the German Air Service and having had enough of living in mud and being shot at, he applied for a transfer.

Two months later, in the July, Dörr was transferred to the German Air Service and sent to the flying school at Döberitz. After completing his initial training he was sent to *Flieger-Ersatz-Abteilung* 3 at Gotha to complete his training. On graduating he was posted to *Armee-Flugpark* B on the Western Front before being assigned on 18 March, 1916, to *Flieger-Abteilung* (Fl.Abt.) 68. On 7 April Gustav Dörr was awarded the Iron Cross 2nd Class and ten days later the Iron Cross 1st Class. Dörr celebrated the awards by shooting his first victim, a Sopwith 1½ Strutter whilst on patrol over Verdun. The short period in time between the 2nd and 1st Class awards was probably because the 2nd Class had been recommended much earlier when Dörr was with the infantry and had taken much longer than anticipated in coming through.

Then one month later, at the beginning of May, he was transferred to *Flieger-Abteilung* (Fl.Abt.)6 which at the end of May was redesignated *Flieger-Abteilung* (A) (Fl.Abt.)257. During the next few months Dörr and his observer *Leutnant* Hans Bohn carried a number of reconnaissance missions over the Front line, then in June 1917, they were attacked by

fighters during which his observer was killed and Dörr suffered serious injuries when the aircraft crash landed from a height of 4,000 feet. Dörr suffered serious injuries to his face, breaking his jaw in six places.

On returning to Fl.Abt. 257 in September, Dörr was transferred to *Flieger-Ersatz-Abteilung* (FEA) 1 at Altenburg testing single-seater aircraft. The following five months were like a holiday for Gustav Dörr, but he craved for the excitement of battle, so in February 1918 he was transferred to *Jagdstaffel* (*Jasta*) 45.

On 17 March 1918 he scored his first victory when he shot down a Sopwith 1½ Strutter over Verdun followed by a SPAD VII and Breuget XIV in consecutive months. It was during the latter engagement that he himself was shot up by another Breguet and was lucky to escape after his aircraft caught fire. He managed to land the aircraft and escape with minor burns.

Informal shot of Gustav Dörr.

By the end of August he had raised his tally to twenty-three and was awarded the Golden Military Merit Cross, the highest Prussian award that could be given to an NCO. The following month, after he had added another five to his tally, his efforts were recognised when he was promoted to *Leutnant*. He was also recommended for the *Orden Pour le Mérite* by *Hauptmann* Hugo Sperrle, *Kommandeur der Flieger der* 7. Armee, but the application never made its way through the bureaucratic maze before the Armistice came and the war was over.

Gustav Dörr had raised his tally to thirty-five by the end of the war and was killed in a flying accident in 1928.

Awards

Golden Military Merit Cross
Iron Cross 2nd Class
Iron Cross 1st Class

Wound Badge in Black
Pilot's Badge – German Army

Victory log

1918

17 Mar	Sopwith 1¹/₂ Strutter	Verdun
11 Apr	SPAD VII (*Escadrille Spa* 163)	Tracy le Mont
28 May	Breguet XIV	Vendeuil
12 Jun	SPAD XI (*Escadrille Spa* 266)	Haraumont
28 Jun	SPAD XIII (*Escadrille Spa* 159)	Villers-Cotterets
28 Jun	SPAD VII (*Escadrille Spa* 159)	Villers-Cotterets
5 Jul	Breguet XIV	Brumetz
8 Jul	Breguet XIV (*Escadrille* Br 224)	Villers-Cotterets
15 Jul	SPAD VII (*Escadrille Spa* 154)	Comblizy
15 Jul	Breguet XIV (*Escadrille Br* 234)	Comblizy
18 Jul	SPAD XIII (*Escadrille Spa* 82)	Pernant
18 Jul	Breguet XIV (*Escadrille Br* 104)	Montigny
21 Jul	SPAD 2 (*Escadrille Spa* 77)	Neuilly
24 Jul	SPAD XIII (*Escadrille Spa* 99)	Pernant
25 Jul	Breguet XIV (*Escadrille Br* 219)	La Croix
29 Jul	Breguet XIV (*Escadrille Br* 216)	Fere-en-Tardenois
30 Jul	SPAD VII (*Escadrille Spa* 83)	Coincy
1 Aug	Nieuport 28 (27th Sqn USAS)	Bruyeres
4 Aug	Breguet XIV (*Escadrille Br* 44)	Nampteil
11 Aug	Breguet XIV (*Escadrille Br* 108)	Braisne
21 Aug.	SPAD XIII (*Escadrille Spa* 23)	Rosnay
21 Aug	SPAD XIII (*Escadrille Spa* 160)	Rosnay
24 Aug	Salmson 2A2 (*Escadrille Sal* 18)	Vezaponin
2 Sep	SPAD XI (*Escadrille Spa* 20)	Ormes
2 Sep	SPAD XI (*Escadrille Spa* 20)	Reims
4 Sep	SPAD VII (*Escadrille Spa* 83)	N Fismes
14 Sep	SPAD XI (*Escadrille Sal* 280)	Blanzy
16 Sep	SPAD VII (*Escadrille Spa* 12)	Fismes
24 Sep	SPAD VII (*Escadrille Spa* 462)	Soissons
26 Sep	SPAD XI (*Escadrille Spa* 265)	Fismes
3 Oct	Salmson 2A2 (*Escadrille Sal* 106)	Coucy le Chateau
5 Oct	Salmson 2A2 (*Escadrille Sal* 264)	Brimont
9 Oct	Breguet XIV (*Escadrille Br* 29)	Coucy le Chateau
27 Oct	SPAD XI (*Escadrille Spa* 90)	Amifontaine
30 Oct	Salmson 2A2 (*Escadrille Sal* 267)	Missy

Total victories claimed: 35

CHAPTER NINETEEN

Hauptmann Eduard Ritter von Schleich – 'The Black Knight' (1888 – 1945)

Unlike the majority of the pilots covered in this book, almost nothing is known of the early life of Eduard Schleich who was born in Munich, Bavaria, on the 9 August, 1888. He first came to prominence when his military career began in 1908, and he joined the 11th Bavarian Infantry Regiment. He rapidly climbed the promotion ladder and within the first year had reached the rank of Colour Sergeant by the age of twenty and the following year was accepted as a *Fahnrich* (Cadet). He received his commission as *Leutnant* two years later and placed on the reserve list. At the outbreak of war he was called up to join his old regiment and within months was in the thick of the action. During one particularly fierce battle on the 25 August, 1914, when the British Army retreated from Mons, he was severely wounded and returned to Munich to recuperate and convalesce.

It was while convalescing that the thought of returning to the Front and becoming cannon fodder prompted him to decided upon a career change and he applied to be transferred to the German Air Service. He was accepted and in May 1915, posted to Flieger-Ersatz-Abteilung (FEA) 1 at Schleissheim for training. On the 11 September, 1915, on completion of his flying training, he was awarded his Bavarian pilot's badge. It is important to note that it was the award of the Bavarian pilot's badge that was to be the cause of certain problems later.

His first posting was to *Feldflieger-Abteilung* (FFl.Abt.)2b in the October of 1915 and after a number of reconnaissance flights, was badly wounded once again during an encounter with Allied fighters in February 1916. In September 1916, after recuperating instead of being returned to his operational unit, he was in command of *Fliegerschule* I, where he became a flying instructor. Early in February 1917, he was transferred to a Bavarian escort unit *Schutzstaffel* 28b as its commanding officer. The elation didn't last long and he soon became bored sitting behind a desk. Within weeks he had written

Hauptmann *Ritter von Schleich.*

numerous letters to the *Kommandeur der Flieger* (Kofl) headquarters requesting that he be transferred to a single-seater fighter unit. There are a couple of stories how his transfer came about, one was that because of the shortage of aircraft he was unable to lead his unit, but had to 'fly' a desk and that was not what he wanted, the other was that his unit had captured a Nieuport Scout intact and Schleich, after flying it, had become enamoured with the idea of flying a single-seater.

Even though he had been an instructor, he was posted to fighter training school at Famars, near Valenciennes, but his instructor, *Leutnant* Böhme, announced after two weeks instruction, that he could teach him no more and suggested that he posted to a fighter unit.

His first posting was to *Jasta* 21 as deputy leader on the 21 May, 1917, with the rank of *Oberleutnant*. Within a day of arriving he was given command of the squadron without having scored a single victory, when the leader, *Hauptmann* Schlieben, took up his new post as a staff officer with *Idflieg*. Schleich resolved the problem four days later by scoring his first victory on the 25 May, when, whilst on patrol over Moronvillers, he shot down a SPAD VII.

His second victory came on the 17 June, a Sopwith $1^1/_2$ Strutter, and he was given command of the squadron permanently. This was followed by two more, a French Caudron and an observation balloon. During this month the *Jasta* lost a couple of their up and coming young pilots and as a mark of respect to them Schleich had his Albatros painted all-over black. This was to result in him being dubbed 'The Black Knight'.

Eduard Ritter von Schleich with two of his fellow pilots

In the following four months Schleich and raised his tally to twenty-five, but his command came under attack for the lack of results from his other pilots. After one escapade concerning three of his pilots, which got him a severe reprimand, he assembled all the pilots together and threatened them that unless they showed more offensive spirit, they would be removed from the squadron and sent away in disgrace. Within days the pilots starting scoring victories and the pressure from above eased. But the success was not without its losses. In the July, the squadron had moved to Chassogne-Ferme, near Verdun and during one skirmish with the enemy, Schleich's friend *Leutnant* Limpert was killed.

It was then that the problems started. It has to be remembered that there still existed in Germany a feudal system and the fact that *Jasta* 21 was a Prussian unit that had just been designated a Saxon unit and was now being commanded by a Bavarian, caused what can only be described as a source embarrassment to the senior members of the old military guard who still held positions of high authority in the German military machine. His command was put under the microscope and any

infringement, no matter how minor, was leapt upon by the powers that be.

Schleich, although a commanding officer, was not adverse to having his own extremely foolish moments. One such incident happened after a SPAD had been forced down intact. Schleich had the aircraft painted in German markings and headed for the front, where he actually joined up with a French squadron on patrol. It took quite a few minutes before the French pilots realised what was happening, but before they could react, Schleich had headed back for his own lines only to be fired upon by German anti-aircraft fire. Fortunately their aim was bad and he landed back safely at his own airfield. Kofl headquarters were not amused and severely reprimanded him for the escapade.

The rest of the squadron was performing well, among them were

Oberleutnant *von Schleich (second right) when taking over* Jasta *21*

Leutnant Emil Thuy and *Leutnant* Karl Thom who were both later awarded the *Pour le Mérite*. Just after achieving his twenty-fifth victory, Schleich fell ill to dysentery. He was rushed to hospital in a serious condition. It was then that the problems started.

After recovering from his illness, Shleich was told that Prussian bureaucracy had taken advantage of his enforced absence and had him removed. They decreed that no Bavarian should serve in a Prussian unit, let alone command one. With the amount of in-fighting that was going on, it was at times like these one wonders who the Germans were actually fighting! A number of the Prussian pilots, who had served under Schleich, voiced their objections to the way their leader had been treated. So in an effort to calm the situation down, Schleich was given command of *Jasta* 32 an all-Bavarian squadron on the 23 October, 1917, his tally by this time had risen to thirty-five.

On 4 December, 1917, Eduard Schleich was awarded the *Orden Pour le Mérite* in recognition of his services, but did not receive the customary Knight's Cross with Swords of the Royal Hohenzollern House Order that usually went with it.

The following month, on 12 January, 1918, he was assigned back to *Fliegerschule* I as its commander. Then in preparation for Germany's last big push in March, he was given command of *Jagdgruppe* Nr. 8, which consisted of Bavarian *Jastas* 23b, 34b and 35b. It was not until the end of 1918 that he learned that he had been awarded the Knight's Cross of the Military Max-Joseph Order, The Saxon's Knights Cross, the Albrecht Order 2nd Class and the Bavarian Military Merit Order 4th Class with Crown and Swords. With these awards came the promotion to *Hauptmann* and the title of nobility *Ritter* von Schleich. He remained in control of *Jagdgruppe* 8. until the end of the war and ended his war by being a member of the Armistice Committee.

In the 1920's he joined Lufthansa and stayed until the rise of Nazism, when he joined the Luftwaffe in 1933. He even visited Britain in the black uniform of the Waffen SS. During the war he rose to the rank of *Generaloberst* commanding combat units. He later took up a post in occupied Denmark, before becoming *General de Fliegers* in Norway. He was taken prisoner at the end of the war by the Allies and interned in a prisoner-of-war camp for high ranking officers. It was there that he died following a short illness.

Awards

Orden Pour le Mérite
Knight's Cross of the Bavarian Military Max-Joseph Order
Bavarian Military Merit Order 4th Class with Swords
Iron Cross 2nd Class
Iron Cross 1st Class
Knight 2nd Class of the Saxon Albert Order
Bavarian Prinzregent Luitpold Medal in Bronze
Wound Badge in Black

Pilot's Badge – Bavarian
Austro-Hungarian Field Pilot's Badge (Karl Pattern)

Victory log

1917

25 May	SPAD VII (No. 19 Sqn RFC)	Moronvillers
17 Jun	Sopwith 1½ Strutter	Thuizy-Prosnes
21 Jun	Caudron G 4	W Auberive
29 Jun	Balloon	W Guyancourt
12 Jul	AR 2 Dorand (*Escadrille* F 8)	E Dicklebush
13 Jul	AR 2 Dorand (*Escadrille* F 70)	W Cuisy
22 Aug	Caudron G 6 (*Escadrille* C 42)	Borrus Wood
26 Aug	SPAD VII (No. 23 Sqn RFC)	S Esnes
3 Sep	AR 2 Dorand (*Escadrille* F 16)	Fort de Hesse
3 Sep	SPAD VII (No 19 Sqn RFC)	S Foret de Hesse
4 Sep	AR 2 Dorand (*Escadrille* F 20)	S Vaquois
5 Sep	SPAD VII (*Escadrille* N 15)	Vauquois
6 Sep	Nieuport XII (*Escadrille* N 65)	Vauquois
11 Sep	AR 2 Dorand (*Reserve Général de l'Aviation*)	Verdun
15 Sep	Caudron G 4	Parois
16 Sep	Caudron G 6 (*Escadrille* C105)	Hessenwal
16 Sep	SPAD VII (No. 19 Sqn RFC)	Hessenwald
18 Sep	Caudron G 6	Verdun
19 Sep	Caudron G 6 (*Escadrille* C 64)	NE Verdun
20 Sep	Nieuport XII (No. 1 Sqn RFC)	N Verdun
21 Sep	Caudron G 4	W Verdun
21 Sep	AR 2 Dorand	Verdun
24 Sep	AR 2 Dorand (*Escadrille* F 59)	W Verdun
24 Sep	SPA VII (No. 19 Sqn RFC)	SW Verdun
29 Sep	SPAD VII	Bethelainville

1918

8 May	SE 5a (No. 1 Sqn RAF)	Auchenvillers
8 May	SE 5a (No. 1 Sqn RAF)	Auchenvillers
8 May	SE 5a (No. 74 Sqn RAF)	Auchenvillers
11 Jun	DH 9 (No. 103 Sqn RAF)	Englebeimer
11 Jun	Sopwith Camel (No. 73 Sqn RAF)	Englebeimer
2 Sep	RE 8 (No. 6 Sqn RAF)	Bapaume
5 Sep	Sopwith Camel (No. 45 Sqn RAF	Douai
9 Sep	Sopwith Camel	Queant
16 Sep	AWFK 8 (No. 2 Sqn RAF)	Marquion
1 Oct	Breguet XIV	Fort de Mondon

Total victories claimed: 35

CHAPTER TWENTY

Leutnant Emil Thuy
(1894 – 1930)

The son of a local schoolteacher, Emil Thuy was born on the 11 March, 1894, in Hagen, Westphalia. Like many other young men at the time his early childhood was uneventful, but it was to become completely changed in August, 1914, with the outbreak of war. Emil Thuy immediately volunteered for front-line duty and was duly enlisted in the 3rd Rhineland Pioneer Regiment. In October 1914, after very basic training, his regiment was sent to the Western Front. Within a matter of weeks Emil Thuy was badly wounded in action and was returned to Germany. Whilst in hospital in soon realised that he was unfit for further service and was discharged from the army.

Determined not to be excluded from the war, on release from hospital, Emil Thuy applied for the German Army Air Service and was accepted. Such was the need for men at the time medicals were not much more

Leutnant Emil Thuy with members of Jagdgruppe 7.

Leutnant *Emil Thuy*

than cursory glances. After completing his training he was awarded his certificate and pilots badge and on the 10 July, 1915, was posted to *Flieger-Abteilung* (Fl.Abt (A)). 53 as a reconnaissance pilot with the rank of *Gefreiter*. After a number of dangerous missions he was awarded the Iron Cross 2nd Class on the 7 August, 1915.

Typical of the flamboyancy of Thuy, his Albatros C.I had a large white circle with a large black 'T' in it, flanked by one black and one white band, painted on either side of the fuselage. There is no doubt that Thuy wanted to be noticed by the enemy and showed his audaciousness by flaunting his distinctively marked aircraft in front of them at every opportunity.

On 8 September, after some extensive combat flying training, he scored his first victory on and was promoted to *Unteroffizier* later the same month. Two months later, on 10 November, 1915, Emil Thuy was awarded the Iron Cross 1st Class and in the same month his request for fighter pilot training was granted. At the end of December 1915 he was promoted to *Vizefeldwebel* and three months later, on 26 March, 1916, given a commission to *Leutnant*.

The formation of an all-fighter *Jagdstaffeln* in the summer of 1916 saw Emil Thuy posted to *Jastaschule* for fighter pilot training and he graduated on the 28 January, 1917. he was assigned to *Jasta* 21 and opened his tally on the 16 April, 1917, when he shot down a Caudron whilst on patrol over N. Berry-au-Bac. His tally had risen to fifteen by the 24 September, 1917.

Leutnant *Emil Thuy with pilots of Jasta 26.*

Emil Thuy's tally had risen to seventeen by the end of 1917. Then on the 26 September, 1916, he was made commander of *Jasta* 28 and was awarded the Knight's Cross with Swords of the Royal Hohenzollern House Order on the 6 November, 1917. *Jasta* 28 was in the thick of the fighting against the Royal Flying Corps and Royal Naval Air Service in Flanders. The unit had lost three of its leaders in almost as many months. On 21 August, whilst under the command of *Hauptmann* Otto Hartmann, six pilots from *Jasta* 28 shared a total of eight victories during one fierce battle.

Leutnant *Emil Thuy with his* Ehrenbecher *awarded to him for his first victory.*

Whilst on patrol on the 2 February, 1918, he and other members of his unit were attacked by Allied fighters. Although badly wounded, Thuy was able to make his way back to his field. He was in hospital for several weeks, but on the 21 February he was able to get back in command of his *Jasta*. By the end of May he had raised his tally to twenty-one and was awarded the Knight's Cross of the Military Merit Order of Württemburg. On the 6 June, 1918, he became the leader of *Jagdagruppe* Nr. 7, which consisted of *Jastas* 28, 33, 57 and 58 and on the 30 June was awarded Germany's highest award, the *Pour le Mérite*.

At the end of the war Emil Thuy became a flying instructor as soon as the Luftwaffe began to reform, he became an instructor at a Luftwaffe flying school near Smolensk, Russia and was killed on 11 June, 1930, in a flying training accident.

Awards

Orden Pour le Mérite
Knight's Cross with Swords of the Royal Hohenzollern House Order
Iron Cross 2nd Class
Iron Cross 1st Class
Knight of the Württemburg Military Merit Order
Knight 2nd Class with Swords of the Württemburg Friedrich Order
Pilot's Badge – German Army

Victory log

1917

16 Apr	Caudron G 4 (*Escadrille* C 228)	N Berry-au-Bac
26 Jun	SPAD VII (*Escadrille* N 124)	Cauroy
13 Jul	SPAD (No. 23 Sqn RFC)	S Avocourt
10 Aug	Balloon (French Balloon Cie 80)	Montzeville
17 Aug	SPAD VII (*Escadrille* N 103)	S Hill 304
19 Aug	SPAD VII (*Escadrille* N 15)	Chattancourt
21 Aug	AR 2 Dorand	SW Avocourt
5 Sep	SPAD VII (*Escadrille* N 15)	Bethelainville
7 Sep	SPAD VII	S Hill 304
11 Sep	SPAD XIII (*Escadrille Spa* 75)	Forges Wood
18 Sep	Caudron G 4	Mort Homme
18 Sep	SPAD VII (*Escadrille* N 84)	S Chattancourt
22 Sep	SPAD VII (*Escadrille* N 65)	Hill 304
24 Sep	SPAD VII (*Escadrille* N 124)	N Hill 304
30 Nov	Sopwith Camel (No. 3 Sqn RFC)	E Ypres
28 Dec	DH 4 (No. 25 Sqn RFC)	Gheluvelt

1918

29 Jan	Sopwith Camel (No. 70 Sqn RFC)	Poelcapelle
18 Mar	Sopwith Camel (No. 10 Sqn RNAS)	W Swevezeele
8 May	DH 9 (No. 206 Sqn RAF)	Zillebeke Lake

14 May	Sopwith Camel (No. 4 Sqn AFC)	N Kemmel Ridge
20 Jun	Sopwith Camel (No. 209 Sqn RAF)	W Cerisy
28 Jun	Sopwith Camel (No. 209 Sqn RAF)	Morcourt
4 Jul	Sopwith Camel (No. 209 Sqn RAF)	SW Cerisy
14 Jul	SPAD VII (*Escadrille Spa* 62)	
24 Aug	SE 5a (No. 12 Sqn RAF)	Tilloy
25 Aug	RE 8 (No. 12 Sqn RAF)	Eterpigny
25 Aug	Sopwith Camel (No. 73 Sqn RAF)	Courcelles
15 Sep	Sopwith Camel (No. 204 Sqn RAF)	
16 Sep	SE 5a (No. 84 Sqn RAF)	
22 Sep	SE 5a (No. 56 Sqn RAF)	Vitry
27 Sep	SE 5a (No. 40 Sqn RAF)	Souchy-Couchy
5 Oct	Aircraft Unknown	
14 Oct	Aircraft Unknown	
14 Oct	Aircraft Unknown	

Total victories claimed: 35

CHAPTER TWENTY-ONE

Leutnant Joseph Veltjens

(1894 – 1943)

Joseph Veltjens was born on the 2 June, 1894 in a small village west of Duisberg in Saxony. An uneventful childhood led to him joining the army at the age of twenty, when on the 3 August, 1914, he enlisted in the Kaiserin-Augusta Guards Regiment Nr. 4. Three months later he was attached to the Lieb-Grenadier Regiment Nr. 8 and later transferred to the 8th Korps-Kraftwagen Kolonne. During this period he received a number of rapid promotions culminating in reaching the rank of *Vizefeldwebel* and the award off the Iron Cross 2nd Class.

At the end of October 1915, Veltjens applied for transfer to the German Army Air Service and was accepted. He was sent to flying school and at the end of December 1915, he was awarded his pilot's certificate and badge. On the 10 May, 1916, he was posted to *Flieger-Abteilung* (Fl.Abt.) 23 a fighter detachment of *Kampfeinsitzer-Kommando-Vaux* becoming a protégé of Rudolf Berthold. There he carried out the duties of a reconnaissance pilot, where, after carrying out a large number of

Leutnant *Josef Veltjens in the cockpit of his rumpler CI*

missions, he was commissioned *Leutnant* at the end of 1916, in recognition of his skills in this field of flying. At the beginning of 1917, he applied for *Jastaschule* for training as a fighter pilot and was accepted. On completion of the course he was posted to *Jasta* 14, where the following month on the 14 April, he scored his first victory by shooting down a SPAD whilst patrolling over Craonne in his Albatros.

Leutnant *Josef Veltjens in the centre of a group of* Jasta 15 pilots.

On 24 July, 1917, Joseph Veltjens was awarded the Knight 2nd Class with Swords of the Saxon Albert Order for his service with Fl.Abt. 23. With his tally at five, he was posted on the 15 August to *Jasta* 18, where by the end of 1917 he had raised it to nine and had been awarded the Knight's Cross 2nd Class with Swords from Saxony.

On the 20 March, 1918, Veltjens was posted to *Jasta* 15, where on the 18 May he took command and celebrated it by shooting down a French Breguet XIV bomber over Cauny. This brought his tally to thirteen and with it came the Iron Cross 1st Class, the Albert Order and the Knight's Cross with Swords of the Royal Hohenzollern House Order on the 20 May. Veltjens continued to score victories freely and by the end of August 1918, had raised his tally to thirty-one. His aircraft was always instantly recognisable by the large white barbed arrow painted on the sides of the fuselage. His efforts were recognised and he was awarded Germany's highest honour, the *Orden Pour le Mérite*. At the end of the war Joseph Veltjens had a total of thirty-five 'kills' to his credit.

During World War Two, Veltjens joined the Luftwaffe with the rank of *Oberst* (Colonel) flying transport aircraft and was at one time Hermann Göring's emissary to Finland. He died in 1943 when the Junkers Ju 52-3m which he was flying, was shot down over Yugoslavia by resistance

fighters.

Awards

Orden Pour le Mérite
Knight's Cross with Swords of the Royal Hohenzollern House
Iron Cross 2nd Class
Iron Cross 1st Class
Knight 2nd Class with Swords of the Saxon Albert Order
Bremen Hanseatic Cross
Wound Badge in Black
Pilot's Badge – German Army

Victory log
1917

14 Apr	SPAD VII	Craonne
4 May	Farman (*Escadrille* F 55)	N Bailly
5 May	SPAD VII (No. 23 Sqn RFC)	Bailly
31 May	SPAD VII (*Escadrille* N 26)	Oulches Wood
1 Jun	SPAD VII (*Escadrille* N 75)	Moulins
16 Sep	RE 8 (No. 4 Sqn RFC)	NW Boisinghe
20 Sep	RE 8 (No. 9 Sqn RFC)	W Hooge
28 Sep	BF 2b (No. 20 Sqn RFC)	E Hollebeke
30 Sep	Sopwith Pup (No. 66 Sqn RFC)	Ploegsteert Wood
15 Nov	SE 5a (No. 65 Sqn RFC)	Langemearc

1918

18 Feb	Sopwith Camel (No. 8 Sqn RNAS)	Voilaines

10 Apr	AWFK 8 (No. 35 Sqn RAF)	Rouvrel
10 May	SPAD XIII (*Escadrille Spa* 94)	Braches
18 May	Breguet XIV (*Escadrille Br* 45)	Cauny
29 May	SPAD XIII (*Escadrille Spa* 98)	S Soissons
2 Jun	Breguet XIV (*Escadrille Br* 226)	SW Soissons
6 Jun	SE 5a (No. 32 Sqn RAF)	SW Montdidier
7 Jun	DH 9 (No. 49 Sqn RAF)	S Noyon
9 Jun	AR 2 Dorand	S Mery
11 Jun	DH 9 (No. 49 Sqn RAF)	W Courcelles
11 Jun	DH 9 (No. 49 Sqn RAF)	W Tricot
12 Jun	Sopwith Camel (No. 43 Sqn RAF)	NE Compiegne
16 Jun	DH 4 (No. 27 Sqn RAF)	Erches
25 Jun	Breguet XIV (*Escadrille Br* 134)	Roy
10 Aug	SPAD XIII (95th Aero Sqn USAS)	Beauvraignes
10 Aug	SE 5a (No. 56 Sqn RAF)	Arvillers
11 Aug	Caudron R 9 (*Escadrille R* 239)	Roy
11 Aug	Caudron R 9 (*Escadrille R* 239)	Roye
11 Aug	SE 5a (No. 92 Sqn RAF)	Nesle
16 Aug	SPAD 2 (*Escadrille Spa* 87)	S Noyon
16 Aug	SPAD XIII (*Escadrille Spa* 88)	W Lassigny
17 Aug	SPAD XIII (*Escadrille Spa* 100)	Roye
1 Oct	SPAD XIII (*Escadrille Spa* 315)	SE Buzancy
3 Oct	Breguet XIV (*Escadrille Br* 282)	Brieulles
4 Oct	SPAD XIII (49th Aero Sqn USAS)	Brieulles
18 Oct	Salmsons 2A2 (12th Aero Sqn USAS)	S Grand Pre

Total victories claimed: 35

CHAPTER TWENTY-TWO

Leutnant Otto Könnecke
(1892 – 1956)

Born in Strasbourg on the 20 September, 1892, the son of a carpenter, Otto Könnecke seemed followed in his fathers footsteps after qualifying from the Building Trade School at Frankfurt am Main in 1909. He became a carpenter's assistant for two years, then in 1911, tired of the mundane life, he volunteered for military service with the Railroad Regiment Nr. 3 at Hanau. After two years he was transferred to *Flieger-Bataillon* 4 at Metz and promoted to *Unteroffizier*. It was at Metz in 1913 that Könnecke took it upon himself to learn to fly and when war was declared the following year, he was already a qualified NCO flying instructor.

Portrait shot of Leutnant Otto Könnecke.

Even though there was a desperate need for pilots at the beginning
of the war, there was an need for instructors was even greater and he
was to stay at Metz as an instructor until the 3 December, 1916, during
which time he awarded the Iron Cross 2nd Class. The Germans at this
point in the war had lost a large number of pilots in France, so pilots
from Macedonia were sent to the Western Front and so new and less
experienced fighter pilots sent to take their place. Otto Könnecke was
one of the inexperienced pilots, battlewise that is, that was posted to
join *Jasta* 25.

On the 9 January, 1917, Könnecke claimed his first 'kill', but it was   Leutnant *Otto Könnecke*
unconfirmed. The following month he opened his tally on the 5   *with his mechanics of*
February when, whilst on patrol over N W Moglia, he shot down a Henry   Jasta 5
Farman from the Serbian Air Park No. 30. He was awarded the
Bulgarian Soldier's Cross for Bravery 1st Class the same day and two
weeks later the Iron Cross 1st Class.

The following day, 6 February, 1917, he notched up his third victory
by shooting down another Farman from the Serbian *Escadrille* F 98. In
March 1917, Könnecke, like many pilots before him, was posted back to
the Western Front to join *Armee-Flug-Park* (AFP).2 as a reconnaissance
pilot. In April he joined *Jasta* 5 and it was there that he joined up with
two other NCO pilots, Fritz Rumey and Joseph Mai, the three of them
later became known as the 'Golden Triumvirate' and between them had
scored 109 victories by the end of the war.

By the end of 1917, Otto Könnecke, in his distinctive Albatros D.V
with its green fuselage and tail edged in red, and a black and white
checkerboard marker edged in red just ahead of the black cross on the
fuselage, had raised his tally to eleven.

Könnecke continued to score steadily, then on the 12 May with his
score standing at eighteen confirmed, his skill and dedication was

recognised by the High Command and he was awarded the Golden Military Merit Cross. This was followed on the 15 June with promotion to the rank of *Leutnant*. Then on the 20 July, with his tally standing at twenty-three, he was awarded the Knight's Cross with Swords of the Royal Hohenzollern House Order. One month later with his tally at thirty-two, came Germany's highest honour, the *Orden Pour le Mérite*.

Leutnant Otto Könnecke finished the war with a tally of thirty-five. There were three unconfirmed victories whilst he was with *Jasta* 5 but this applied to most fighter pilots during the war

In 1926, he joined the newly formed Lufthansa as a pilot, then in 1935 with the birth of the Luftwaffe he enlisted and became the commandant of the flying schools with the rank of *Major*. He died in Germany on the 25 January, 1956.

Group of pilots including Josef Mai and Fritz Rumey (top left) and Leutnant Otto Könnecke, *with light collar in the middle row.*

Awards

Orden Pour le Mérite
Knight's Cross with Swords of the Royal Hohenzollern House Order
Prussian Golden Military Merit Cross
Iron Cross 2nd Class
Iron Cross 1st Class
Bulgarian Soldier's Cross for Bravery 1st Class
Pilot's Badge

Victory log

1917

5 Feb	Farman (Serbian Air Park No.30)	NW Mogila
6 Feb	Farman (Serbian *Escadrille* F 98)	Monastir
28 May	FE 2b (No. 25 Sqn RFC)	Beaumont
4 Jun	FE 2b (No. 22 Sqn RFC)	S Vendhuil
10 Aug	DH 5 (No. 59 Sqn RFC)	Malaisse-ferme
18 Aug	DH 5 (No. 32 Sqn RFC)	Ribecourt
21 Aug	RE 8 (No. 24 Sqn RFC)	NW Vaucelles Wood
17 Oct	Sopwith 2	Origny
22 Nov	Sopwith Camel (No. 59 Sqn RFC)	Anneux
23 Nov	DH 5 (No. 46 Sqn RFC)	Fontaine
5 Dec	Sopwith Camel (No. 3 Sqn RFC)	Seranvillers

1918

28 Jan	SE 5a (No. 11 Sqn RFC)	Tilloy
17 Mar	DH 4 (No. 57 Sqn RFC)	Graincourt
23 Mar	BF 2b (No. 22 Sqn RFC)	Hervilly
24 Mar	RE 8 (No. 53 Sqn RFC)	
1 Apr	SE 5a (No. 56 Sqn RAF)	Albert
11 Apr	SE 5a (No. 60 Sqn RAF)	Bapaume
12 Apr	SE 5a (No. 84 Sqn RAF)	N Albert
19 May	DH 9 (No. 49 Sqn RAF)	Villers Bretonneaux
30 May	DH 9 (No. 49 Sqn RAF)	Dernancourt
30 May	Sopwith Camel (No. 4 Sqn AFC)	Ribecourt
9 Jul	BF 2b (No. 48 Sqn RAF)	NE Albert
19 Jul	Sopwith Camel (No. 70 Sqn RAF)	NE Etinehem
8 Aug	BF 2b (No. 48 Sqn RAF)	Mericourt
8 Aug	SE 5a (No. 24 Sqn RAF)	W Mericourt
8 Aug	SE 5a (No. 24 Sqn RAF)	NW Roman Camp
9 Aug	SE 5a (No. 41 Sqn RAF)	Estrees
9 Aug	BF 2b (No. 11 Sqn RAF)	St Just
9 Aug	SE 5a (No. 41 Sqn RAF)	Estrees
12 Aug	Sopwith Scout (No. 104 Sqn RAF)	
14 Aug	BF 2b (No. 11 Sqn RAF)	Vert Galand
24 Aug	SE 5a (No. 56 Sqn RAF)	NE Bapaume
18 Oct	SE 5a (No. 25 Sqn RAF)	Le Cateau
1 Nov	DH 4 (No. 64 Sqn RAF)	
4 Nov	DH 4 (No. 57 Sqn RAF)	Mormal Wood

Total victories claimed: 33

CHAPTER TWENTY-THREE

Oberleutnant Kurt Wolff
(1895 – 1917)

Born on the 6 February, 1895, in the village of Greifswald, Pomerania, Kurt Wolff was the son of a local farmer. When he became seventeen Kurt Wolff joined the Eisenbahn Regiment Nr. 4 as a cadet where he served as an *Unteroffizer* in the field. On the 17 April, 1915, after seeing action in the war he was promoted to *Leutnant*, but his thoughts were on other things and asked to be transferred to aviation. Initially the regiment were reluctant to let him go, but the need for fighter pilots was

Portrait shot of Leutnant
Kurt Wolff.

Kurt Wolff deep in conversation with Manfred von Richthofen.

greater and he was transferred in July 1915.

His first flight was nearly his last, when his instructor misjudged a landing in their LVG and crashed. The instructor was killed outright but Wolff suffered nothing more than a dislocated shoulder. Fortunately it did not deter him and he made rapid progress, receiving his pilot's badge at the end of December. He was assigned to a *Kampfgeschwader* (KG) unit at Verdun flying Albatros Scouts against ground troops. As the battle fronts moved so did the units and after some months in the Verdun area his unit was moved to the Somme where once again they were soon in the thick of the action against the Allied ground troops.

Then on the 5 November, 1916, he was posted to *Jasta* 11, where he carried out a number of sorties against Allied aircraft but failed to score one victory. It wasn't until the 14 January, 1917, when command of the *Jasta* was taken over by Manfred von Richthofen that things started to change. Under Richthofen's guidance and tutelage, Kurt Wolff began to take his toll on the enemy aircraft. Within a couple of weeks of Richthofen taking command, Kurt Wolff had secured his first victory, a BE 2d, No. 5856, of 16 Squadron, RFC, over Givenchy on the 6 March, 1917. In a remarkable seven week period Kurt Wolff had taken his tally to twenty-seven.

Then on the 26 April, 1917, he was awarded the Knight's Cross with Swords of the Royal Hohenzollern House Order and one week later, on the 4 May, came Germany's highest award the *Orden Pour le Mérite*.

Kurt Wolff took over command of *Jasta* 29 after its *Staffelführer Leutnant* Ludwig Dorheim had been shot down and killed by the French ace Rene Dorme on 29 April. Wolff's luck ran temporarily, when on the 11 July he ran into a Sopwith Triplane from No. 10 Squadron, RNAS, and was shot in the hand. Managing to fly his Fokker Triplane with one hand he was able to return to his base. The injury kept Kurt Wolff on the ground for two months, but on the 11 September he resumed command

Leutnant Kurt Wolff taking off in his new Albatros D III.

Fokker Dr I in which Kurt Wolff was killed on 15/9/'17

of *Jasta* 29 and returned to the air. In July he returned to *Jasta* 11 to take over command from *Leutnant* Karl Allmenröder, who was returning from an unsuccessful sortie against Allied aircraft, when his plane was hit by machine gun fire from the ground and crashed into the ground killing him instantly.

The following day, orders came through confirming Kurt Wolff's promotion to *Oberleutnant*.

On the 15 September whilst on patrol over Moorslede in Manfred von Richthofen's Fokker Triplane with other members of his *Jasta*, he encountered Sopwith Camels from Nos 10 and 70 Squadrons, RNAS. After a brief dogfight, his Fokker Dr.I, No. FI 102/17, suffered sustained machine gun fire from a Sopwith Camel flown by Flight Sub-Lieutenant N M McGregor. Kurt Wolff's aircraft spun out of control and crashed just north of Wervicq killing him instantly. He was just twenty-two years

old.
Awards

Orden Pour le Mérite
Knight's Cross with Swords of the Royal Hohenzollern House Order
Bavarian Military Merit Order 4th Class with Swords
Iron Cross 2nd Class
Iron Cross 1st Class
Pilot's Badge – German Army

Victory log

1917

6 Mar	BE 2d (No. 16 Sqn RFC)	Givenchy
9 Mar	FE 8 (No. 40 Sqn RFC)	Anna
17 Mar	Sopwith 1½ Strutter (No. 43 Sqn RFC)	SW Athies
30 Mar	Nieuport XVII (No. 60 Sqn RFC)	E Gavrelle
31 Mar	FE 2b (No. 11 Sqn RFC)	Gavrelle
6 Apr	RE 8 (No. 59 Sqn RFC)	Bois Bernard
7 Apr	Nieuport XVII (No. 60 Sqn RFC)	Mercatel
8 Apr	DH 4 (No. 55 Sqn RFC)	NE Blecourt
11 Apr	BF 2a (No. 48 Sqn RFC)	N Fismes
13 Apr	RE 8 (No. 59 Sqn RFC)	N Vitry
13 Apr	FE 2b (No. 11 Sqn RFC)	S Bailleul
13 Apr	Nieuport XVII (No. 29 Sqn RFC)	S Monchy
13 Apr	Martinsyde G100 (No. 27 Sqn RFC)	Rouvroy
14 Apr	Nieuport XVII (No. 60 sqn RFC)	SE Drocourt
14 Apr	SPAD VII (No. 19 Sqn RFC)	E Bailleul
16 Apr	Nieuport XVII (No. 60 Sqn RFC)	NE Roeux
21 Apr	BE 2g (No. 16 Sqn RFC)	W Willerval
21 Apr	Nieuport XXIII (No. 29 Sqn RFC)	E Fresnes
22 Apr	FE 2b (No. 11 Sqn RFC)	Hendecourt
22 Apr	Morane Parasol (No. 3 Sqn RFC)	Havrincourt
26 Apr	BE 2g (No. 5 Sqn RFC)	E Gavrelle
27 Apr	FE 2b (No. 11 Sqn RFC)	S Gavrelle
28 Apr	BE 2g (No. 5 Sqn RFC)	S Oppy
29 Apr	SPAD VII (No. 19 Sqn RFC)	Sailly
29 Apr	FE 2b (No. 18 Sqn RFC)	S Pronville
29 Apr	BE 2f (No. 16 Sqn RFC)	W Gravelle
30 Apr	BE 2e (No. 13 Sqn RFC)	W Fresnes
1 May	Sopwith Triplane (No. 8 Sqn RNAS)	S Seclin
1 May	FE 2b (No. 25 Sqn RFC)	S Bois Bernard
13 May	SPAD VII (*Escadrille* N 37)	Beine
27 Jun	Nieuport XXIII (No. 29 Sqn RFC)	SW Noyelles
6 Jul	RE 8 (No. 4 Sqn RFC)	Zillebeke
7 Jul	Sopwith Triplane (No. 1 Sqn RNAS)	Comines

Total victories claimed: 33

CHAPTER TWENTY-FOUR

Oberleutnant Heinrich Claudius Kroll (1894 – 1930)

The son of a schoolmaster, Heinrich Kroll was born on the 3 November, 1894, at Flatsby, Flensberg, near Kiel. Kroll seemed to be destined to follow in his fathers footsteps and was studying to become a schoolmaster, when the First World War broke out. He immediately volunteered to join the army and serve with Fusilier Regiment Nr. 86, but was sent to join the Reserve Infantry Regiment Nr. 92 at the Front. With only the barest of training he was soon in the thick of the action. He proved to be an extremely able soldier and within a year had been

Leutnant *Kroll wearing his newly awarded* Pour le Mérite.

awarded the Iron Cross 2nd Class and granted a commission to *Leutnant*.

Kroll had been watching the birth of the German Air Service with great interest and late in 1915, applied for a transfer. After a number of requests he was finally accepted and in January 1916, was sent to flying training school. After graduating at the end of April, Kroll was posted to *Flieger-Abteilung* (Fl.Abt.) 17 as a reconnaissance pilot flying Rumpler two-seaters. At his own request he asked for training as a fighter pilot and was sent to *Jastaschule*. On completion of his training, he was posted to *Jasta* 9 at the beginning of November 1916.

His first encounter with the enemy was not a memorable one and during his first mission on the 24 November his aircraft was shot up and he was forced to land. He was unharmed but his pride was dented somewhat. He continued to fly patrols and on the 12 February, 1917, he was awarded the Iron Cross 1st Class. On the 1 May, 1917, he opened his tally by shooting down a SPAD whilst on patrol in his Albatros over W Moronvillers. By the end of the month he had increased his tally to five confirmed and one un-confirmed. The fifth victory was particularly pleasing to him, as it was the French ace Rene Dorme, who had twenty-three German pilots and their aircraft to his credit.

Kroll was given command of *Jasta* 24 on the 1 July and celebrated it by claiming his sixth victim, an SE 5 of 56 Squadron, RFC, on the 20 July. Seven days later he was shot down in flames during a battle over Menin, this time it was 56 Squadron getting their own back. Miraculously he was able to land the flaming Albatros D.V and walk away unhurt. Kroll continued to steadily score victories and by the end of the year had raised his tally to fifteen. The new year started well for Heinrich Kroll scoring four more victories in the January raising his tally to nineteen. After his twentieth victory, he was awarded the Knight's Cross of the Hohenzollern House Order on the 22, February 1918. The following month, 29 March, he was awarded Germany's highest honour, the *Pour le Mérite* and promoted to *Oberleutnant*. Another award on the 18 June, the Knight's Cross 2nd Class with Swords of the Order of Albert, brought more recognition. On the 27 July Kroll had another lucky escape, when he was again shot down with his aircraft in flames and once again he walked away unhurt. But his luck changed on the 14 August when he was attacked whilst on patrol and was badly injured in his shoulder. The injury was so bad that it effectively ended his combat career and he was able to sit the war out. Command of *Jasta* 24 was passed to *Oberleutnant* Hasso von Wedel, although the *Jasta's* most successful pilot next to Kroll was *Offizier-Stellvertrer* Altemeier with twenty-one victories, but he was a non-commissioned officer and as such could not command a *Jasta*.

In 1928 he joined the Hamburg Flying Club, after successfully operating a business. One year later he closed the business down and became a commercial pilot, returning to the world he knew best. Heinrich Kroll died

Leutnant *Heinrich Kroll* *with his Fokker D VII*

in Hamburg on the 21 February, 1930, of pneumonia.

Awards

Orden Pour le Mérite
Knight's Cross with Swords of the Royal Hohenzollern House Order
Knight 2nd Class with Swords of the Albert Order
Iron Cross 2nd Class
Iron Cross 1st Class
Wound Badge in Black
Pilot's Badge – German Army

Victory log

1917

1 May	Nieuport XXIII (*Escadrille* N 88)	W Moronvillers
7 May	SPAD VII (*Escadrille* N 75)	E Auberive
7 May	SPAD VII (*Escadrille* N 75)	St Hilaire-le-Grand
20 May	SPAD VII (*Escadrille* N 82)	St Hilaire-le-Petit
25 May	SPAD VII (*Escadrille* Spa 3)	Fort de la Pompelle
20 Jul	SE 5 (No. 56 Sqn RFC)	S Moronvillers
12 Aug	Sopwith Triplane	N Ypres
15 Aug	FE 2d (No. 20 Sqn RFC)	N Ypres
9 Sep	Sopwith Triplane (No.1 Sqn RNAS)	NW Bellewaarde Lake
12 Sep	SPAD VII (No. 23 Sqn RFC)	SW Linselles
20 Sep	SPAD VII (No. 19 Sqn RFC)	W Zonnebeke
25 Sep	Sopwith Pup (No. 54 Sqn TFC)	SW Langemarck
12 Nov	Sopwith Camel (No. 65 Sqn RFC)	NE Armentieres
13 Nov	Sopwith Camel (No. 45 Sqn RFC)	N Zillebeke Lake
4 Dec	SE 5a	E Cantaing

1918

13 Jan	SE 5a (No. 84 Sqn RFC)	Flesquieres
25 Jan	BF 2b (No. 22 Sqn RFC)	NW St Quentin
29 Jan	Sopwith Camel (No. 3 Sqn RFC)	S St Quentin
30 Jan	BF 2b (No. 22 Sqn RFC)	Hesbecourt
18 Feb	Sopwith Camel (No. 70 Sqn RF)	Vendeuil-Rumigny
17 Mar	Sopwith Camel (No. 80 Sqn RFC)	W St Quentin
22 Mar	RE 8 (No. 53 Sqn RFC)	Genlis Wood
1 Apr	SPAD VII (Escadrille Spa 155)	NW Noyon
31 May	Breguet XIV (*Escadrille Br* 131)	Compiegne
7 Jun	SPAD XIII (*Escadrille Spa* 78)	Foret de Laigne
9 Jun	SPAD XIII (*Escadrille Spa* 88)	Moreuil-Ellincourt
9 Jun	SPAD XIII (*Escadrille Spa* 88)	Moreuil-Ellincourt
29 Jun	RE 8 (No. 53 Sqn RAF)	W Villers-Brettoneux
29 Jun	SE 5a	W Villers-Brettoneux
5 Jul	SPAD VII (*Escadrille Spa* 93)	S Cournay
8 Aug	RE 8 (No. 8 Sqn RAF)	W Villers-Brettoneaux
8 Aug	SE 5a (No. 60 Sqn RAF)	W Villers-Brettoneaux
9 Aug	SE 5a (No. 41 Sqn RAF)	W Le Quesnel

Total victories claimed: 33

CHAPTER TWENTY-FIVE

Leutnant Heinrich Bongartz
(1892 – 1946)

Heinrich Bongartz was born in Gelsenkirchen, Westphalia on the 31 January, 1892, the son of a schoolteacher. Throughout his education it was assumed that he would follow the family tradition and become a schoolteacher. But like many other boys of his generation, his life was to affected by the actions of a young Bosnian man by the name of Gavrilo Princip, who, on the morning of the 28 June, 1914, was to commit an act that was to affect the lives of millions of other people.

On leaving school, Bongartz when to college and trained as a teacher. Then in August 1914 at the outbreak of war, he volunteered for the army and joined Infantry Regiment Nr. 16, then later the Reserve Infantry Regiment Nr. 13 with the rank of Sturmoffizier. Throughout 1915 Bongartz saw some of the heaviest fighting of the war whilst the regiment was stationed on the Western Front near Verdun. His bravery and leadership qualities during this period did not go unnoticed and in March 1916 it earned him a commission to *Leutnant* and the award of the Iron Cross 2nd Class. By this time the fighting in the mud and cold had taken its toll on him, so he applied for transfer to the German Army Air Service. Reluctantly his unit let him go but he had been accepted and was posted for training as a pilot to *Flieger-Abteilung* (Fl.Abt.) 5 in the autumn of 1916. On completion of his training in the October, he was posted to *Kaghol* 5 as a reconnaissance and scouting pilot.

At the beginning of January 1917, he was posted to *Kasta* 27 (later became *Schusta* 8) where he stayed until the beginning of April 1917, when he was posted to *Jasta* 36. Within days of arriving at *Jasta* 36, Bongartz had opened his tally when he shot down a SPAD VII from *Spa* 31, whilst on patrol over Viry. By the end of the month his score had increased to four and he continued to score steadily until the 13 July, when with his tally standing at 11, he was badly wounded in the upper and lower arms during a battle with Allied fighters. The wound put him out of commission for two months, then on the 26 September he celebrated his return by shooting down a Sopwith Triplane over Houthulst Forest.

At the end of September Bongartz was appointed the Commanding
Officer of *Jasta* 36 and during the following two months he added
another fourteen victories to his total, bringing the number of victories
claimed to twenty-five. For this he was awarded the Knight's Cross with

Swords of the Hohenzollern House Order. Bongartz finished the year by shooting down another two Allied fighters and bringing raising his tally to twenty-seven. Then on the 23 December, 1917, he was awarded Germany's highest honour, the *Orden Pour le Mérite*, from the Kaiser himself during a field review of the troops.

1918 started quietly for Bongartz, with only one victory, a Sopwith Camel whilst on patrol over Poelcapelle on 29 January. Two more were added in February and three in March took his score to thirty-three, then on the 30 March he was wounded when hit by 'friendly anti-aircraft fire' whilst returning from a sortie. The following month on the 25 April he was slightly wounded again but on the 27 April he was very seriously wounded. Whilst on patrol over Kemmel Hill, he

Heinrich Bongartz (second from left) after receiving his Pour le Mérite.

clashed with fighters from No. 74 Squadron, RFC, and during the
mêlée, he was hit in the head. His aircraft crashed near Kemmel Hill
and he was taken unconscious to hospital. On reaching hospital it was
discovered that the bullet had passed right through his left temple,
then his eye and nose. The wounds were so serious that he lost his left
eye and finished his wartime career. He later took over as Director of
the Aeroplane Inspectorate at Aldershof, where he stayed until the
end of the war and helped to deactivate the German Army Flying
Corps.

Although the First World War was over there was a post-war
revolution going on and Bongartz found himself fighting against the
Spartacists, a group of German left-wingers who formed the nucleus

*Celebration of Bruno
Loerzer's award of the
PLM. Bongartz is third
from left.*

of the German Communist Party. Once again he was wounded, this time in the leg and seriously. This was the final straw and the wound finally finished his military career and he was invalided out. But Bongartz could not stay away from aviation and became the Director of German Air Trade (*Deutschen Lufttreederei*) a department that was concerned with using airships for trade and transport. In January 1921 he was involved in a crash and again was seriously injured but recovered later in the year. Heinrich Bongartz died of a heart attack on the 23 January, 1946.

Awards

Orden Pour le Mérite
Knight's Cross with Swords of the Royal Hohenzollern House Order
Iron Cross 2nd Class
Iron Cross 1st Class
Pilot's Badge – German Army
Wound Badge in Silver

Victory log

1917

6 Apr	SPAD VI (*Escadrille Spa* 31)	Vitry
13 Apr	Salmson-Moineau (*Escadrille* F 72)	Cormicy
27 Apr	Balloon	Berry-au-Bac
27 Apr	Balloon	SE Thillois
2 May	Caudron (*Escadrille* C 28)	Reims
20 May	Balloon	Bouvancourt
20 May	Balloon (59 *Cie Aérostiers*)	Villers-Marmery
23 May	Balloon (54 *Cie Aérostiers*)	W Prunay
7 Jul	FE 2d (No. 20 Sqn RFC)	Ypres
11 Jul	Sopwith Triplane (No.10 Sqn RNAS)	Tenbrien
12 Jul	Sopwith Triplane (No.10 Sqn RNAS)	SE Zillebeke
26 Sep	Sopwith Triplane(No.1 Sqn RNAS)	Houthulst Forest
10 Oct	DH0 4 (No. 57 Sqn RFC)	Westroosebeke
14 Oct	RE 8 (No. 21 Sqn RFC)	Zonnebeke
17 Oct	DH 4 (No. 57 Sqn RFC)	Houthulst Forest
18 Oct	RE 8 (No. 9 Sqn RFC)	Molenhoek
27 Oct	Sopwith Camel (No. 70 Sqn RFC)	Roulers
31 Oct	RE 8 (No. 53 Sqn RFC)	S Polecapelle
31 Oct	SPAD 7 (No. 23 Sqn RFC)	Neuville
31 Oct	SPAD 7 (No. 23 Sqn RFC)	Rouler
8 Nov	BF 2b (No. 22 Sqn RFC)	Ledegheim
12 Nov	RE 8 (No. 5 Sqn RFC)	E Merken
15 Nov	Nieuport Scout (No. 29 Sqn RFC)	NE Zillebeke Lake
23 Nov	Sopwith Camel (No. 65 Sqn RFC)	Becelaere
23 Nov	Sopwith Camel (No. 65 Sqn RFC)	Becelaere
29 No	BF 2b (No. 206 Sqn RFC)	Moorslede

| 2 Dec | DH 4 (No. 57 Sqn RFC) | NE Moorslede |
| 18 Dec | Sopwith Camel (No. 65 Sqn RFC) | Roulers |

1918

29 Jan	Sopwith Camel (No. 70 Sqn RFC)	Poelcapelle
5 Feb	DH 4 (No. 25 Sqn RFC)	Thielt
5 Feb	DH 4 (No. 25 Sqn RFC)	Oudenburg
23 Mar	Sopwith Camel (No. 46 Sqn RFC)	Lagincourt
27 Mar	DH 4 (No. 25 Sqn RFC)	Albert
27 Mar	Sopwith Camel (No. 3 Sqn RFC)	SW Albert

Total victories claimed: 34

CHAPTER TWENTY-SIX

Leutnant Hermann Frommherz (1891 – 1964)

Hermann Frommherz was born on 10 August, 1891, at Waldshut, Baden a small town near the border with Switzerland. On leaving school he became an engineering student at the University of Stuttgart. Whilst there he became a reservist with the Mecklenburg Jaeger-Battalion Nr. 14 in 1911 and when war was declared in 1914 he was sent to France with the Ersatz Bataillon Infanteri-Regiment Nr. 113. In December 1914 he was transferred to Reserve Infantry Regiment Nr. 250 and promoted to *Vizefeldwebel*. Then in the January of 1915 he was sent to the Russian Front and in February after being involved in heavy fighting, he was awarded the Iron Cross 2nd Class. Two months later he was transferred back to the Ersatz Bataillon Infanteri Regiment Nr. 113 where he saw more heavy fighting. Deciding that fighting on the ground in thick mud and atrocious conditions, Hermann Frommherz applied for a transfer to the newly created German Army Air Service.

On 1 June, 1915, his application was successful and he was transferred and commenced his basic flying training at *Flieger-Ersatz-Abteilung* (FEA) 7 at Cologne. On completion of this he was sent *Fliegerschule* at Freiburg on 31 July for further training and then on to FEA 9 at Darmstadt for advanced training. On completion of this he was posted to *Kampfstaffel* 20 of *Kaghol* 4 and promoted to *Offizier-Stellvertrer*. His training continued under the guidance of more experienced pilots and he was involved in the Fronts of Verdun and the Somme. Then on 1 August 1916 he was promoted to *Leutnant*. At the end of November he was posted to Bulgaria when *Kasta* 20 was amalgamated into *Kaghol* 1, and flew sorties first in Romania and then in Salonika and Macedonia. On 3 March 1917 he was posted to *Jasta* 2 and one month later scored his first victory when he shot down a SPAD VII from No. 23 Squadron over Cuvillers. Three days later he scored his second victory when he shot down a BE 2e over Ribecourt and received the Iron Cross 1st Class. On 1 May after returning from a sortie his aircraft crashed whilst landing and Frommherz suffered severe injuries.

Studio portrait of
Leutnant *Hermann*
Frommherz.

After recuperating Hermann Frommherz became an instructor with *Flieger-Ersatz-Abteilung* (FEA) 3 at Lubeck. He quickly became bored with instructing and rejoined *Jasta* 2 on 1 March, 1918, but it wasn't until the 3 June that he claimed his third victory, a SPAD VII over Acienville. By the end of July he had raised his tally to ten and was given command of *Jasta* 27, when Hermann Göring replaced *Hauptmann* Wilhelm Reinhard as commander of *Jagdegeschwader* 1, when the latter had been shot down

(Above) Leutnant
*Hermann Frommherz at the
Lübeck Flying School when
an instructor. (Below)
Frommherz second from left
on back row. Bernert and
Voss are in the middle row.*

and killed. In addition to the command, Frommherz was awarded the Knight's Cross with Swords of the Royal Hohenzollern House Order.

In the next two months, he had raised his tally to twenty-six this included three Sopwith Camels of the 148th Aero Squadron, USAS on the 26 September. By this time the tide of war had turned and the Germans were fighting a retreating battle, although in the air they still retained a degree of superiority. Four 'kills' in October and three in

November brought Frommherz's total to thirty-two and the nomination for the highest accolade, the *Orden Pour le Mérite*. It was unfortunate that the nomination, which had been approved in every quarter, was still in the pipeline when the war ended and was never awarded. So incensed was Frommherz that he continued to badger the authorities for this, the highest military award and one that he richly deserved, but to no avail so he managed to purchase one and had many photographs taken showing him wearing the *Orden Pour le Mérite*.

After the war Frommherz served with the German Police Aviation Service until 1925, then in Russia, and in 1931 went to China to teach fighter tactics to Chiang-Kai-shek's newly formed air force. During the Second World War he joined the Luftwaffe commanding No. 1 Gruppe of *Jagdegeschwader* 134 and achieved the rank of *Generalmajor*. Hermann Frommherz died in December 1964 in his home town of Waldshut.

Awards

Iron Cross 2nd Class.
Iron Cross 1st Class.
Lübeck Hanseatic Cross
Knight's Cross with Swords of the Royal Hohenzollern House Order.
Knight's Cross of the Military Karl Friedrich Merit Order.
Knight's Cross of the Saxon Military St. Henry Order.
Knight's Cross 2nd Class with Swords of the Zähringen Lion Order.

Victory log

1917

11 Apr	SPAD VII (No. 23 Sqn RFC)	Cullvillers
14 Apr	BE 2c (No. 9 Sqn RFC)	Ribencourt

1918

3 Jun	SPAD VII (*Escadrille Spa* 37)	Acienville
9 Jun	SPAD VII (*Escadrille Spa* 89)	Vauxbin
5 Jul	Nieuport 28 (95th Aero Sqn USAS)	Courchamps
15 Jul	Nieuport 28 (95th Aero Sqn USAS)	Chateau-Thierry
17 Jul	BF 2b	Vassy, Soilly
24 Jul	SPAD XIII (*Escadrille Spa* 83)	Acy
25 Jul	Sopwith Camel (No. 43 Sqn RAF)	Mareuil
28 Jul	Salmson 2A2 (12th Aero Sqn USAS)	Sergy
9 Aug	DH 9 (No. 107 Sqn RAF)	Herleville
13 Aug	SE 5a (No. 2 Sqn AFC)	Rouvroy
26 Aug	Sopwith Camel (148th Aero Sqn USAS)	Sapignes
26 Aug	Sopwith Camel (17th Aero Sqn USAS)	Vaulx
26 Aug	Sopwith Camel (17th Aero Sqn USAS)	NE Beugny
27 Aug	Bf 2b(No. 22 Sqn RAF)	Graincourt
2 Sep	BF 2b (No. 22 Sqn RAF)	Hamel
3 Sep	RE 8 (No. 12 Sqn RAF)	Beugnatre
3 Sep	RE 8 (No. 12 Sqn RAF)	Beugny
4 Sep	Sopwith Camel (No. 18 Sqn RAF)	Recourt
5 Sep	Sopwith Camel (No. 4 Sqn AFC)	Marquion
17 Sep	DH 9	

20 Sep	Sopwith Camel (No. 60 Sqn RAF)	Marcoing
22 Sep	Sopwith Camel (17th Aero Sqn USAS)	NE Beugny
27 Sep	SE 5a (No. 40 Sqn RAF)	
27 Sep	SE 5a(No. 40 Sqn RAF)	
28 Oct	Sopwith Camel (No. 70 Sqn RAF)	Quartes
28 Oct	BF 2b (N. Flight)	
29 Oct	RE 8 (No. 42 Sqn RAF)	
30 Oct	Sopwith Dolphin (No. 19 Sqn RAF)	Mons
4 Nov	BF 2b (No. 62 Sqn RAF)	
4 Nov	BF 2b (No. 62 Sqn RAF)	

Total victories claimed:

CHAPTER TWENTY-SEVEN

Leutnant Paul Billik
(1891 – ?)

Paul Billik was born in Haatsch, Schlesien on 27 March, 1891. Nothing is known of his childhood or whether or not he served in the German Army prior to joining the *Fliegertruppe* but in May 1916 he attended the flight training school at Posen. On completing his initial training he was assigned to *Schutzstaffel* 4 on 4 January, 1917, to complete his training. After qualifying on 26 March he was posted to *Jasta* 12, his fighter unit

Portrait shot of Leutnant
Paul Billick

and almost immediately was into the action. On 30 March he claimed his first victory a Sopwith Pup over Roumaucourt. Two weeks later he shot down his second victim a SPAD VII whilst on patrol over Izel, but it was to be another month before he could claim his third, a Nieuport XVII from No. 19 Squadron, RFC, over Bullencourt. Four days later number four victim crashed to earth, another Nieuport XVII from No. 29 Squadron, RFC, and with it came the award of the Iron Cross 1st Class. There is no record of him having the Iron Cross 2nd Class, but it follows that he must have had the award, possibly during the period before joining the *Fliegertruppe*.

Leutnant *Paul Billick (seated far right) with members of* Jasta *12.* Oberleutnant *Ritter von Tutschek is seated on the extreme left.*

On the 4 July 1917 *Leutnant* Paul Billik was posted to *Jasta* 7 where he remained until the end of the year where he added another three to his tally. Then suddenly on 28 December, 1917, came an order naming him *Staffelführer* of the newly created *Jasta* 52. Based initially at Braunschweig, the *Jasta* became operational on 9 January and moved to an airfield at Pecq on the 6 *Armee* Front. During January Paul Billik started to lick his new command into shape and by the end of January it was ready. The first contact with the British came on the 30 January when two of the Allied aircraft fell to the guns of *Jasta* 52. Billik's first victories with his new *Jasta* came on the 9 March when he shot down two SE 5as after intercepting them whilst they were on a reconnaissance mission. Two more at the end of the month brought his total to twelve. By the end of May his tally had risen to eighteen and under his command, *Jasta* 52 was beginning to make a name for itself. In the following three months Paul Billik claimed another thirteen aircraft bringing his total thirty-one and an obvious candidate for the *Orden Pour le Mérite*. He had already received the Knight's Cross with Swords of the Hohenzollern House Order on the 25 July, usually a precursor to the *Pour le Mérite*.

Then on 10 August whilst on patrol his flight was attacked by British fighters and his aircraft suffered a number of hits to the engine forcing him to crash-land behind enemy lines. Paul Billik was captured and made a prisoner-of-war. Because he had been captured he was never awarded the *Orden Pour le Mérite*, an award he so richly deserved. It seems unfair when Rudolf Windisch, who was also shot down and made a prisoner-of-war, was awarded the *Orden Pour le Mérite* and his tally of victories only stood at twenty-two.

After the war Paul Billik returned to his home town and continued

Leutnant *Paul Billik of* Jasta *12 studying his garishly marked Albatros D III.*

flying. He was killed in a flying accident whilst testing a Junkers F.13.

Awards

Knight's Cross with Swords of the Royal Hohenzollern House Order
Iron Cross 2nd Class
Iron Cross 1st Class
Pilot's Badge – German Army

Victory log
1917

30 Apr	Sopwith Pup (No. 3 Sqn RNAS)	Roumancourt
12 May	SPAD VII (No. 19 Sqn RFC)	Izel
29 Jun	Nieuport XVII (No. 29 Sqn RFC)	Bullencourt

3 Jul	Nieuport XVII (*Escadrille* N 77)	SW Villers
18 Aug	Sopwith Camel (No. 4 Sqn RNAS)	Vladsloo
3 Sep	Sopwith Camel (No. 45 Sqn RFC)	Dixmuiden
6 Sep	SPAD VII (No. 23 Sqn RFC)	Schaep Baillie
12 Dec.	Sopwith Camel (No. 10 Sqn RNAS)	Keyem

1918

9 Mar	SE 5a (No. 40 Sqn RFC)	E Dourges
9 Mar	SE 5a (No. 40 Sqn RFC)	Noyelle sous Lens
28 Mar	Sopwith Camel (No. 4 Sqn AFC)	Fampaux-Arras
28 Mar	Sopwith Camel (No. 43 Sqn RFC)	Sailly
7 Apr	Sopwith Camel (No. 208 Sqn RAF)	Steinwäldchen
3 May	Sopwith Camel (No. 46 Sqn RAF)	W Estaires

Total victories claimed: 31

CHAPTER TWENTY-EIGHT

Oberleutnant Karl Bolle
(1893 – 1955)

The only son of an academic, Karl Bolle was born in Berlin on 20 June, 1893. In 1912 he went to Oxford University to read economics, but , just before the outbreak of the First World War, Karl Bolle returned to Germany. He joined a cavalry unit, the Kürassier-Regiment von Seydlitz (Magdeburgisches) Nr. 7, with the rank of *Leutnant* and almost immediately was in France fighting on the Western Front. The regiment was moved to the Eastern Front at the beginning of 1915, and found themselves fighting in Poland and Courland. At the end of 1915, Bolle was awarded the Iron Cross 2nd Class, but by this time he had decided that he had had enough of the cold and the mud and applied for transfer to the newly formed German Army Air Service. His application was accepted and in February 1916 he was posted to the Johannisthal field for his initial flying training. He was then posted to *Flieger-Ersatz-Abteilung* (Fl.Abt.) 5 in Hanover, for continuation training and from there posted to the *Kampfgeschwadern*.

After completing his training in July 1916, Karl Bolle was awarded his pilot's badge and posted to *Kampfgeschwader* (KG).4 as a reconnaissance pilot. In October 1916, whilst on a reconnaissance mission, his aircraft was attacked by five French fighters. Although badly wounded, he managed to land his crippled aircraft behind German lines. Dragging his observer from the wreckage, he crawled across open ground with him to safety, whilst his aircraft was destroyed by enemy fire. Upon being released from hospital at the beginning of April 1917, Bolle, was posted to *Kampfstaffel* 23, where for a short period he flew as an observer with Lothar von Richthofen, brother of the Red Baron. At the end of April he found that the application he had made some months earlier to transfer to single-seater fighters had been accepted, and he was posted to *Jastaschule* at the beginning of 1917.

After graduating in July 1917, he was posted to *Jasta* 28, where he came under the tutelage of *Offizier-Stellvertreter* Max Müller. The commanding officer at that time was *Leutnant* Karl-Emil Schäfer, holder of the coveted *Orden Pour le Mérite*. On 8 August he opened his tally by

shooting down a DH 4 from 57 Squadron, RFC, whilst on patrol over
Kachtem. His second, a Martinsyde G100 bomber from 27 Squadron,
RFC, was shot down over Seclin on 21 August. Bolle was awarded the
Friedrich Order Knight 2nd Class with Swords on 6 September, 1917, for
his bravery. It wasn't until 18 December that he scored his next victory,
a Sopwith Camel from 65 Squadron, RFC. Bolle scored his fourth victory
on 29, January, 1918, when he shot down another Sopwith Camel from

65 Squadron. The following day he raised his tally to five by shooting down a DH 4 from No. 5 Squadron, RNAS.

During his time with *Jasta* 28, Bolle served under a succession of experienced commanding officers, among them *Leutnant* Karl-Emil Schäfer and *Leutnant* Emil Thuy. No young pilot could have wished for better tutors than these seasoned veterans.

Despite his relative inexperience, Bolle was given command of *Jasta* Boelcke on 20 February, 1918 and promoted to *Oberleutnant*. The reason behind this appointment was that the unit had lost its two previous leaders within a short time of each other. First *Leutnant* Walter von Bülow was shot down and killed on 6 January, then *Leutnant* Max Müller took over temporarily, (while it was debated whether or not a Bavarian could take command of a Prussian unit) but was killed three days later when his aircraft was seen to go down in flames. His successor was *Leutnant* von Höhne who lasted less than a month, admitting that he wasn't up to the job of commanding such a high profile *Jasta*. To be fair to von Höhne he was still recovering from a serious wound received a year previously. Bolle was assigned and immediately set about making it one of the best, but it was to be two months before Bolle himself got back into the air and started scoring again. On 3 April he shot down a DH 9 bomber whilst on patrol over Frezenberg, and on 25 April a Sopwith Camel, raising his tally to seven.

Leutnant *Karl Bolle about to board his Fokker Triplane.*

The next three months of the war in the air were frantic ones as the Allies started making their big push and the skies were cluttered with aircraft. A further twenty-one Allied aircraft,By the end of July, brought Bolle's tally to twenty-eight, but at an even greater cost to his own squadrons.

He was promoted to *Rittmeister* at the beginning of August and awarded the Order of Max Joseph, the Mecklenburg Military Cross of Merit with Swords and the Knight's Cross with Swords of the Hohenzollern House Order. Then on 28 August, 1918, he received the ultimate accolade, the *Pour le Mérite*, Germany's highest award. Bolle continued to fight on and by the end of the war had raised his score to thirty-six.

When the war ended Karl Bolle left the army and became a flying instructor, then in the early 1920's was appointed Director of the German Transportation Flying School, in charge of all pilot training. At the beginning of the Second World War, Bolle became special advisor to the Luftwaffe, a post he held throughout the war. He died in Berlin on 9 October, 1955, at the age of sixty-two.

The elite of the German fighter pilots: Oblt. *von Dostler (far left), Manfred von Richthofen in fur coat, Rudolf Berthold in doorway and Karl Bolle to Berthold's left*

Awards

Orden Pour le Mérite
Knight's Cross with Swords of the Royal Hohenzollern House Order
Iron Cross 1st Class
Iron Cross 2nd Class
Knight 2nd Class with Swords of the Württemberg Friedrich Order
Mecklenburg-Schwerin Military Merit Cross 2nd Class
Wound Badge in Black – Germany.
Pilot's Badge, Army – Germany.

Victory log

1917

8 Aug	DH 4 (No. 57 Sqn RFC)	Kachtem
21 Aug	Martinsyde G.100 (No. 27 Sqn RFC)	N Seclin
18 Dec	Sopwith Camel (No. 65 Sqn RFC)	NW Staden

1918

29 Jan	Sopwith Camel (No. 70 Sqn RFC)	E Polecapelle
30 Jan	DH 4 (No. 5 Sqn RNAS)	E Wilskerke
3 Apr	AWFK 8 (No. 35 Sqn RAF)	Frezenberg
25 Apr	Sopwith Camel (No. 73 Sqn RAF)	Nieuvekerke
3 May	Sopwith Camel (No. 73 Sqn RAF)	S Bailleul
8 May	SE 5 (No.1 Sqn RAF)	St. Eloi
8 May	Sopwith Camel (No. 43 Sqn RAF)	Steenwerk
19 May	DH 9 (No. 206 Sqn RAF)	Zonnebeke
29 May	SPAD VII (*Escadrille Spa* 99)	Soissons
3 Jun	SPAD VII (*Escadrille Spa* 89)	Fauborg
4 Jun	Breguet XIV (*Escadrille Br* 108)	Fresnes
9 Jun	SPAD XIII (*Escadrille Spa* 90)	Dampleux
14 Jun	Breguet XIV (*Escadrille Br* 29)	Laversine
16 Jun	DH 9 (No. 27 Sqn RAF)	Bus
24 Jun	Breguet XIV (*Escadrille Br* 21)	Saponay
28 Jun	SPAD XIII (*Escadrille Spa* 162)	Longpont
5 Jul	Nieuport 28 (95th Aero Sqn USAS)	Courchamps
15 Jul	Sopwith Camel (No. 43 Sqn RAF)	Dormans
17 Jul	DH 9 (No. 211 Sqn RAF)	Soilly
18 Jul	SPAD (*Escadrille Spa* 159)	Quesnoy
18 Jul	Breguet XIV (*Escadrille Br* 104)	Ferme
22 Jul	Sopwith Camel (No. 73 Sqn RAF)	Quesnoy
25 Jul	Sopwith Camel (No. 43 Sqn RAF)	Fere-en-Tardenois
28 Jul	Salmson 2A2 (12th Aero Sqn USAS)	Villers-sur-Fere
31 Jul	SPAD XIII (*Escadrille Spa* 88)	Courtemain
9 Aug.	RE 8 (No. 6 Sqn RAF)	Rosieres
11 Aug	Salmson 2A2 (88th Aero Sqn USAS)	Fismes
26 Aug	Sopwith Camel (17th Aero Sqn USAS)	W Beugny

1 Nov	SE 5 (No. 32 Sqn RAF)	W Harchies
4 Nov	Sopwith Snipe (No. 4 Sqn AFC)	Englefontaine
4 Nov	Sopwith Snipe (No. 4 Sqn AFC)	Englefontaine
4 Nov	Sopwith Snipe (No. 4 Sqn AFC)	Tournai
4 Nov	Sopwith Snipe (No. 4 Sqn AFC)	Escanaffles

Total victories claimed: 31

CHAPTER TWENTY-NINE

Oberleutnant zur See Gotthard Sachsenberg (1891 – 1961)

Oberleutnant *Gotthard Sachsenberg getting instruction on the Fokker Eindecker.*

Gotthard Sachsenberg was born in Rossau on the 6 December, 1891. His childhood, like many others, was an uneventful one. Then in 1913, at the age of twenty-two, he joined the Imperial German Navy as a sea cadet aboard the cruiser Hertha. In the spring of 1914 he was posted aboard the battleship *Pommern* with a promotion to *Fähnrich*, however Sachsenberg had other ideas and when Germany declared war, almost immediately Sachsenberg volunteered for aviation duties in the newly formed Air Service. His decision to transfer may have saved his life, because at the Battle of Jutland, the *Pommern* was blown apart by the two British battle-cruisers HMS *Fortune* and HMS *Ardent* with the loss of almost all the crew.

Sachsenberg wanted to be a pilot and applied specifically for that, but the need for observers was just as great and he was assigned to observer school. After training he was posted to *Marine Flieger-Abteilung* (Fl.Abt.)2, where after ten missions he was awarded the Iron Cross 2nd Class. Then on 26 April, 1915, came the award of the Iron Cross 1st Class. On 18 September, 1915, his promotion to *Leutnant zur See* came through and with it a new posting, back to observer training school, this time as an instructor. In the meantime Sachsenberg had applied for pilot training which was approved. Whilst he was waiting for the posting to come through he took advantage of his position at the flying school to polish up his flying skills with the aid of some of the pilots. He was posted to *Jastaschule* at Mannheim for training in the February and after graduating in February 1916, returned to his old unit *Marine* Fl.Abt.2 flying Fokker E.IIIs from Mariakerke.

Gotthard Sachsenberg standing alongside a new LVG C II.

A lull in the fighting in that area during 1916 resulted in Sachsenberg having no success as a fighter pilot, but he continued to carry out observation duties. Then in May of 1917, he was given command of *Marine-Feldjasta* I (MFJ.I) in the April, and the war suddenly escalated. He scored his first victory, a Belgian Farman over Dixmude on 1 May, 1917, and the same day a Belgian Sopwith 1½ Strutter over Oudercappelle. On the 20 August, after six victories, he received the Knight's Cross with Swords of the Hohenzollern House Order. By the end of the 1917 he had raised his tally to eight and was awarded the Iron Cross 1st Class and the Knight 1st Class with Swords House of the Order of Albert the Bear.

The beginning of 1918 saw the war hotting up and by the end of April, Nr. I *Marine-Feldjasta* received a special commendation for having shot down fifty enemy aircraft and Sachsenberg was singled out for his leadership.

In August, Sachsenberg's tally had risen to twenty-four and he was awarded Germany's highest honour, the *Orden Pour le Mérite*.

Other honours continued to come his way, the Friedrich Cross 1st and 2nd Class of Anhalt; Friedrich-August Cross 1st and 2nd Class of Oldenburg and the Hanseatic Cross of Hamburg. At the end of the war his tally stood at thirty-one the last one being scored when he flew with the *Marine Freikorps* MJG. I in the Baltic. In 1920 the long overdue promotion to *Oberleutnant zur See* came through.

Oberleutnant zur See Gotthard Sachsenberg died on the 23 August, 1961, at the age of seventy.

Oberleutnant *Gotthard Sachsenberg when commander of 1* Marine Feldflieger-Abteilung

Awards

Orden Pour le Mérite
Knight's Cross with Swords of the Royal Hohenzollern House Order
Knight 1st Class with Swords of the Anhalt House Order of Albert the Bear
Iron Cross 2nd Class
Iron Cross 1st Class
Anhalt Friedrich Cross 1st Class
Anhalt Friedrich Cross 2nd Class
Oldenburg Friedrich-August Cross 1st Class

Oldenburg Friedrich-August Cross 2nd Class
Hamburg Hanseatic Cross
Ottoman Empire War Medal
Pilot's Badge (Navy)
Observer's Badge (Navy)
Austro-Hungarian Field Pilot's Badge (Karl Pattern)

Victory log

1917

1 May	Farman (Belgian 4m *Escadrille*)	Dixmude
1 May	Sopwith 1½ Strutter (Belgian 4m *Escadrille*)	Oudercapelle
12 May	Sopwith Pup (No. 4 Sqn RNAS)	Zeebrugge
7 Jun	FE 2d (No. 20 Sqn RFC)	St Eloi
7 Jun	Sopwith Pup (No. 3 Sqn RNAS)	Potyz
9 Aug	SPAD VII (No. 23 Sqn RFC)	NE Lampernisse
18 Nov	Sopwith Camel	Nieuport

1918

17 Mar	Breguet XIV (*Escadrille Br* 213)	Pervsye
25 Apr	Sopwith Camel (No. 54 Sqn RFC)	Avecapelle
21 May	DH 4 (No. 211 Sqn RAF)	Mariakerke
29 May	DH 9	SW Nieuwscapelle
2 Jun	SPAD XIII (*Escadrille Spa* 155)	Middlekereke
12 Jun	DH 9 (No. 218 Sqn RAF)	Ostende
13 Jul	SPAD XIII (*Escadrille Spa* 84)	Westende
16 Jul	SPAD XIII (*Escadrille Spa* 153)	Zeebrugge
16 Jul	DH 9 (No. 202 Sqn RAF)	Uberschwemm
16 Jul	DH 4 (No. 202 Sqn RAF)	Middlekerke
29 Jul	Sopwith Camel (No.73 Sqn RAF)	Pervsye
12 Aug	Sopwith Camel (17th Aero Sqn USAS)	Ostende
12 Aug	DH 9 (No. 206 Sqn RAF)	Ostende
16 Aug	Sopwith Camel (No. 213 Sqn RAF)	Zeebrugge
16 Aug	DH 9 (No. 211 Sqn RAF)	Cadzand
21 Aug	DH 9 (No. 107 Sqn RAF)	Zeebrugge
2 Sep	DH 9 (No. 206 Sqn RAF)	Dunkirk
23 Oct	DH 9 (No. 108 Sqn RAF)	Vosselaere
23 Oct	Sopwith Camel (No. 204 Sqn RAF)	Bellen-Ursel
23 Oct	Sopwith Camel (No. 204 Sqn RAF)	Bellen-Ursel
26 Oct	Sopwith Camel (No. 65 Sqn RAF)	Essenghem
28 Oct	DH 9 (No. 27 Sqn RAF)	Deinze
29 Oct	RE 8 (No. 4 Sqn)	

Total victories claimed: 31

CHAPTER THIRTY

Leutnant Carl Allmenröder (1896 – 1917)

The son of a Lutheran Pastor, Carl Allmenröder was born on the 23 May, 1896, in the small town of Wald, near Solingen. He had a very strict upbringing and an intensive education which was instrumental in his choosing to become a doctor, but his studies were interrupted by the outbreak of war. He immediately enlisted in the German Army and joined the Ostfriesisches Feldartillerie-Regiment Nr. 62. On completion of his training he was posted to 1.Posensches Feldartillerie-Regiment Nr. 20, but within months he returned to the Nr. 62. He saw active service in Poland during which he was awarded the Iron Cross 2nd Class at the beginning of March 1915. On the 30 March he was awarded a commission. At the beginning of August his leadership resulted in him being awarded the Friedrich August Cross 1st Class.

During this period Carl Allmenröder discovered that his brother Willi had also enlisted in the German Army and together they applied, and were accepted, for the German Air Service on 29 March, 1916. They reported to *Flieger-Ersatz-Abteilung* (FEA) 5 at the Halberstadt Flying School near Hanover to begin pilot training. On completion of their flying training they were both posted to *Artillerie-Flieger-Abteilung* (Fl.Abt.(A)) 227 and in November 1916 to *Jasta* 11 (Royal Prussian). *Jasta* 11 was led by *Oberleutnant* Rudolf Lang and had been created one month earlier. A number of other pilots joined the *Jasta*, among them *Leutnant* Konstantin Krefft, *Leutnant* Kurt Wolf, *Leutnant* Georg Simon and *Vizefeldwebel* Sebastian Festner, all of whom were destined to leave their mark. On 15 January, 1917, *Oberleutnant* Lang's place was taken by the already legendary Manfred von Richthofen and the *Jasta* was to become the second highest scoring *Jasta* in the German Air Service.

Within a week Manfred von Richthofen had sent the standard of what he expected of the pilots in his *Jasta*, when he shot down two aircraft on the 23 and 24 January and three more in February. This gave a great deal of encouragement to the other pilots and Carl Allmenröder scored his first victory on the 16 February, 1917, when he shot down a BE 2c of 16 Squadron, RFC. The *Jasta's* strength was further enhanced by the

arrival of *Leutnant* Karl Emil Schäfer and Manfred's brother Lothar von Richthofen.

Allmenröder had raised his tally to four by the end of March and had been awarded the Iron Cross 1st Class. A victory over a BE 2 of 13 Squadron, RFC, over Lens during the Battle of Arras at the beginning of April boded well for Allmenröder. This was followed on the 25, 26 and 27 when he shot three aircraft down on consecutive days bringing his tally to eight. This success was marred by the news that his brother Willi, who had scored two victories, had been severely wounded in a dog-fight and had been invalided out of the German Air Service.

Karl Allmenröder of Jasta *11 beside the red fuselage of his Albatros D III.*

The *Jasta* lost one of their top pilots on 25 April when Sebastian Festner was shot down and killed. Karl Emil Schäfer on the other hand was increasing his tally daily and was awarded the Knight's Cross with Swords of the Royal Hohenzollern House Order and the *Orden Pour le Mérite* in an unprecedented step when they were awarded together.

Manfred von Richthofen went on leave in April and left command of *Jasta* 11 to his brother Lothar. Kurt Wolff in the meantime had been assigned to take over *Jasta* 29, whose commander, *Oberleutnant* Ludwig Dornheim had just been killed in action. Then Lothar von Richthofen, returning from a sortie, was hit by groundfire and badly injured. This in effect left Carl Allmenröder as the leader of *Jasta* 11, a role he took on until the return of Manfred von Richthofen

The month of May turned out to be one of the most successful for Carl Allmenröder when he scored thirteen victories in the month bringing his tally to twenty-one. Four more at the beginning of June highlighted his relentless pursuit of the enemy and brought his tally to twenty-five. On the 6 June, he was awarded the Knight's Cross of the House of Hohenzollern Order and the following day the coveted *Orden Pour le Mérite*. Manfred von Richthofen was delighted, four of the men under his command had been awarded the coveted award.

Although June was to start dramatically well for Carl Allmenröder, it was to end tragically. On the 18, 24, 25 and 26, four more British aircraft were to fall before his guns, bringing his tally to twenty-nine.

Then at 0945 on the 27 June his patrol was returning from an unsuccessful sortie against Allied aircraft, when his plane was hit by machine gun fire from the ground and crashed into the ground killing him instantly. He was posthumously awarded the Oldenburg Friedrich August Cross 1st and 2nd Class and the Bayern Military Kronen Order 4th Class on the 20 July, 1917.

In one eyewitness report in a newspaper called the *Wüppertaler General Anzieger*, part of what was said to have happened to Allmenröder was reported:

Infantryman Max Feuerstein of the 4th Company of the Bavarian 6th Reserve was in   a grenade shelter when a flock of English fliers arrived at the Front. They went back and forth at low altitude like a swarm of hornets. Then Blood-red single-seater   fighters,   well known by every soldier in Flanders, shot like lightning below the English hornets. The first blue-white-red cockade pulled out toward its own lines, burning in a cloud of black smoke. Fleeing, the enemy sought its own territory. A red arrow shot out after it. Then the red arrow came back from the other side. Artillery and machine gun fire

Funeral procession of Karl Allmenröder

directed at it created a roar that exploded around the plane. Gripping fear came over the field grays in the cratered field as the red machine veered and then spun. One wing broke off. A plume of smoke trailed behind. A tongue of fire shot out of the aircraft explosive like. It shuddered, fell and crashed out of control into the depths. The splintered machine with its doomed occupant fell into the mud in a nearby bunker. Barely two hundred metres in front of the first English positions the red Albatros had bored itself into the ground enveloped in fire and smoke.

Carl Allmenröder was just twenty-one years old.

Awards

Orden Pour le Mérite
Knight's Cross with Swords of the Royal Hohenzollern House Order
Iron Cross 2nd Class
Iron Cross 1st Class
Oldenburg Friedrich-August Cross 1st Class
Oldenburg Friedrich-August Cross 2nd Class
Bayern Military Kronen Order 4th Class
Pilot's Badge

Victory log

1917

16 Feb	BE 2c (No. 16 Sqn RFC)	Roeux
9 Mar	FE 8 (No. 40 sqn RFC)	Hulluch
17 Mar	Sopwith 1½ Strutter (No. 43 Sqn RFC)	Athies-Oppey
21 Mar	Sopwith 1½ Strutter (No. 43 Sqn RFC)	Loos
30 Mar	Nieuport 17 (No. 40 Sqn RFC)	Bailleul-Arras
2 Apr	BE 2 (No. 13 Sqn RFC)	Lens
25 Apr	BE 2e (No. 12 Sqn RFC)	Guemappe
26 Apr	BE 2g (No. 16 Sqn RFC)	Vimy
27 Apr	BE 2c (No. 2 Sqn RFC)	Athies-Fampoux
7 May	BE 2c (No. 13 Sqn RFC)	Fresnoy
10 May	Sopwith Pup (No. 66 Sqn RFC)	Vitry
13 May	RE 8 (No. 16 Sqn RFC)	Arleux
13 May	Nieuport XXIII (No. 29 Sqn RFC)	Ostricourt
14 May	BE 2e (No. 8 Sqn RFC)	Guemappe
18 May	BE 2e (No. 12 Sqn RFC)	Monchy
19 May	Sopwith Camel (No. 12 Sqn RFC)	Bethune
24 May	FE 2b (No. 11 Sqn RFC)	Boiry
24 May	Sopwith 1½ Strutter (No. 43 Sqn RFC)	Izel-Ferme
25 May	Nieuport XXIII (No. 60 Sqn RFC)	Bois de Vert
25 May	DH 4 (No. 55 Sqn RFC)	Monchy
28 May	SE 5 (No. 60 Sqn RFC)	Feuchy-Tilloy
29 May	BE 2 (No. 5 Sqn RFC)	Oppy
3 Jun	SE 5 (No. 60 Sqn RFC)	Monchy

4 Jun	RE 8 (No. 21 Sqn RFC)	Cagnicourt
4 Jun	SE 5 (No. 29 Sqn RFC)	Monchy
5 Jun	Sopwith 1½ Strutter (No. 45 Sqn RFC)	Ypres
18 Jun	Nieuport XVII (No. 1 Sqn RFC)	Verlorenhoek
24 Jun	Sopwith Triplane (No. 10 Sqn RNAS)	Polygonwald
25 Jun	Sopwith Triplane (No. 10 Sqn RNAS)	Quesnoy
26 Jun	Nieuport Scout (No. 1 Sqn RFC)	Ypres

Total victories claimed: 30

CHAPTER THIRTY-ONE

Leutnant Carl Degelow
(1891 – 1970)

Carl Degelow was born on 5 January, 1891, in Munsterdorf, Germany and throughout his childhood had the urge to travel which resulted in him going to America when he was twenty-one. He worked at various jobs throughout the United States from Chicago to El Paso, Texas, then On hearing that there was possibly going to be a war in Europe, returned to Germany and arrived back just prior to the start of the First World War.

Almost immediately on his arrival Carl Degelow joined the Nassauischen Infantrie-Regiment Nr. 88 and after some preliminary training was sent to the Western Front. His regiment was in action within

Leutnant *Carl Degelow*

weeks of being there and Degelow showed his leadership qualities. Within three months he had been promoted from *Gefreiter* to *Unteroffizier* and had been awarded the Iron Cross 2nd Class. At the beginning of 1915, the regiment was posted to the Russian Front and once again Degelow showed his leadership qualities by leading a succession of offensives against the Russians, for which he was promoted to *Vizefeldwebel* and awarded the Iron Cross 1st Class. It was on one of theses offensives against the Russians, that Degelow was badly wounded in the arm. On 31 July whilst in hospital, he was awarded a commission to *Leutnant*, but his inclinations were to get away from the mud and cold of the Russian Front, so he applied for a transfer to the German Army

Air Service.

Leutnant Carl Degelow returned to the Russian Front on release from hospital and for the next nine months was involved in some of the bitterest battles on that Front. Then in the April of 1916, the welcome news came that his transfer had come through and he was posted to flying school back in Germany. He graduated at the beginning of 1917, and was assigned to *Flieger-Abteilung* (A)(Fl.Abt.)216 on the Somme as a reconnaissance pilot. For the next couple of months, Degelow with his observer *Leutnant* Kurten, flew artillery support and reconnaissance missions in their Albatros CV. Then on 22 May 1917, whilst on an artillery support flight over SW Braye, they were attacked by a Caudron G.IV. During the ensuing fight they managed to get the better of it and shoot it down, but unfortunately it was unconfirmed. Three days later, whilst on another reconnaissance mission over Bailly-Braye, they were attacked by another Caudron G.IV, and shot it down. This time it was confirmed and Degelow opened his tally.

Tired of flying reconnaissance missions Carl Degelow applied for transfer to single-seater fighters and was posted to *Jasta* 36 for training.

Leutnant *Carl Degelow (extreme left) with a slightly battered British pilot who had just been shot down.*

Within days of starting the course he had been returned to his unit after accidentally shooting an airmen during a mock combat exercise. It happened as he carried out a strafing attack on a ground target which was out of bounds for the exercise. An observer on the ground, *Leutnant* Kreuzer, suddenly saw an aircraft diving towards him, then bullets started hitting the ground around him and one struck him in the foot. He was rushed to hospital for emergency surgery and Degelow was rushed back to his unit.

Carl Degelow completed his single-seater training some weeks later. He was posted to *Jasta* 7 on 17 August, 1917, where he notched up another two victories, but again they were unconfirmed. But a victory over a BF2b of 20 Squadron, RFC, on 25 January, 1918, a Sopwith Camel from 54 Squadron, RFC, on 21 April, and an RE 8 from No. 7 Squadron, RFC, on 16 May, raised his tally to four. On 16 May, 1918 Carl Degelow was posted to *Jasta* 40 and two months later took command on 11 July. He celebrated his appointment to commander, by shooting down six more aircraft in July bringing his score to thirteen.

On the 9 August, 1918, he was awarded the Knight's Cross with Swords of the Hohenzollern House Order for his dedication to duty and for making his *Jasta* one of the highest scoring *Jastas* of the German Army Air Service. He celebrated the award by shooting down another six Allied aircraft in the month of September as if to prove the point. By the end of October he had shot down another ten Allied aircraft, raising his total to twenty-nine. The total rose to thirty on 4 November 1918, when he shot down a DH 9 near the Dutch border. Then on 9 November, 1918, he was awarded Germany's highest award, the *Orden Pour le Mérite*, he was to be the last member of the German Army Air Service to receive the prestigious award.

After the war Degelow created the Hamburg Zeitfretwillingen Korps and fought against the communists in the post-war revolution. At the beginning of the Second World War, he joined the Luftwaffe becoming a Major. After surviving a second world war, Degelow went into business

Leutnant Carl Degelow when CO of Jasta *40.*

becoming a director of a concrete factory in Pommerania and died in Hamburg on 9 November, 1970.

Awards

Orden Pour le Mérite
Knight's Cross with Swords of the Royal Hohenzollern Hose Order
Iron Cross 2nd Class
Iron Cross 1st Class
Wound Badge in Black
Pilot's Badge – German Army

Victory log

1917

25 May	Caudron G.IV (Escadrille C 27)	Bailly-Braye

1918

25 Jan	BF 2b (No. 20 Sqn RFC)	Courtemarck
21 Apr	Sopwith Camel (No.54 Sqn RAF)	E Armentieres
16 May	RE 8 (No. 7 Sqn RAF)	Vlamertinghe
18 Jun	SE 5a (No. 29 Sqn RAF)	Vieux Berquin
25 Jun	Sopwith Camel (No. 54 Sqn RAF)	Zandvoorde
27 Jun	SE 5a (No. 29 Sqn RAF)	La Creue
2 Jul	SE 5a (No. 29 Sqn RAF)	Kruisstraat
13 Jul	SE 5a (No. 85 Sqn RAF)	Erquighem
14 Jul	SE 5a (No. 85 Sqn RAF)	SE Vieux Berquin
14 Jul	SE 5a (No. 64 Sqn RAF)	W Merville
22 Jul	BF 2b (No. 62 Sqn RAF)	Lestrem
25 Jul	Sopwith Camel (No. 208 Sqn RAF)	Wystschaete
18 Sep	Balloon (Balloon Company 36-17-2)	Poperinghe
20 Sep	BF 2b (No. 48 Sqn RAF)	N Annapes
21 Sep	RE 8 (No. 7 Sqn RAF)	N. Ypres
24 Sep	SE 5a (No. 41 Sqn RAF)	Zillebeke Lake
27 Sep	BF 2b (No. 99 Sqn RAF)	Valenciennes
28 Sep	Sopwith Camel (No. 70 Sqn RAF)	Armentieres
1 Oct	SE 5a (N0. 74 Sqn RAF)	Menin
2 Oct	Sopwith Camel (No. 213 Sqn RAF)	Roulers
3 Oct	SPAD XIII (*Escadrille Spa* 82)	Roulers
4 Oct	Sopwith Camel (No. 213 Sqn RAF)	Roulers
5 Oct	DH 9 (No. 211 Sqn RAF)	Ghent
7 Oct	Sopwith Camel (No. 65 Sqn RAF)	Ghent
8 Oct	Sopwith Camel (No. 210 Sqn RAF)	Ypres
26 Oct	SPAD XIII (*Escadrille Spa* 161)	Ghent
27 Oct	Sopwith Camel (No. 204 Sqn RAF)	Wynghene
30 Oct	SE 5a (No. 32 Sqn RAF)	Courtrai
4 Nov	DH 9 (No. 103 Sqn RAF)	Abancourt

CHAPTER THIRTY-TWO

Leutnant Josef Mai
(1887 – 1982)

Josef Mai was born and educated in Berlin on 3 March, 1887. Very little is known of his early years, although it is believed he served in the army before applying for a transfer to the German Army Air Service in May 1915 at the age of twenty-eight. This was unusual as most of the Air Service personnel were in their late teens or early twenties. He applied

Leutnant *Josef Mai.*

to become a pilot and was accepted and after completing his training at *Jastaschule* 1 at Johannisthal, near Berlin, he was assigned to *Kampstaffel* (Kasta) 29 of *Kampfgeschwader* (KG) 5 with the rank of *Vizefeldwebel*.

In February 1916 he applied for fighter-pilot training and was accepted and sent to *Jastaschule*. On graduating 28 July, 1916, he was promoted to *Offizier-Stellvertreter* and posted to *Jasta* 5 which was under the command of *Leutnant* Hans Berr. There he joined two other non-commissioned officers, *Vizefeldwebel* Otto Könnecke and *Vizefeldwebel* Fritz Rumey. They were to become known as the 'golden triumvirate' as all were later awarded the Golden Military Merit Cross and collectively have a score of 108 confirmed victories. These three were to become the backbone of the *Jasta* 5 and became instrumental in helping the *Jasta* to become the third highest scoring *Jasta* in the German Army Air Service.

It wasn't until 20 August, 1917, that Mai, flying in an Albatros D.V, scored his first victory when he shot down a Sopwith Camel from No. 70 Squadron, RFC, over Rumaucourt whilst on patrol. His second came five days later and the award of the Iron Cross 2nd Class. In November he added a further a three, a Sopwith Camel from No. 3 Squadron, RFC, a BF 2b and an SE5a from No. 56 Squadron, RFC. The *Jasta* went through

Leutnant *Josef Mai of Jasta 5 together with his ground crew.*

Vzfw Josef Mai (third from left) with Vzfw Fritz Rumey (second from right)

a relatively quiet period until January 1918 when Mai shot down two BF 2bs both from No. 11 Squadron, RFC. January also saw the award of the Iron Cross 1st Class and the promotion to Unteroffizier.

His next three victories during March and April were carried out in his Albatros D.V, then the *Jasta* was re-equipped with the Fokker Dr.I Triplane. After his thirteenth victory he was awarded the Golden Military Merit Cross or *Pour le Mérite für Unteroffiziere*, as it was called by non-commissioned officers. His two fellow NCOs had by this time been promoted to *Leutnant* and were about to be awarded the *Orden Pour le Mérite*, but it wasn't until 27 September, 1918, that Josef Mai was to be promoted to officer rank. August and September of 1918 saw Josef Mai claim thirteen victories all of which were confirmed and on 27 September his promotion to *Leutnant* was approved and his nomination for the *Orden Pour le Mérite* recommended for approval. By the end of the war he had shot down thirty Allied aircraft

When the war ended Josef Mai's *Orden Pour le Mérite* award was still in the pipeline and that is where it stayed. Little is known of Josef Mai's activities during the Second World War but it is believed he became an instructor at one of the Luftwaffe's flying schools.

Joseph Mai was a perfect example of one of Germany's top fighter pilots who received just three awards in recognition of his services to his country compared to Max Immelmann who was given thirteen awards for just fifteen victories – half of what Joseph Mai scored

He died on 18 January, 1982, at the age of ninety-four.

Awards

Golden Military Merit Cross
Iron Cross 2nd Class
Iron Cross 1st Class
Wound Badge in Black

Pilot's Badge – German Army

Victory log

1917

20 Aug	Sopwith Camel (No. 70 Sqn RFC)	Rumaucaourt
25 Aug	DH 5 (No. 41 Sqn RFC)	Selvigny
20 Nov	Sopwith Camel (No. 3 Sqn RFC)	W Estourmel
22 Nov	BF 2b (No. 11 Sqn RFC)	Cantaing-Anneux
30 Nov	SE 5a (No. 56 Sqn RFC)	Le Pave

1918

13 Jan	BF 2b (No. 11 Sqn RFC)	W Gonnelieu
28 Jan	BF 2b (No. 11 Sqn RFC)	Bourlon Wood
8 Mar	DH 4 (No. 27 Sqn RFC)	Fresnoy le Grand
16 Mar	DH 4 (No. 5 Sqn RNAS)	St Benin
25 Apr	Sopwith Camel (No. 65 Sqn RAF)	Dommart
2 May	Sopwith Camel (No. 65 Sqn RAF)	Morcourt
15 May	BF 2b (No. 11 Sqn RFC)	Contalmaison
20 May	Sopwith Camel (No. 65 Sqn RAF)	Morlancourt
2 Jun	Sopwith Camel (No. 65 Sqn RAF)	S Hangard
27 Jun	Sopwith Camel (No. 70 Sqn RAF)	Thiepval
5 Jul	BF 2b (No. 48 Sqn RAF)	Guillemont
20 Jul	DH 4 (No. 57 Sqn RAF)	Achiet le Petit
8 Aug	BF 2b (No. 48 Sqn RAF)	Mericourt
8 Aug	DH 9 (No. 27 Sqn RAF)	Ham
12 Aug	Sopwith Camel (No. 209 Sqn RAF)	Maricourt
19 Aug	BF 2b (No. 48 Sqn RAF)	Lihons
19 Aug	BF 2b (No. 48 Sqn RAF)	Lihons
19 Aug	SE 5a (No. 56 Sqn RAF)	Le Translov
3 Sep	BF 2b (No. 20 Sqn RAF)	Bertincourt
5 Sep	SE 5a (No. 64 Sqn RAF)	Bugnicourt
17 Sep	Sopwith Camel (No. 46 Sqn RAF)	SW Hermies
21 Sep	DH 4 (No. 205 Sqn RAF)	Le Catelet
24 Sep	DH 9 (No. 49 Sqn RAF)	S Beauvois
29 Sep	BF 2b (No. 20 Sqn RAF)	E Caudry

Total victories claimed: 30

CHAPTER THIRTY-THREE

Leutnant Ulrich Neckel
(1898 – 1928)

Born in Bavaria on 23 January, 1898, Ulrich Neckel like many other children at that time had a normal carefree childhood. When the First World War began, Neckel was sixteen and was always seeking adventure so he volunteered for the army. He joined the Holstein Feld-Artillerie Regiment Nr. 24 as an artillery man and on completing the training in January 1915, he was sent to the Eastern Front and was in action immediately. During the next six months Neckel distinguished himself several times under fire for which he was awarded the Iron Cross 2nd Class. The terrible conditions and strain of the Eastern Front was beginning to take their toll on Neckel and made him think of ways of getting out of the cold and the mud. In September 1916 Neckel applied for transfer to the German Army Air Service and was accepted. He was then sent to the flying school at Gotha in November 1916 and after completing his training graduated as a pilot in February 1917.

Joining the Air Service was one of the reasons Neckel used to get away from the Eastern Front, but then to his dismay he found he was posted back there to join *Flieger-Abteilung* (Fl.Abt.) 25. After completing a number of reconnaissance missions he applied for training as a fighter pilot and in August 1917, was sent to *Jastaschule* at Valenciennes. After graduating at the beginning of September, he was promoted to *Gefreiter* and posted to *Jasta* 12.

On 21 September, 1917, Neckel was on patrol over E. Monchy-le-Preux when he shot down a Sopwith Pup from 46 Squadron, RFC, and opened his tally. Seven days later he shot down a D.H.5 from No. 41 Squadron, RFC, increasing his score to two, followed on the 18 October by another DH5 from No. 41 squadron. His total stayed at three until the end of the year.

By the end of April 1918 Neckel had raised his tally to ten and been awarded a commission to *Leutnant* in recognition of his rapid success. The end of July saw his score doubled and with it came the award of the the Iron Cross 1st Class. Neckel continued his scoring and by the end of August he was transferred to *Jasta* 19 and awarded the Knight's Cross

with Swords of the Hohenzollern House Order. On 1 September he was given command of *Jasta* 6 in Jadgeschwader 1. with his score standing at twenty-four. It was during this period that he was awarded first the Mecklenburg-Schwerin Military Merit Cross 1st Class and then the Mecklenburg-Schwerin Military Merit Cross 2nd Class

During one incident on 18 October, the *Jasta* was involved in combat

Leutnant Ulrich Neckel with a laurel wreath celebrating his 20th victory.

with Allied fighters and Neckel's wingman, *Leutnant* Noltenius who had recently joined the *Jasta*, was accused later of not keeping up with his leader in the middle of a fight. The charge was vehemently denied by Noltenius and appears to be without foundation, but suffice to say that he was transferred to *Jasta* 11 two days later. Noltenius it appears had a history of quarrels in his previous *Jasta* complaining that he was being continually upstaged and having his claims for aircraft shot down turned in favour of more senior pilots. On 8 November, 1918, Ulrich Neckel was awarded Prussia's highest honour the *Orden Pour le Mérite*.

At the end of the war, *Leutnant* Ulrich Neckel's score stood at twenty-nine, but not long after he contracted tuberculosis and after a very long illness, died in Italy on the 11 May, 1928.

Awards

Orden Pour le Mérite
Knight's Cross with Swords of the Royal Hohenzollern House Order
Mecklenburg-Schwerin Military Merit Cross 1st Class
Mecklenburg-Schwerin Military Merit Cross 2nd Class
Iron Cross 2nd Class
Iron Cross 1st Class
Pilot's Badge

Victory log

1917

21 Sep	Sopwith Pup (No. 46 Sqn RFC)	E Monchy le Preux
28 Sep	DH 5 (No. 41 Sqn RFC)	Biache Station
18 Oct	DH 5 (No. 2 Sqn RFC)	NE Boursies

1918

18 Jan	AWFK.8 (No. 70 Sqn RFC)	Loos
26 Feb	SE 5a (No. 24 Sqn RFC)	E Vauxaillon
28 Feb	SE 5a (No. 84 Sqn RFC)	St Gobain Woods
23 Mar	Sopwith Camel (No. 70 Sqn RFC)	Ham
31 Mar	SPAD XIII (*Escadrille Spa* 57)	W Montdidier
12 Apr	SPAD XIII (*Escadrille Spa* 86)	E Arvillers
21 Apr	Breguet XIV (*Escadrille Br* 220)	Bussy
14 Jun	Sopwith Camel (No. 80 Sqn RAF)	Drelincourt
14 Jun	Sopwith Camel (No. 80 Sqn RAF)	Drelincourt
16 Jun	Sopwith Camel (No. 80 Sqn RAF)	Drelincourt
17 Jun	SPAD XIII (*Escadrille Spa* 37)	W Roye
25 Jun	BF 2b (No. 48 Sqn RAF)	E Albert
25 Jun	Sopwith Camel (No. 201 Sqn RAF)	E Villers Bretonneux
27 Jun	BF 2b (No. 48 Sqn RAF)	Villers Bretonneaux
27 Jun	SE 5a (No. 84 Sqn RAF)	Villers Brettoneaux
3 Jul	Sopwith Camel	Roye
7 Jul	Sopwith Camel (No. 209 Sqn RAF)	NE Warfusee
11 Aug	SPAD XIII (*Escadrille Spa* 37)	N Roye
13 Aug	Sopwith Camel (No. 201 Sqn RAF)	Le Quesnel
14 Aug	SE 5a (No. 92 Sqn RAF)	Chaulnes
21 Aug	SPAD XIII (*Escadrille Spa* 160)	Quierzy
15 Sep	BF 2b (No. 20 Sqn RAF)	Estrees
23 Oct	Salmson 2A2 (1st Observation Sqn USAS)	
30 Oct	SPAD XIII (22nd Aero Sqn USAS)	
31 Oct	Salmson 2A2 (27th Aero Sqn USAS)	
6 Nov.	SPAD XIII (28th Aero Sqn USAS)	Bethelainville

Total victories claimed: 29

CHAPTER THIRTY-FOUR

Leutnant Karl Emil Schäfer
(1891 – 1917)

K arl Emil Schäfer was born into a middle class family on the 17 December, 1891, in Krefeld, Bavaria. Almost nothing is known of his childhood years, but what is known is that in 1909 he served a years compulsory service in the army with the 10th Jaeger Regiment. On being discharged from the army Schäfer retuned to his home but then in the summer of 1914 he went first to London and then to Paris, and was there when the First World War broke out. Experiencing some difficulties because of his German nationality Schäfer managed to return to Germany and was almost immediately assigned to the 7th Jäger Reserve Regiment at Bückeburg. Within weeks of joining the regiment was into action and on the 19 September won the Iron Cross 2nd Class and promotion to *Vizefeldwebel*. Within days of receiving the award and the promotion, he was badly wounded by an explosive bullet in the thigh during a particularly intensive push forward and was hospitalised for six

Leutnant *Karl Schäfer in his Albatros D I.*

months. It was whilst in hospital that he decided that life in the infantry
was not for him and considered a move to the newly formed German
Army Air Service.

On release from hospital in March, Schäfer rejoined his unit and two
months later was granted a commission to *Leutnant*. One month later he
was awarded the Iron Cross 1st Class and the Military Merit Order 4th

Class with Swords from Bavaria. At the beginning of September Schäfer requested a transfer to the German Army Air Service for training as a pilot. His request was approved and on 16 January 1916 he was posted to *Flieger-Ersatz-Abteilung* (FEA) 8 at Graudenz. At the end of January he was sent to Köslin for flying training. Schäfer completed his flying training after only three months training was awarded his pilot's badge and certificate. He was then posted back to FEA 8 to be given his frontline assignment.

Schäfer, and his observer *Leutnant* Freiherr von Grone, joined *Kampfstaffel* 8 of *Kampfgeschwader* (KG).2 and on 30 July, 1916, was sent to the Eastern Front. Almost immediately his unit was sent to help plug the gap caused by the Russian Southwest Army Group smashing their way through the Austrian Fourth and Seventh Armies. Based at Kowel in the Ukraine, the unit flew reconnaissance and bombing missions, the latter against troop concentrations and railway junctions, for the next six months. It was whilst on the Eastern Front that Schäfer met Manfred von Richthofen and became friends.

Then the unit was moved to the Western Front and Schäfer joined *Kasta* II of KG.2. On the 22 January he scored his first victory, when he shot down a French Caudron over W. Pont-a-Mousson. It was to be the

Leutnant Karl Schäfer in front of his Albatros D III.

start of a remarkable but short career. Schäfer wrote to von Richthofen when he heard that the latter had been given command of a fighter *Jasta* and asked if he could join him. The answer was short and precise – Yes. Schäfer was posted to join Manfred von Richthofen's *Jasta* II on the 21 February, 1917, and made his mark by shooting down eight aircraft in the following month of March – five of them in two days.

At the beginning of April, after being 'bounced' by British fighters, he had been forced to carry out an emergency landing and had been slightly injured, but by the end of April he had raised his tally to twenty-three and had been awarded the Knight's Cross with Swords of the Royal Hohenzollern House Order and the nations most prestigious award the *Orden Pour le Mérite*. He was then given command of *Jasta* 28.

The propeller of Karl Schäfer's Albatros D III after its machine gun interruptor gear malfunctioned

During the following month of May, Schäfer raised his tally to twenty-nine. On the 4 June he shot down a DH 4 from 55 Squadron RFC bringing his tally to thirty. Just after 1600 hrs on the 5 June, 1917, he and other members of *Jasta* 28, engaged FE 2d fighters of 20 Squadron, RFC. After a short but vicious fight, Schäfer was shot down by FE 2d, A6469, flown by Lieutenant H L Satchell and his Observer T A Lewis. The following is the official report by the RFC of Karl Schäfer's demise.

In the afternoon of the 5th a formation of seven FE 2ds of No. 20 Squadron had a running fight with about fifteen Albatros Scouts over the Ypres-Menin road. The German leader in a red Albatros, attacked one of the FEs and mortally wounded its pilot, Lieutenant W W Sawden, who dived for home closely pursued by the Albatros. Another of the FE 2ds (pilot, Lieutenant L Satchell, observer, Second Lieutenant T A M S Lewis) went to the assistance of Lieutenant Sawden and engaged the red Albatros in a combat lasting fifteen minutes. The German pilot showed exceptional skill and tenacity, but, eventually a burst of bullets from the FE 2d at very close range shattered a part of the Albatros which broke up in the air and crashed near Zandvoorde. The pilot proved to be *Leutnant* Karl Schäfer, one of the foremost German fighting pilots who had, at the time of his death, thirty Allied aeroplanes to his credit.

Karl Schäfer was twenty-six years old.

Awards

Orden Pour le Mérite
Iron Cross 2nd Class
Iron Cross 1st Class
Bavarian Military Merit Order 4th Class with Swords
Knight's Cross with Swords of the Royal Hohenzollern House Order
Schaumburg-Lippe Cross for Faithful Service 2nd Class
Pilot's Badge – German Army

Victory log

1917

22 Jan.	Caudron G 4 (*Escadrille* C 224)	W Pont-a-Masson
4 Mar	Sopwith 1½ Strutter (No. 43 Sqn RFC)	SW haisnes
6 Mar	Sopwith 1½ Strutter (No. 43 Sqn RFC)	Lens
6 Mar	Sopwith 1½ Strutter (No. 43 Sqn RFC)	Lens
9 Mar	FE 8 (No. 40 Sqn RFC)	Faschoda
9 Mar	FE 8 (No. 40 Sqn RFC)	Pont-a-Vendin
11 Mar	BE 2c (No. 2 Sqn RFC)	Loosbogen
24 Mar	Sopwith 1½ Strutter (No. 70 Sqn RFC)	Arras
3 Apr	FE 2d (No. 25 Sqn RFC)	S Lens
6 Apr	BE 2 (No. 16 Sqn RFC)	Givenchy
6 Apr	BE 2 (No. 2 Sqn RFC)	Vimy
7 Apr	Nieuport XXIII (No. 60 Sqn RFC)	Mecatal
8 Apr	DH 4 (No. 55 Sqn RFC)	Epinoy
9 Apr	BE 2d (No. 4 Sqn RFC)	Aise Roulette
11 Apr	BF 2a (No. 48 Sqn RFC)	Fampoux
11 Apr	BE 2e (No. 8 Sqn RFC)	Arras
13 Apr	FE 2b (No. 25 Sqn RFC)	Le Point du Jour
14 Apr	FE 2b (No. 25 Sqn RFC)	Lievin-Elu
14 Apr	BF 2d (No. 2 Sqn RFC)	La Coulette
21 Apr	Nieuport Scout (No. 29 Sqn RFC)	E Fresnes
22 Apr	FE 2b (No. 11 Sqn RFC)	NW Monchy-Tilloy
25 Apr	FE 2b (No. 25 Sqn RFC)	Bailleul
25 Apr	BF 2a (No. 48 Sqn RFC)	Bahnoff Roeux

1 May	Farman (Belgian 4me *Escadrille*)	Dixmude
1 May	Nieuport Scout (No. 1 Sqn RFC)	E Poperinghe
9 May	Sopwith 1½ Strutter (No. 45 Sqn RFC)	Warneton
18 May	FE 2d (No. 20 Sqn RFC)	Hollebeke
23 May	FE 2d (No.20 Sqn RFC)	Warneton
23 May	Sopwith Pup (No. 46 Sqn RFC)	Wytschaetebogen
4 Jun	DH 4 (No. 55 Sqn RFC)	Moorslede

Total victories claimed: 30

CHAPTER THIRTY-FIVE

Leutnant Walter von Bülow-Bothkamp (1894 – 1918)

The son of a very wealthy landowner, Walter von Bülow-Bothkamp was born on 24 April, 1894, at Borby, Near Eckernforde, Holstein. The Bülow-Bothkamp family had a strong military tradition so it was expected that he would join the army. But von Bülow was a very bright pupil and when he finished school he broke with family tradition and went to study law at Heidleberg University.

When war was declared Walter von Bülow-Bothkamp joined the famous Saxon Braunschweigisches Husaren-Regiment Nr.18, the 'Death's Head' Hussars, whose commander had once been the legendary *Feldmarschall* August von Mackensen. The Hussars were one of the first regiments into action, then later, early in 1915, they saw heavy fighting in the Alsace Region. During numerous actions Walter von Bülow-Bothkamp stood out from the rest of the men and after a series of skirmishes, in which he distinguished himself, was awarded the Iron Cross 2nd Class and given a field commission to *Leutnant*.

But even at this early stage of the war, von Bülow-Bothkamp could see that the days of the Hussars were numbered. The days of the cavalry charging with sabres drawn and wearing elaborate colourful uniforms were gone – mechanisation had taken over. He applied for transfer to the newly formed German Army Air Service in the spring of 1915 and was accepted. At the beginning of June he was posted to Valenciennes for pilot training, and on graduating was assigned to *Feldflieger-Abteilung* 22 (FFl.Abt. 22) flying reconnaissance missions in twin-engined AEG G.II biplanes.

His first victory came on 10 October, 1915, when, whilst flying on a reconnaissance mission over Metz, he shot down a Voisin. A second victory the next day, a Maurice Farman whilst patrolling the Champagne region, gained him the Iron Cross 1st Class.

With the winter of 1916 well and truly settled in, *Leutnant* Walter von Bülow-Bothkamp was posted to *Flieger-Abteilung* 300 (Pascha) in Palestine. As far as the weather was concerned, it was a welcome relief, but there was very little action. Von Bülow-Bothkamp's next victory

Studio portrait of
Leutnant *Walter von
Bülow with his pet dog.*

wasn't until the 8 August, when on a reconnaissance flight he shot down an EA over El Arish, Suez. This was followed on 17 September by two Sopwith Babys, the first one was from the seaplane carrier *Ben-my-Chree*, again over El Arish. It is not known where the other Sopwith came from. He was awarded the Turkish War Medal, and posted back to the Western Front to join *Jasta* 18 on 7 December of 1916, after he had written numerous requests to be transferred back to where the action was.

On 23 January, 1917, Walter von Bülow-Bothkamp took his tally to six, when he shot down a Sopwith $1^{1}/_{2}$ Strutter from 45 Squadron, RFC, followed by an FE 8 from 41 Squadron, RFC, whilst patrolling over Gheluvelt in his Albatros D.V. By the end of April, he had his score had increased to twelve and in recognition of this was awarded the Knight's Cross with Swords of the Hohenzollern House Order and the Saxon

Military St Henry Order. Then on the 10 May, 1917, he was appointed commander of *Jasta* 36. This had come about due to the commanding officer, *Leutnant* Albert Dossenbach, being injured during a bombing raid on the airfield. Dossenbach's wound kept him in hospital for the next couple of months and on his release was given a temporary post at Idflieg before taking over command of *Jasta* 10.

Walter von Bülow-Bothkamp celebrated the appointment on 20 May, when, accompanied by *Leutnant* Heinrich Bongartz and *Leutnant*

Leutnant *Walter von Bülow, CO of* Jagdstaffel *36. L-R: Unknown,* Vzfw *Patzer,* Ltn *Bongartz,* Unteroffizzier *Neumann,* Ltn. *Furmann, Walter von Bülow,* Ltn *Hoyer,* Ltn *Harry von Bülow,* Ltn *Müller,* Ltn *Von Haebler,* Ltn *Quandt and* Ltn *Böhning.*

Theodor Quandt, they shot down seven balloons in the vicinity of Bouvancourt. By the beginning of October 1917, von Bülow-Bothkamp had raised his tally to twenty-one and then, on 8 October 1917, he was awarded Germany's highest honour, the *Orden Pour le Mérite*. Von Bülow's score kept mounting and when on 13 December he was made commander of *Jasta* 2 'Boelcke', it stood at twenty-eight.

His appointment as commander of the famous 'Boelcke' *Jasta* was unfortunately for him to be very short. On 6 January, 1918, whilst on patrol in his Albatros DV over Ypres, east of Paschendale, he was jumped by British fighters from No.'s 23 and 70 Squadron, RFC. After a brief skirmish, *Leutnant* Walter von Bülow's aircraft spun out of control and crashed into the Allied front line trenches. His body was recovered by the Allies and buried with full military honours. He was aged just twenty-four.

Awards

Orden Pour le Mérite
Royal Hohenzollern House Order, Knight's Cross with Swords
Iron Cross 1st Class
Iron Cross 2nd Class
Military St. Henry Order, Knight
Ottoman Empire War Medal
Pilot's Badge, Army – Germany

Victory log

1915

10 Oct	Voisin (*Escadrille* VB 114)	Metz
11 Oct	Farman	

1916

8 Aug	Unknown Aircraft	El Arish
17 Sep	Sopwith Baby (HMS *Ben-my-Chree*)	El Arish

1917

23 Jan	Sopwith 1½ Strutter (No. 45 Sqn RFC)	Ghelvelt
23 Jan	FE 8 (No.41 Sqn RFC)	Bixschoote
26 Jan	Sopwith 1½ Strutter (No. 45 Sqn RFC)	Recham
7 Feb	Sopwith 1½ Strutter (No. 45 Sqn RFC)	Linselles
11 Mar	Balloon (Kite Balloon Section)	N Armentieres
7 Apr	FE 2d (20 Sqn RFC)	S Plegsteert
8 Apr	Nieuport XII (No. 46 Sqn RFC)	Ypres
24 Apr	FE 2d (No. 20 Sqn RFC)	Ypres
7 May	FE 2d (No. 20 Sqn RFC)	Menin
21 May	Balloon (77 *Cie d'Aérostieres*)	Bouvancourt
21 May	Balloon (53 *Cie d'Aérostieres*)	Bouvancourt
6 Jul	SPAD VII (No. 23 Sqn RFC)	St. Julien
7 Jul	FE 2d (No. 20 Sqn RFC)	Hooge
3 Sep	Sopwith Camel (No. 70 Sqn RFC)	Tenbrielen
13 Sep	Sopwith Camel (No. 10 Sqn RNAS)	Nr. Becelaere
23 Sep	Nieuport XXIII (No. 29 Sqn RFC)	Warneton
26 Sep	RE 8 (No. 21 Sqn RFC)	Polygon Wood
18 Oct	SPAD VII (*Escadrille Spa* 73)	E. Passchendale
24 Oct	SPAD (No. 19 Sqn RFC)	Linselles
24 Oct	SPAD (No. 19 Sqn RFC)	Houthem
8 Nov	SPAD (No. 19 Sqn RFC)	W. Moorslede
23 Nov	Sopwith Camel (No. 65 Sqn RFC)	Passchendale
2 Dec	BF 2b (20 Sqn RFC)	Becelaere

Total victories claimed: 28

CHAPTER THIRTY-SIX

Leutnant Walter Blume
(1896 – 1964)

Born in Hirschberg, a village at the foot of the Silesian mountains on the 10 January, 1896, Walter Blume, after graduating from school in 1911, took an apprenticeship as a tool maker in a machine factory. In 1914, when the war erupted in Europe, Blume immediately enlisted in the Silesian Jaeger Battalion Nr. 5 and was posted to East Prussia. The battalion had only been at the front a matter of months, when during heavy fighting near the town of Lyck, Blume was severely wounded. Whilst in hospital Blume considered his position and decided to apply for transfer, on his release, to the newly formed German Army Air Service.

Blume was to be just one of many German pilots who transferred to the Army Air Service after being wounded in battles on the ground. A number also joined even after they had been discharged from the army because their wounds were deemed to be serious enough to invalid them out.

Walter Blume's application was approved and on 30 June, 1915, he reported to the Flying Reserve Unit at Grossenhaim for initial training and then posted to the Flying School at Leipzig-Mockau for the completion of his training. Upon graduating and receiving his pilots badge, Blume was assigned to the Research and Exercise Field West Unit near St Quentin on the Western Front. At the beginning of March he was posted to the Army Aeroplane Park A at Strassburg to await a posting to another unit. His posting to *Feldflieger Abteilung* (FFl.Abt.) Nr. 65 as a reconnaissance pilot came on 18 June, then one month later was posted to *Feldflieger Abteilung* (FFl.Abt.) 280. Being a reconnaissance pilot was not quite what Blume had in mind, but he quickly distinguished himself and was awarded the Iron Cross 2nd Class on the 24 July, followed one month later, on 23 August, 1916, to promotion to *Vizefeldwebel*. Then on 31 January, 1917, he was given a commission to *Leutnant* der Reserve.

At the beginning of March 1917, Bruno Loerzer and Hermann Göring formed the nucleus of *Jasta* 26, a fighter unit, and Walter Blume was selected by them to be one of the pilots. One month later, after conversion and tactical training, the squadron was ready and was assigned to the St Quentin area. The *Jasta* was in action within days of arriving and took part in some of the heaviest aerial fighting of the war.

Whilst on patrol over Gouzencourt, on the 10 May, Blume opened his tally when he shot down a DH 4 from 55 Squadron, RFC. By the end of November he had raised his score to six and had been awarded the Iron Cross 1st Class. Then on the 29 November during a patrol, his flight encountered some Bristol fighters from 48 Squadron, RFC and during the skirmish Blume was hit in the chest. Despite considerable damage to his aircraft and fighting waves of unconciousness and pain, Blume managed to keep control of his aircraft, and guide it back to his base. It was only due the skill of the surgeons and the consequent nursing care that Blume survived.

Walter Blume returned to the Front on the 5 March, 1918, and was given command of *Jasta* 9 and assigned to the Champagne Front. Within days Blume was in the skies and back with a vengeance. The next month was barren in terms of 'kills' but then on 21 April whilst on patrol over Chiry-Ourscamp, he shot down a SPAD VII from *Escadrille Spa* 12, taking his total of 'kills' to seven. Ten more victories in the following three months brought his tally to seventeen. The shooting down of a SPAD XVI from *Escadrille Spa* 385 over Bazoches on the 6 August,

Leutnant *Walter Blume (second from left) standing in front of the steps with members of* Jagdgruppe 5.

brought the award of the Knight's Cross with Swords of the Hohenzollern House Order. At the beginning of October, Blume score stood at twenty-six. A victory on the 2 October followed by another on the 8 October, a Sopwith Camel from 209 Squadron over Remaucourt, gave him his 28th victory and the *Jasta's* 100th. On returning to his field, Blume discovered that he had been awarded Germany's highest award, the *Orden Pour le Mérite*.

The end of the war came and Blume returned home and completed his engineering studies. He was offered a position as a designer with the Arado and Albatros aviation companies and was responsible for contributing to many of the designs of aircraft used in the Second World War. He died on the 27 May, 1964, one of the few World War One fighter pilots to survive.

Awards

Orden Pour le Mérite
Knight's Cross with Swords of the Royal Hohenzollern House Order
Iron Cross 2nd Class
Iron Cross 1st Class
Wound Badge in Black
Pilot's Badge – German Army

Victory log
1917

10 May	DH 4 (No. 55 Sqn RFC)	Gouzencourt
28 May	Sopwith Pup (No. 66 Sqn RFC)	Malincourt
11 Jul	Sopwith Triplane (No. 10 Sqn RNAS)	Comines
14 Aug	DH 4 (No. 55 Sqn RFC)	Hollebeke
24 Oct	Sopwith Triplane (No. 1 Sqn RNAS)	Zillebeke Lake
5 Nov	RE 8 (No. 6 Sqn RFC)	Zillebeke

1918

21 Apr	SPAD VII (*Escadrille Spa* 12)	W. Chivry
16 May	SPAD VII (*Escadrille Spa* 3)	SE Elincourt
30 May	SPAD VII (*Escadrille Spa* 77)	
13 Jun	Breguet XIV (*Escadrille Br* 35)	St Pierre Aigle
28 Jun	SPAD (Escadrille Spa 88)	
15 Jul	Nieuport XXVII (*Groupe de d'Entrainment*)	S. Mareuil
16 Jul	Nieuport (147th Aero Sqn USAS)	
18 Jul	SE 5a (No. 32 Sqn RAF)	
21 Jul	SPAD XIII (*Escadrille Spa* 77)	
25 Jul	Sopwith Camel (No. 433 Sqn RAF)	
31 Jul	SPAD 2 (*Escadrille Spa* 88)	Olizy
6 Aug	SPAD XVI (*Escadrille Spa* 285)	S. Bazoches
21 Aug	SPAD XIII (*Escadrille Spa* 160)	Missy-aux-Bois
24 Aug	SPAD 2 (*Escadrille Spa* 87)	N. Soissons

31 Aug	SPAD XIII (*Escadrille Spa* 77)	E. Juvigny
31 Aug	SPAD VII (*Escadrille Spa* 89)	E. Pont St. Mard
3 Sep	SPAD VII (*Escadrille Spa* 91)	S Fismes
14 Sep	SPAD 2 (*Escadrille Sal* 280)	S. Laffaux
14 Sep	SPAD (GC. 20)	Braye
26 Sep	SPAD VII (*Escadrille Spa* 265)	Tahure
2 Oct	SPAD (*Escadrille Spa* 150)	Gueux
8 Oct	Sopwith Camel (No. 209 Sqn RAF)	N. Remancourt

Total victories claimed: 28

CHAPTER THIRTY-SEVEN

Oberleutnant Friedrich Ritter von Röth (1893 – 1918/19)

Born in Nuremburg on the 29 September, 1893, of a military family, Frederick von Röth started his military career at the outbreak of war. He volunteered to join the 8th Bavarian Field Artillery Regiment and because of his background was immediately promoted to *Unteroffizier*. In almost the first action his regiment was involved, Röth was seriously injured and spent almost a year in hospital. It was during his time in hospital that he received his commission to *Leutnant*, and it was whilst lying in hospital seeing other soldiers being brought in from the Front that he considered a career move to the German Army Air Service. On being released from hospital he made enquiries and after being told he could return to his regiment, Röth applied for transfer to the German Army Air Service and to be considered for pilot training.

He was posted *Flieger-Ersatz-Abteilung* (FEA) 1. to start training but after just a few weeks was severely injured again in a flying accident. The accident put him back in hospital for almost a year, but on release he returned to FEA.1 to continue his training and was able to qualify as a pilot in February 1917. His first assignment was to *Flieger-Erstaz-Abteilung* (FEA) 3 where he stayed for the next four months. Then followed a posting to *Armee-Flug-Park* B for six weeks.

Röth was then assigned to *Flieger-Abteilung* (A)(Fl.Abt.) 296b on the 1 April, 1917, and carried out a number of reconnaissance sorties. In recognition for his services, he was awarded the Bavarian Military Merit Order 4th Class with Swords in June 1917. Then began a series of moves to different *Jastas*. Firstly to *Jastaschule* 1, on the 10 September, then to *Jasta* 34 on the 17th and to *Jasta* 23b on the 4 October. Further awards came his away on 1 November, when he was awarded the Iron Cross 1st Class for his dedication to his role as a reconnaissance pilot.

At the end of January 1918, Röth turned into an attacking aggressive pilot, when on the 25 January he attacked and shot down three reconnaissance balloons in the one day and all within ten minutes of each other. He was awarded the Knight's Cross of the Military Max-Joseph Order in recognition of this dangerous mission. The granting of this

Leutnant *Freidrich Ritter von Röth leaning on the wing of his Albatros DV.*

award allowed Röth to use the title 'Ritter' giving rise to his name being changed to Friedrich Ritter von Röth. The following month, 25 February, he was given another award, the Knight's Cross with Swords of the Hohenzollern House Order. Usually the recipient of this order had at least twelve victories to his credit, but Röth only had three balloons and the fact that Röth had never shot down one aircraft at this point in time, gave rise to stories about him having defective eyesight. These stories arose from his poor marksmanship when engaging the enemy, so, then it is claimed, he turned to the more static observation balloons.

Although the shooting down one of these balloons could prove to be extremely dangerous if the attacker happened to be close when the balloon exploded.

The following day, the 26th, Röth dispelled these rumours by claiming his first aircraft when he shot down an RE 8. One month later he shot down two more balloons and then on the 1 April shot down four balloons in one day.

Leutnant von Röth in the cockpit of his Albatros DVa whilst his mechanics check his engine.

On the 29 April 1918, Friedrich Röth took command of *Jasta* 16b and by this time he had raised his tally to ten, nine of which were balloons the other being the RE 8 of No.16 Squadron, RFC. On 29 May Röth surpassed even his score for one day, when he shot down five British balloons in an incredible fifteen minutes. Three of the balloons were hit on his first pass. Ten British balloons were up on this particular day and Röth, his guns armed with a mixture of phosphorus incendiary and half ball ammunition, swept into attack whilst under heavy anti-aircraft fire. At one point Röth's attack was interrupted by the arrival of a SPAD, but after a brief exchange of fire the SPAD broke away and retreated. Röth continued to wreak havoc as the balloon crews frantically tried to wind their balloons down, the observers by this time had all taken to their parachutes. As the fifth balloon plunged earthwards in flames, Röth spotted three British fighters closing in on him and decided that it was time for him to leave.

Interestingly enough such an exploit would have normally been met with some form of recognition followed by an award on some sorts, but nothing ever came of it. It may have contributed to his consideration for the *Orden Pour le Mérite*.

During the next couple of months he added another RE 8 and a couple of balloons, three of them along the Belgian Front line, making his *Jasta* one of the most successful. Then on the 19 August, Röth was promoted to *Oberleutnant* and having reached the 'magic' number of twenty-two 'kills' and was awarded the *Orden Pour le Mérite* on the 9 September, 1918. His promotion to *Oberleutnant* was a considerable

Three 'Aces' L-R: Kissenberth, Schleich, Röth

achievement from someone who had risen from the ranks at the age of twenty-four.

As the German Army retreated and the war reached its final conclusion, Röth scored four more victories when he shot down three balloons and a DH 9, but was wounded in the foot.

On the cessation of hostilities his tally had risen to twenty-eight, twenty of which were observation balloons and all scored in multiples of two or three during probing expeditions over enemy lines.

Röth returned to Nuremburg bitter and disillusioned at Germany's defeat. It was something that he could not come to terms with and suffered a nervous breakdown. He had been convinced that Germany was unbeatable, then on New Year's Eve 1918/19 at the age of twenty-five, he committed suicide.

Awards

Orden Pour le Mérite
Knight's Cross with Swords of the Royal Hohenzollern House Order
Knight's Cross of the Military Max-Joseph Order
Iron Cross 2nd Class
Iron Cross 1st Class
Bavarian Military Merit Order 4th Class with Swords
Pilot's Badge

Victory log

1918

25 Jan	Balloon (French Balloon Cie. 55)	Recicourt
25 Jan	Balloon (French Balloon Cie. 59)	Betheleville
25 Jan	Balloon (French Balloon Cie. 80)	Framerville
26 Feb	RE 8 (No. 16 Sqn RFC)	Mericourt
21 Mar	Balloon (British Balloon 44-19-3)	Marcoing
21 Mar	Balloon (British Balloon 1-18-3)	Beugny
1 Apr	Balloon (British Balloon 10-2-1)	Cambrin
1 Apr	Balloon (British Balloon 8-1-1)	Hulloch
1 Apr	Balloon (British Balloon 20-1-1)	Loos
1 Apr	Balloon (British Balloon 24-2-1)	S Loos
29 May	Balloon (No. 1 Belgiam Balloon Co.)	Dixmude-Poperinghue
29 May	Balloon (No. 4 Belgian Balloon Co.)	Dixmude-Poperinghue
29 May	Balloon (British Balloon 25-5-2)	Dixmude-Poperinghue
29 May	Balloon (British Balloon 39-8-2)	Dixmude-Hazebrouk
25 Jul	BF 2b (No. 20 Sqn RAF)	Gheluvelt
29 Jul	DH 9 (No. 206 Sqn RAF)	Gheluvelt
30 Jul	BF 2b (No. 20 Sqn RAF)	S Ypres
12 Aug	SE 5a (No. 85 Sqn RAF)	Langemarck
13 Aug	Balloon (No. 6 Belgian Balloon Co.)	Lampernisse
13 Aug	Balloon (No. 2 Belgian Balloon Co.)	Lampernisse
13 Aug	Balloon (No. 3 Belgian Balloon Co.)	Lampernisse

4 Sep	DH 9 (No. 107 Sqn RAF)	Neuf Berquin
8 Oct	RE 8 (No.7 Sqn RAF)	Gheluvelt
10 Oct	Balloon (British Balloon 38-7-2)	Staden-Ypres
10 Oct	Balloon (French Balloon CIE.25)	Staden-Ypres
10 Oct	Balloon (Frnech Balloon CIE.91)	Staden-Ypres
14 Oct	DH 9 (No. 108 Sqn RAF)	Ledeghem

Total victories claimed: 27

CHAPTER THIRTY-EIGHT

Leutnant Hans Kirschtein
(1896 – 1918)

Leutnant Hans Kirschstein was born in Koblenz on 5 August, 1896. At the outbreak of war he joined the 3rd Pioneer Battalion and was soon in action, first in Poland then in France. In the spring of 1915 his battalion was shipped to Galicia, Macedonia, and it was here that Kirschstein contracted malaria. He was shipped back to Germany for treatment and convalescence, returning to Galicia in the December. It was while in hospital that Kirschstein started to make enquiries about the newly formed German Army Air Service. In the February of 1916 he applied for transfer to aviation and was accepted. At the beginning of May he was posted to the flying school at Schliessheim, and after

Leutnant Hans Kirchstein and his mechanics with their Fokker Dr 1. The aircraft was later sent to Jasta 4 where it was flown by Ernst Udet.

Leutnant *Hans Kirchstein*

graduating was posted to bomber squadron FA.19. During the battles in
Flanders he became notorious amongst the Allies for his low level
strafing runs on tanks. He was also one of the first pilots to carry out a
bombing run on Dover, for which he received the Iron Cross 2nd Class.

During 1917, Kirschstein flew with FA.256 and FA.3 building his
reputation as he went along. Then at the beginning of February 1918
he asked to be posted to a fighter squadron and was sent to *Jastaschule*

for conversion training. On 13 March, 1918, after graduating, he was posted to *Jasta* 6 in the Richthofen Circus. Within five days he had opened his tally by shooting down a Sopwith Camel from 54 Squadron, RFC, on the 18 March, and by the end of the month had raised it to three. He received the Iron Cross 1st Class in the May, followed by the Knight's Cross with Swords of the Hohenzollern House Order.

On 10 June Kirschstein took over the command of *Jasta* 6 with his tally at twenty-four. By the end of June 1918 Kirschstein had raised his tally to twenty-seven, and on 24 June 1918 received Germany's highest award, the *Pour le Mérite*. But his delight was to be short lived. One month later, on 11 July, Kirschstein took his personal Fokker to the Aircraft Park at Fismes for its annual complete overhaul. With him, flying a Hannover CL.II, was a new pilot, *Leutnant* Johannes Markgraf, who had joined *Jasta* 6 one week previously and he was to fly Kirschstein back to the squadron. Just after taking off on the return flight the Hannover crashed, killing both men instantly. It was revealed later at a board of inquiry, that Markgraf had never flown a Hannover before, and as nothing else appeared to contribute to the crash, it was deemed to be pilot error.

Awards

Orden Pour le Mérite
Knight's Cross with Swords of the Royal Hohenzollern House Order
Iron Cross 1st Class
Iron Cross 2nd Class

Victory log

1918

18 Mar	Sopwith Camel (No. 54 Sqn RFC)	Vaux-Andigny
27 Mar	AWKF 8 (No. 2 Sqn RFC)	SW Albert
27 Mar	Sopwith Camel (No. 3 Sqn RFC)	NE Albert
2 Apr	SE 5a (No. 60 Sqn RFC)	W Habonnieres
6 Apr	Sopwith Camel (No. 43 Sqn RFC)	NE Wartisse
7 Apr	Sopwith Camel (No. 73 Sqn RFC)	S Proyart
3 May	SPAD VII (*Escadrille Spa* 96)	W.Pozieres
10 May	Sopwith Camel (No. 80 Sqn RFC)	Chipilly
15 May	Sopwith Camel (No. 209 Sqn RFC)	E Demuin
15 May	BF 2b (No. 48 Sqn RFC)	SE Caix
15 May	BF 2b (No. 11 Sqn RFC)	Orvillers
16 May	BF 2b (No. 62 Sqn RFC)	Sailly-le-Sec
16 May	SE 5a (No. 56 Sqn RFC)	Contalmaison
17 May	Breguet XIV (*Escadrille* GB 5)	Cappy
18 May	Breguet XIV (*Escadrille Br* 45)	E Caix
30 May	Breguet XIV (*Escadrille Br* 29)	Grand Rozoy
2 Jun	SPAD 2 (*Escadrille Spa* 98)	Cugny

2 Jun	Breguet XIV (*Escadrille Br* 226)	Troesnes
3 Jun	Breguet XIV (*Escadrille Br* 127)	Epaux-Bezu
3 Jun	Breguet XIV (*Escadrille Br* 117)	Fere-en-Tardenois
5 Jun	SPAD VII (*Escadrille Spa* 163)	Villamont
5 Jun	Breguet XIV (*Escadrille Br* 227)	Ambleny
5 Jun	SPAD VII (*Escadrille Spa* 94)	Chezy-en-Orxois
7 Jun	SPAD 2 (*Escadrille Spa* 86)	Montgobert
14 Jun	Balloon (29 *Cie d'Aérostiers*)	Villers Cotterets
14 Jun	SPAD XIII (*Escadrille Spa* 99)	Villers Cotterets
24 Jun	Breguet XIV (*Escadrille Br* 128)	Oulchy le Chateau

Total victories claimed: 27

CHAPTER THIRTY-NINE

Oberleutnant Fritz Otto Bernert
(1893 – 1918)

Fritz Bernert was born on the 6 March, 1893, the son of the *Burgermeister* of Ratibor, Upper Silesia. He joined the 173rd Infantry Regiment as a cadet on leaving school, where he served for the next six years and was commissioned as a *Leutnant* just after the outbreak of the First World War. His infantry regiment was one of those who were sent to the Front almost as the war started and were soon in action. In November 1914, Bernert was wounded during some bitter fighting and was awarded the Iron Cross 2nd Class for his part in the action. He quickly recovered and was back with his regiment at the end of the 1914 when he was wounded twice more, fortunately none of the wounds proved to be too serious. At the very end of December 1914, during a particularly heavy close-quarter hand-to-hand fight, he received a bayonet wound to his left arm which severed the main nerve. He was deemed to be unfit for further military duties, but the taste of battle was in his blood and he applied to join the German Army Air Service as a Observer.

Somehow Fritz Bernert passed the medical examination for the Air Service, how is a mystery, but he did, and in February 1915 was sent for training. I think the need for more men was one of the reasons why the vast majority of medicals at the beginning of the war, were no more that cursory glances to see if the applicant had the required number of arms, legs, hands, feet and eyes. After graduating as an observer Bernert was posted to *Feldflieger-Abteilung* (FFl.Abt.) 27 and for six months carried out reconnaissance and scouting missions. Then in the July of 1915, Bernert was posted to FFl.Abt. 71 but he was tired of being just an observer and was looking toward flying the aircraft himself and so applied for pilot training. In the November his application was accepted and he was posted to *Jastaschule* 1 for training. Again somehow he was able to conceal the fact that he only had one arm that was fully functional and another that had very limited mobility. In addition to this he wore glasses, being one of only three *Jasta* pilots in the German Army Air Service who were known to wear glasses. Despite these handicaps Fritz Bernert graduated at the end of March 1916, and was assigned to Kek Vaux. On 17 April he

opened his tally by shooting down a Nieuport fighter.

A lull in the action during the summer months of 1916, appeared in Fritz Bernert's sector enabling the *Jasta* to get some well earned rest and carry out necessary maintenance on all their aircraft. The in the last part of August he was posted to *Jasta* 4. Bernert claimed his second victory on the 6 September and the first official victory of *Jasta* 4, when he shot down a Caudron whilst on patrol east of Peronne. A third victory, a Nieuport fighter over Allenes on the 11 September, followed by a Caudron on 21 October raised his tally to four. On 9 November he shot down three aircraft – two DH 2s and an FE 8, bringing his total at the end of the year to seven.

On 25 January Fritz Bernert was awarded the Iron Cross 1st Class, the Saxon Albert Order, Knight 2nd Class with Swords and Knight's Cross with Swords of the Hohenzollern House Order, and was posted to *Jasta* 2. As if to celebrate, Bernert opened his score with his new *Jasta* by shooting down a Sopwith Camel whilst on patrol over Ecourt-Mory, this brought his tally to eight, on 1 March, 1917, and a BE 2d at the end of March seemed to set the scene for April, when on consecutive days starting on the 1st, Bernert scored four victories. He continued to score almost daily, then on the 23 April he was awarded Germany's highest accolade, the *Orden Pour le Mérite*. As if to celebrate this honour, the following day, the

Oberleutnant *Otto Bernert (back row second on left) with pilots of* Jasta *4.*

24 April, Bernert claimed five victories in the one day, three BE 2es (all from No. 9 Squadron RFC), a DH 4 and a Sopwith 1$^{1}/_{2}$ Strutter. He had shot down fifteen enemy aircraft in April bringing his total to twenty-four.

On the 1 May, Fritz Bernert was appointed *Staffelführer* to *Jasta* 6 and celebrated the appointment by shooting down a Nieuport whilst on patrol over St Quentin the following day bringing his tally to twenty-four. Bernert added three more victories to his score by the end of May raising his total of kills to twenty-seven. It was whilst with *Jasta* 6 that Bernert was injured in a crash and was sent back to *Jasta* 2 (*Jasta* Boelcke) on 9 June, 1917, to take over as commander. It was a very tired and physically worn out Bernert that took over command of *Jasta* Boelcke. He was suffering from the remnants of the various injuries he had sustained over the years, but he still managed to lead his *Jasta* into battle with courage and determination.

He continued to fly but with no more successes and on the 18 August was wounded once again. On his release from hospital in the November, he was deemed to be unfit for flying duties and was assigned to the office

Bareheaded Oberleutnant *Otto Bernert with pilots of* Jasta *Boelcke*

of the Inspector of the Flying Service with a promotion to *Oberleutnant*. In September of 1918, Fritz Otto Bernert was taken ill with influenza and died in hospital in his hometown on the 18 October, 1918.

Awards

Orden Pour le Mérite
Knight's Cross with Swords of the Royal Hohenzollern House Order
Iron Cross 2nd Class
Iron Cross 1st Class
Knight 2nd Class with Swords of the Albert Order
Pilot's Badge – German Army

Victory log

1916

17 Apr	Nieuport	Not known
6 Sep	Caudron G 4 (*Escadrille* C 28)	Dompiere
11 Sep	Nieuport (*Groupe de Divisions d'Entrainment*)	Allenes
21 Oct	Caudron G 4 (*Escadrille* C 28)	Chaulnes
9 Nov	DH 2 (No. 29 Sqn RFC)	Le Sars
9 Nov	DH 2 (No. 40 Sqn RFC)	Haplincourt
9 Nov	FE 8 (No. 29 Sqn RFC)	Martinpuich

1917

19 Mar	Sopwith Camel	Ecourt-Mory
24 Mar	BE 2e (No. 15 Sqn RFC)	Pronville
1 Apr	Balloon (Balloon Company 4-13-5)	Villers-au-Flers
2 Apr	Nieuport (No. 60 Sqn RFC)	Queant
3 Apr	Balloon (Balloon Company 13-17-5)	Ervillers
3 Apr	Balloon (Balloon Company 18-17-5)	NW Bapaume
6 Apr	RE 8 (No. 59 Sqn RFC)	Roeux
7 Apr	Nieuport (No. 29 Sqn RFC)	Roeux
8 Apr	RE 8 (No. 59 Sqn RFC)	Remy
8 Apr	Bf 2a (No. 48 Sqn RFC)	Eterpigny
11 Apr	SPAD VII (*Escadrille* N 73)	Arras
11 Apr	Morane Parasol (No. 3 Sqn RFC)	NW Lagincourt
24 Apr	Sopwith 1½ Strutter (No. 70 Sqn RFC)	Vaucelles
24 Apr	BE 2e (No. 9 Sqn RFC)	N.Joncourt
24 Apr	BE 2e (No. 9 Sqn RFC)	Bellincourt
24 Apr	BE 2e (No. 9 Sqn)	Boni
24 Apr	DH 4 (No. 55 Sqn)	Levergies
2 May	Nieuport XVII (*Escadrille* N 80)	St. Quentin
4 May	Balloon (Balloon Company 14-14-4)	Hervilly-Nauroy
7 May	BE 2e (No. 7 Sqn RFC)	Pontreut
19 May	FE 2b (No. 22 Sqn RFC)	Villers Guislane

Total victories claimed: 27

CHAPTER FORTY

Leutnant Otto Fruhner
(1893 – 1965)

Otto Fruhner was born in Brieg, Schleisen on 6 September, 1893. On leaving school he became apprenticed as a mechanic which culminated in him joining the German Army Air Service on 20 November, 1914. Because of his background he was assigned a mechanics post and sent to *Feldflieger-Ersatz-Abteilung* (FEA) 4 at Posen. Over the next twelve months Fruhner became increasingly interested in flying and applied several times to be considered for entry into flying school. He was posted to FEA at Graudenz in the August and finally in November 1915 he was accepted and assigned to flying school at Köslin for training. On completion of his training in the May of 1916 he returned to FEA Graudenz whilst it was decided what unit he was going to be posted to. Fruhner was assigned to *Flieger Abteilung* 51 on the Eastern Front flying two-seater reconnaissance flights. In August he was awarded the Iron Cross 2nd Class and promoted to *Unteroffizier*. At the beginning of July 1917 Fruhner decided to apply for single-seater fighter training and was sent to *Jastaschule* 1. Within the month he had completed the course and was assigned to Bruno Loerzer's *Jasta* 26.

Vzfw Otto Fruhner – 7th from left – with fellow pilots of Jasta 26 *The British pilot in the centre of the group is Cyril Ball, brother of British ace Albert Ball*

Fruhner was coached by Loerzer and steadily improved, then on 3 September he scored his first victories over Flanders, two Sopwith Camels, one in the morning the other in the afternoon. He wasn't to score again until January 1918 when he increased his tally to six. By the end of July 1918 he had scored thirteen victories and had been awarded the Iron Cross 1st Class, the Golden Military Merit Cross and given a commission to *Leutnant*. Over the next three months *Leutnant* Fruhner scored steadily and by the end of September had raised his tally to twenty-seven and had been nominated for the *Orden Pour le Mérite*. Then on the 20 September he was in a mid-air collision with a Sopwith Camel from No. 203 Squadron, RAF, and was forced to bale out. He was to take no more part in the war and because the war ended a couple of months later never received the *Pour le Mérite* he so richly deserved.

In 1935 *Leutnant* Otto Fruhner joined the Luftwaffe and was given the rank of *Major* and put in command of the flying school at Ludwigslust. During the war he reached the rank of *Generalmajor* and survived the war. He died in Austria on 19 June, 1965, at the age of sseventy-two.

Vzfw *Otto Fruhner (left)*
with Vzfw *Otto Esswein.*

Awards

Golden Military Merit Cross
Iron Cross 1st Class
Iron Cross 2nd Class

Victory log

1917

| 3 Sep | Sopwith Pup (No. 46 Sqn RFC) | W Wervicq |
| 3 Sep | Sopwith Camel (No. 70 Sqn RFC) | Zillebeke Lake |

1918

3 Jan	Sopwith Camel (No. 10 Sqn RNAS)	Armentieres
4 Jan	DH 4 (No. 57 Sqn RFC)	Neuville
22 Jan	Sopwith Camel (No. 70 Sqn RFC)	Wervicq
29 Jan	Sopwith Camel (No. 13 Sqn RNAS)	Coucou
3 Feb	Sopwith Camel (No. 9 Sqn RNAS)	SW Poleceapelle
3 Feb	Sopwith Camel (No. 10 Sqn RNAS)	Sleihgen
26 Mar	SE 5a (No. 1 Sqn RFC)	Tamechon Wood
1 Jul	SPAD VII (*Escadrille Spa* 98)	Chateau Thierry

7 Jul	Nieuport 28 (94th Aero Sqn USAS)	S Soissons Ferme
8 Jul	Breguet XIV (*Escadrille Br* 24)	Hartennes
16 Jul	SPAD XIII (*Escadrille Spa* 153)	SW Igny
8 Aug	SE 5a (No. 24 Sqn RAF)	Estrees
13 Aug	SE 5a (No. 60 Sqn RAF)	Foucheres
15 Aug	Sopwith Camel (No. 204 Sqn RAF)	Parvillers
27 Aug	SE 5a (No. 84 Sqn RAF)	Ecourt
30 Aug	SE 5a (No. 64 Sqn RAF)	Inchy
2 Sep	SE 5a (No. 56 Sqn RAF)	Villers
2 Sep	SE 5a (No. 56 Sqn RAF)	Barelle
3 Sep	Sopwith Camel (No. 4 Sqn AFC)	Sin-le-Noble
4 Sep	Sopwith Camel (No. 70 Sqn RAF)	Cantin West
4 Sep	Sopwith Camel (No. 70 Sqn RAF)	S.Douai
4 Sep	Sopwith Camel (No. 70 Sqn RAF)	W. Corbehen
15 Sep	RE 8 (No. 5 Sqn RAF)	Palleul
16 Sep	BF 2b (No. 11 Sqn RAF)	Fontaine
27 Sep	Sopwith Camel (No. 203 Sqn RAF)	E. Cagnicourt

Total victories claimed: 27

CHAPTER FORTY-ONE

Leutnant Karl Thom
(1893 – ?)

Karl Thom was born on the 19 May, 1893, in Freystadt, West Prussia and was just one of the many young men whose life was changed totall by the war. After leaving school at the age of fourteen he had a succession of jobs until he was eighteen, then, in 1911, he joined the army, signing on for three years military service and was assigned to the 5th Hussar Regiment. When war broke out three years later Thom, now an experienced soldier, was posted to the Jaeger Regiment Pferde Nr. 10 on the 4 September, 1914, and promoted to *Unteroffizier*. The regiment was soon in action and in one particularly bitter fight, Thom was seriously injured for which he received the Iron Cross 2nd Class. After being released from hospital in June 1915, he, like many other infantrymen who had been wounded on the Front line, applied for transfer to the German Army Air Service and was accepted.

Thom was sent to pilot training school at Schneidemühl in September 1915, where in the January of 1916 he graduated as a pilot. He first posting was to *Flieger-Abteilung* (A) (Fl.Abt.) 216 who were operating patrols in the Vosges Sector where he carried out reconnaissance missions. On the 16 May, 1916, he crashed on landing and was badly injured. On release from hospital, on 24 July, Thom was promoted to *Vizefeldwebel* and was posted to Roumania in the October to join Fl.Abt. 48 as a reconnaissance pilot.

At the end of October, after flying only two missions, he was shot down and captured, but he managed to escape and made his way back to his unit. For this he was awarded the Iron Cross 1st Class. Thom was tired of just flying reconnaissance missions, even though he realised the importance of them, but he wanted more action – he wanted to be the hunter not the hunted.

Thom had a short spell with *Flieger-Abteilung* (Fl.Abt.) 234 and then on the 24 April, 1917, after a number of requests, he was posted to *Jastaschule* and trained as a fighter pilot. On graduation on 15 May, he was posted to *Jasta* 21. One week later the commanding officer *Hauptmann* Richard Schlieben was replaced by *Oberleutnant* Eduard *Ritter*

Offz-Stv. *Karl Thom when with* Jasta *21.*

von Schleich, who initially had arrived to be the deputy leader. Initially Thom was having trouble when faced with a combat situation which was down to the fact that he was exhausted and rather than compromise his fellow pilots, requested a transfer back to his old unit and back to reconnaissance duties. Schleich, recognising that Thom was in desperate need of a rest, refused his request and sent him on leave.

Within one week of his return he was into the action and opened his score on the 22 August, 1917, when he shot down a French Dorand AR.2 bomber whilst on patrol with his section leader Emil Thuy, over S. Avocourt. He then followed the aircraft down and strafed the wreckage, not once but three times. On his return he expected to be congratulated by Thuy, but instead got an angry verbal reprimand, not for the lack of chivalry, which was also pointed out to him in no uncertain manner, but

(Above) The diminutive figure of Karl Thom in the cockpit of his Fokker D VII. (Below) Leutnant Karl Thom (second from left) with pilots of Jasta 21. *In the centre of the group is* Oberleutnant *Eduard Ritter von Schleich.*

for wasting ammunition. It was also made clear to him that had the unit come under attack he would have had virtually no ammunition left to fight off the attackers.

A suitably chastened Thom gained his second victory two weeks later, when he shot down a Caudron whilst over Foret de Hesse. This time he just watched the aircraft fall to the ground.

By the end of September, his tally had risen to twelve – eleven aircraft in the one month. For this exploit he was awarded the Golden Military Merit Cross, the first airmen to be honoured with the award. One month later the commanding officer of *Jasta* 21, *Oberleutnant* Eduard *Ritter* von Schleich, was unceremoniously removed and replaced by *Oberleutnant*

Oskar Freiherr von Boenigk in one of the purges that seemed to plague the German Air Service at the time. Prussian commanders of Bavarian *Jastas* being replaced by Bavarians and vice versa.

Thom had added two more 'kills' to his tally, when on the 23 December he attacked a balloon and was injured when set upon by defending Allied fighters. He managed to get his crippled aircraft back to his field and was hospitalised for a month as a result of his injuries. On his return to *Jasta* 21 on the 24 January, 1918, he was promoted to

A rather severe looking Leutnant *Karl Thom* *wearing his* Pour le Mérite.

Offizierstellvertreter. Activity in the area went very quiet for the next couple of months and Thom's tally did not increase. Then in June 1918, activity in the area became hectic as the Allies made a huge push forward supported from the air. Thom accounted for six Allied aircraft in this month and by the beginning of August he had raised his tally to twenty-seven, for this he was awarded the Members Cross with Swords of the Royal Hohenzollern House Order. Four days later he was wounded again, only this time severely when his patrol ran into a patrol of SE 5s from the RFC.

Whilst in hospital news came through that he had promoted to *Leutnant* and been nominated for the *Orden Pour le Mérite*. Karl Thom remained in hospital until the beginning of October, then on the 1 November, five days before he returned to *Jasta* 21, he was awarded the prestigious *Orden Pour le Mérite*. Thom stayed with *Jasta* 21 until the Armistice, but again bad luck dogged him, when he was badly injured in a crash the day before the war ended.

During the Second World War, Karl Thom joined the Luftwaffe and held posts in Eastern Germany. He was reported missing whilst visiting the Russian Front and is thought to have been taken prisoner, he was never seen again.

Awards

Orden Pour le Mérite
Members Cross with Swords of the Royal Hohenzollern Order
Prussian Golden Military Merit Cross
Iron Cross 2nd Class
Iron Cross 1st Class
Wound Badge in Silver
Pilot's Badge

Victory log

1917

22 Aug	AR 2 Dorand (*Escadrille* F 211)	S Avocourt
3 Sep	Caudron G.4 (*Escadrille* C 229)	Foret de Hesse
11 Sep	Nieuport XII (No. 1 Sqn RFC)	Verdun
17 Sep	AR 2 Dorand	Morte Homme
18 Sep	SPAD VII (No. 19 Sqn RFC)	W Verdun
18 Sep	AR 2 Dorand (*Escadrille* F 41)	Hessen Wood
18 Sep	Caudron R 4	NE Cumieres
19 Sep	AR 2 Dorand (*Escadrille* F 14)	N Verdun
19 Sep	AR 2 Dorand (*Escadrille* F 14)	E Verdun
22 Sep	AR 2 Dorand (*Escadrille* F 14)	Verdun
22 Sep	AR 2 Dorand (*Escadrille* F 14)	Borrus
26 Sep	Caudron G 4 (*Escadrille* GDE)	S Hessen Wood
29 Oct	SPAD VII	Fleury
1 Dec	Caudron G 6 (*Escadrille* C 10)	Samogneux

1918

11 Jun	Breguet XIV (*Escadrille Br* 217)	S Crepy
14 Jun	SPAD XIII (*Escadrille Spa* 163)	Villers Cotterets
18 Jun	SPAD VII (*Escadrille Spa* 100)	Villers Cottretes
27 Jun	SPAD XIII (*Escadrille Spa* 88)	Crezancy
28 Jun	SPAD VII (*Escadrille Spa* 48)	Bois de Mandry
15 Jul	SPAD XIII (*Escadrille Spa* 87)	SW Pourcy
16 Jul	SPAD XIII (*Escadrille Spa* 87)	S Pourcy
24 Jul	SE 5a (No. 64 Sqn RAF)	Blesmes
24 Jul	SE 5a (No. 64 Sqn RAF)	Courtemont
24 Jul	SE 5a (No. 32 Sqn RAF)	E La Ferte
25 Jul	SE 5a (No. 64 Sqn RAF)	SW Hartennes
1 Aug	SPAD XIII (27th Aero Sqn USAS)	NW Le Charmel
4 Aug	SPAD XIII (*Escadrille Spa* 76)	N Arcy

Total victories claimed: 27

CHAPTER FORTY-TWO

Hauptmann Adolf Ritter von Tutschek (1891 – 1918)

Born in Ingolstadt, Bavaria on the 16 May, 1891, into a military family, Adolf Tutschek, after leaving school surprised no one when he joined the army. His father and grandfather were both military men and in 1910, at the age of ninteen, he joined the 3rd Bavarian Infantry Regiment as a cadet. When the First World War broke out Adolf Tutschek, who had been commissioned in 1912, was assigned to the 40th Bavarian Infantry Regiment and immediately was in action on the Western Front. After a year of intensive fighting his regiment was sent to the Eastern Front where on 2 May, 1915, Tutschek was wounded. Whilst in hospital he was awarded the Iron Cross 1st Class and the Bavarian Military Merit Order 4th Class with Swords for the action he had been wounded in and previous actions on the Western Front. Within days of being discharged from Hospital in the June he was back in action with his regiment.

On the 15 August his name was put forward for the award of the Military Max-Joseph Order which would give him the title of 'Ritter'. The prestigious award had come about during an action that started on 25 July, 1915, when Tutschek volunteered to lead his men on an assault of a key Russian position near the village of Petrilow. After some bitter hand-to-hand fighting the position was captured, and despite heavy counter attacks and dwindling survivors, held out until 10 August when they were relieved.

He was recalled to headquarters on the 17 January, 1916, and promoted to *Oberleutnant*, then ordered back to the Western Front at Verdun. Then on 31 January his award of the Military Max-Joseph Order was approved and made retroactive to 10 August, 1915.

Back in the thick of the fighting at Verdun, von Tutschek was gassed on the 26 March, 1916, and hospitalised for several months. It was while lying in hospital that news came through of another award, the Bavarian Military Merit Order, 4th Class with Swords, but his mind was elsewhere and his thoughts turned to other aspects of enhancing his military career. One of the services that intrigued him, was the German Army Air

Oberleutnant *Ritter von Tutschek.*

Service. He applied for a transfer and was accepted although his own regiment were not at all keen on losing such an experienced infantry officer.

Adolf Ritter von Tutschek reported to *Flieger-Ersatz-Abteilung* (FEA)1 at Schleissheim as a student pilot on the 25 July, 1916. Three months later at the end of October 1916, after qualifying as a pilot, he was posted to *Feldflieger-Abteilung* (FFl.Abt.) 6b to train as a single-seater pilot.

Eight days after completing his single-seater training, he was posted to *Jasta* 2 Boelcke on the 25 January. It was two months before he claimed his first victory when he shot down a DH2 from No. 32 Squadron, RFC, on 6 March. This was followed by a second on 31 March and the award of his Bavarian Pilot's badge. By the end of April 1917 his score had risen to four and the staff officers of the *Luftstreitkräfte* decided that he was ready for command and assigned him to *Jasta* 12 as its commander. Von Tutschek had been given the command, not for his flying prowess and record, but because of the experience he had in command as an infantryman. By the end of July he had raised his tally to twenty-one for which he was awarded the Knight's Cross with Swords of the Royal Hohenzollern House Order on the 11th. This was followed on 3 August, 1917, by the award of the coveted *Orden Pour le Mérite*.

On 11 August, whilst on patrol, Tutschek came under attack from a Sopwith Triplane of No. 8 Naval Squadron flown by Flight Commander C D Booker. He was severely wounded in the arm in the ensuing dogfight and just managed to get his aircraft back to the field. He was rushed to hospital for emergency surgery and after recuperating was

Oberleutnant *Ritter von Tutschek standing on top of the wreckage of his 22nd victim.*

Oberleutnant *Ritter von Tutschek in an informal pose.*

promoted on the 6 December, 1917, to *Hauptmann*. He was also told that he had been nominated for the Commander's Class of the Military Max-Joseph Order, which was unprecedented because it was only normally give to Generals. Adolf von Tutschek was never to receive the award, like many other awards they remained in the pipeline until the war ended and then disappeared. He was also give command of the newly formed *Jagdgeschwader* Nr. II, made up *Jastas* 12, 13, 15 and 19 on the 1 February 1918. It was to be a short-lived command.

Whilst flying in his all-over green Fokker Dr.I, No. 404/17, on 15 March, 1918, he and his flight were attacked by Allied aircraft and von Tutschek was shot down and killed by Lieutenant H B Redler of 24 Squadron, flying in his SE 5a. *Hauptmann* Adolf Ritter von Tutschek was twenty-seven years old when he died and had 27 victories to his credit.

Awards

Orden Pour le Mérite
Knight's Cross of the Bavarian Military Max-Joseph Order
Bavarian Military Merit Order 4th Class with Swords
Bavarian Military Merit Order 4th Class with Crown and Swords
Knight's Cross with Swords of the Royal Hohenzollern House Order
Iron Cross 2nd Class
Iron Cross 1st Class
Bavarian Prinzregent Luitpold Medal in Bronze
Austro-Hungarian Empire Military Merit Cross 3rd Class with War Decoration
Pilot's Badge – German Army

Victory log

1917

6 Mar	DH 2 (No. 32 Sqn RFC)	Beugny
31 Mar	Nieuport (No. 60 Sqn RFC)	NE Lens
6 Apr	FE 2b (No. 57 Sqn RFC)	S Anneux
30 Apr	FE 2d (No. 18 Sqn RFC)	Izel
1 May	Sopwith Pup (No. 3 Sqn RNAS)	Cantaing
4 May	Sopwith Pup (No. 3 Sqn RNAS)	Baralle
11 May	Sopwith Pup (No. 3 Sqn RNAS)	Croiselle
12 May	Sopwith Pup (No. 66 Sqn RFC)	Baralle
19 May	Sopwith Triplane (No. 1 Sqn RNAS)	Dury
20 May	SPAD VII (No. 23 Sqn RFC)	Reincourt
3 Jul	Sopwith 1½ Strutter (No. 43 Sqn RFC)	N Vaulx
11 Jul	RE 8 (No. 5 Sqn RFC)	Thelus
11 Jul	FE 2d (No. 25 Sqn RFC)	Monchy
12 Jul	Balloon (Balloon Company 36-16-1)	NW Lens
13 Jul	Martinsyde G 102 (No. 27 Sqn RFC)	Noeux-les-Mines
15 Jul	Nieuport (No. 60 Sqn RFC)	S Douai
21 Jul	Nieuport (No. 40 Sqn RFC)	S Moeuvres
23 Jul	Balloon	Neuville
28 Jul	Sopwith Triplane (No. 10 Sqn RNAS)	Mericourt
28 Jul	Nieuport 17 (No. 29 Sqn RFC)	NE Lens
29 Jul	SE 5a (No. 60 sqn RFC)	Henin-Lietard

| 11 Aug | BF 2b (No. 22 Sqn RFC) | Biache |
| 11 Aug | BF 2b (No.22 Sqn RFC) | W Courcelles |

1918

26 Feb	SPAD XIII (No. 23 Sqn RFC)	NE Laon
1 Mar	Balloon (*Cie Aérostieres?*)	Terny
5 Mar	SE 5a (No. 24 Sqn RFC)	Nertancourt
10 Mar	SPAD XIII (*Escadrille Spa* 86)	Chavignon

Total victories claimed: 27

CHAPTER FORTY-THREE

Leutnant Kurt Wüsthoff
(1897 – 1926)

Kurt Wüsthoff was born in Aachen on the 27 January, 1897, the son of a local businessman. It was discovered from an early age that he had a natural aptitude for anything mechanical, so it was no surprise that when he was old enough, at the age of 16, he immediately applied to join German Army Air Service. His application was accepted and he sent to the Military Pilot's School at Leipzig. After four months of training he was awarded his pilot's certificate and badge, but because he was too young to send to the front, Wüsthoff was posted to *Flieger-Ersatz-Abteilung* (FEA). 6 at Grossenhain as an instructor. After pressurising his superiors, he managed to get posted to *Kampfgeschwader* (KG).1 in the Flanders Sector. For the next eighteen months, Wüsthoff saw action in such places as Bulgaria; Roumania and Macedonia as a bomber/reconnaissance pilot.

He was posted to *Jasta* 4 in France at the beginning of June 1917, after being promoted to *Vizefeldwebel*. It was with *Jasta* 4 that he scored his first victory, when, whilst flying on patrol over Vormezeele, he attacked and shot down a Sopwith $1^{1}/_{2}$ Strutter from No. 45 Squadron, RAF. Ten days later he scored his second victory when he brought down an observation balloon whilst over Wytschaeteand for this he was awarded the Iron Cross 2nd Class.

He was awarded the Iron Cross 1st Class at the end of July with his tally standing at six. The following month Kurt Wüsthoff was commissioned and awarded the rank of *Leutnant* on the 1 August, 1917. On 20 August, after scoring his seventh victory, Wüsthoff was awarded the Knight's Cross with Swords of the Royal Hohenzollern House Order. He continued to take his toll on the Allied fighters and by the end of November his tally stood at twenty-six. On November 26 he was awarded Germany's highest award, the *Orden Pour le Mérite*.

Wüsthoff became acting commander of *Jasta* 4 in December until the end of February 1918, when he was promoted to *Staffelführer*. He was not a popular commander, considered by many who served under him to be arrogant and lacking in communication skills with his fellow pilots. His skill as a fighter pilot however was without question. Wüsthoff was then

assigned to the staff of *Jagdgeschwader* (JG)1 until the 16 June, then given command of *Jasta* 5. The day after he had assumed command of *Jasta* 5 whilst flying Georg Hantlemann's Fokker D.VIII, he was jumped by fighter aircraft from No. 23 and 24 Squadrons, RAF, and shot down near Cachy. He was badly wounded in both legs and was taken to a French hospital.

Released from the prison hospital in 1920 and returned to Germany on crutches. Wüsthoff maintained that the French doctors had deliberately neglected to give him proper treatment. He was taken to Dresden so that German doctors could look after him and after a number of operations over a period of two years, he was finally able to leave hospital and walk unaided. He found a position with an Austrian car manufacturer and also returned to his first love, flying. During an aerobatic display at an airshow on 18 July, 1926, that had been set up to raise funds for a memorial to Max Immelmann, he crashed and was badly smashed up. Five days later he died from his injuries.

A youthful Kurt Wüsthoff standing in front of his Albatros aircraft.

Awards

Orden Pour le Mérite
Knight's Cross with Swords of the Royal Hohenzollern House Order
Knight 2nd Class with Swords of the Saxon Albert Order
Wound Badge in Black
Iron Cross 2nd Class
Iron Cross 1st Class
Pilot's Badge – German Army

Victory log

1917

15 Jun	Sopwith 1½ Strutter (No. 45 Sqn RFC)	Vormezeele
23 Jun	Balloon (British Balloon 2-5-2)	Wytschaete
11 Jul	Balloon (Balloon Company 25-5-2)	W Wytschaetebogen
16 Jul	Balloon (Balloon Company 38-7-2)	Kemmel
20 Jul	Sopwith Camel (No. 6 Sqn RNAS)	Bcelaere-Gheluvelt
31 Jul	FE 2d (No. 20 Sqn RFC)	Verbrandenmolen
5 Aug	Nieuport XXIII (No. 29 Sqn RFC)	W Ypres
3 Sep	Sopwith Pup (No. 46 Sqn RFC)	Tenbrielen
3 Sep	RE 8 (No. 4 Sqn RFC)	E Zillebeke
4 Sep	Nieuport XXIII (No. 29 Sqn RFC)	NW Polygon Wood
4 Sep	Sopwith Pup (No. 66 Sqn RFC)	S Ypres
5 Sep	Sopwith Camel (No. 45 Sqn RFC)	SE Zillebeke
11 Sep	Sopwith Camel (No. 70 Sqn RFC)	St Julien
12 Sep	Sopwith Camel	Deulemont
13 Sep	Sopwith Triplane (No. 1 Sqn RNAS)	S Wervicq
16 Sep	Sopwith Camel (No. 70 Sqn RFC)	W Staden
20 Sep	SPAD VII (No. 23 Sqn RFC)	Amerika
20 Sep	SPAD VII (No. 23 Sqn RFC)	W Langemarck
22 Sep	Sopwith Camel (No. 45 Sqn RFC)	Langemarck
24 Sep	Sopwith Camel (No. 10 Sqn RNAS)	Moorslede
26 Sep	SPAD VII (No. 23 Sqn)	Becelaere
27 Oct	Sopwith Triplane (No. 1 Sqn RNAS)	Poelcapelle-Hooge
31 Oct	SE 5a (No. 84 Sqn RFC)	N Bellewardersee
5 Nov	Sopwith Camel (No. 45 Sqn RFC)	Poelcapelle
5 Nov	Sopwith Camel (No. 45 Sqn RFC)	S Staden
9 Nov	RE 8 (No. 21 Sqn RFC)	N Bellewardersee

1918

10 Mar	Sopwith Camel (No. 3 Sqn RFC)	La basse-Bethune

Total victories claimed: 27

CHAPTER FORTY-FOUR

Oberleutnant Oskar Freiherr von Boenigk (1893 – 1946)

Oskar Freiherr von Boenigk was born in Siegersdorf, near Bunzlau, Silesia on 25 August, 1893, the son of an army officer. As expected, on leaving school he followed the family tradition and became an army cadet. He was commissioned as a *Leutnant* in the Grenadier-Regiment König Friedrich III on 22 March, 1912. By the time the First World War broke out, Boenigk was a platoon leader with his regiment and was soon in action. In October 1914, during the battle of Longwy, he was badly wounded in the chest and spent many months in hospital. For his part in the battle, he was awarded the Iron Cross 2nd Class and whilst recovering in hospital, was awarded the Knight's Cross 2nd Class with Swords of the Ernestine House Order.

On his return to his unit in the early spring of 1915, Boenigk was soon in action again on the French Front where he was wounded again. He returned after recuperating and fought at Loretto Heights and Arras. Boenigk soon began to weary of the cold and the mud and looked toward the newly formed German Army Air Service. Boenigk applied for transfer to the Air Service and was accepted. He was then posted to the observer school *Flieger-Ersatz-Abteilung* 7 (FEA.7) in Cologne on 20 December 1915 and after training, was posted to *Kampfstaffel* 19 of *Kampfgeschwader* 4 (KG 4) in March 1916.

The next four months were spent on reconnaissance and scouting missions, then he was posted to *Kampfstaffel* S 2.(KA.S 2) carrying out reconnaissance flights during the Battle of the Somme for which he was awarded the Iron Cross 1st Class. At the beginning of January 1917 he applied to *Jastaschule* for training as a pilot and at the end of the course on 24 June 1917, was posted to *Jasta* 4. On the 20 July, whilst on patrol over Tenbrielen, Boenigk shot down a Nieuport Scout from No. 29 Squadron, RFC, flown by the flight commander, Captain Alfred S Shepherd, DSO, MC. He scored his second victory one week later when he shot down a Sopwith Camel from No. 70 Squadron RFC whilst on patrol over Moorslede.

On 18 August 1917, Boenigk was promoted to *Oberleutnant* and at the

Studio portrait of
Oberleutnant *Freiherr*
von Boenigk.

end of September he had taken his score to five and been given temporary command of *Jasta* 4 when the leader, *Oberleutnant* Kurt-Bertram von Döring, was sent to *Jagdgeschwader* Headquarters. Then on 21 October he was given command of *Jasta* 21, when its Bavarian commander, *Oberleutnant* Eduard Ritter von Schleich went on leave and never returned. This was one of the underlying problems that infested the German Air Service – Bavarian or Prussian commanders commanding each others *Jastas*. Although he had been deservedly given command of *Jasta* 21, Boenigk's command was the result of this in-fighting within the Imperial German Air Service. Predominantly, some Bavarian air units were commanded by Prussians and vice-versa. Amongst certain of the nobility within the hierarchy of the air service, these people were actually considered to be 'foreigners' and as such, had no right to be in command of units belonging to other states. What was even more ironic, *Jasta* 21's command was given to Boenigk who was a Saxon. Once the command had been turned over to Boenigk, no Bavarian would ever command a Prussian unit. By the end of the year Boenigk had raised his tally to six.

In December 1917, during an attack on some reconnaissance balloons, Boenigk was hit in the leg and hospitalized. He returned to *Jasta* 21 in

January 1918. Fortunately the pressure of command due to the easing of hostilities, meant that for the first six months of 1918 things for Oskar von Boenigk were very quiet. But at the beginning of June it all changed during the first week. Boenigk claimed six more victories, two SPADs, one Breguet XIV and three balloons, bringing his total to twelve. By the end of August he had increased it to nineteen and had been awarded the Knight's Cross with Swords of the Royal House Order of Hohenzollern. He was also given command of *Jagdgeschwader* 2 (JG.2), comprising of *Jastas* 12, 13, 15 and 19. on 31 August and promoted to *Oberleutnant*. The *Geschwader* was moved to the St Mihiel Front in September to oppose the American forces that were massing there, and by the end of the month Boenigk had raised his personal tally to twenty-six.

Leutnant Oskar Freiherr von Boenigk, seated on the right, with members of Kampstaffel *19 at Montigny le France.*

His efforts were rewarded when, at the beginning of October 1918, Boenigk received the Saxon Albert Order 2nd Class with Swords, the Sax-Ernestine House Order, Knight 2nd Class with Swords and the Prussian Order of St John, Knight of Honour. The last award conferred upon him title 'Freiherr von', making him a knight. Then on 25 October 1918, he was awarded Germany's highest accolade, the *Orden Pour le Mérite*. By the end of the war he had raised his score to twenty-six. But his days of action were not over and he served in the post-war revolution with some distinction.

During the Second World War, Boenigk served in the Luftwaffe as commander of various airfields, then as area commander rising to the rank of GeneralMajor. He was captured by the Russians in May 1945 and died in a prison camp the following year.

Awards

Orden Pour le Mérite
Knight's Cross with Swords of the Royal Hohenzollern House Order
Iron Cross 1st Class
Iron Cross 2nd Class

Knight 2nd Class with Swords of the Albert Order
Knight 2nd Class with Swords of the Ducal Saxe-Ernestine House Order
Knight of Honour of the Order of St. John
Pilot's Badge, Army – Germany
Observer's Badge, Army – Germany.

Post-war Awards

Silesian Eagle, 1st Class

Victory log

1917

20 Jul	Sopwith Camel (No. 6 Sqn RNAS)	NW Tenbrielen
28 Jul	Sopwith Pup (No. 6 Sqn RNAS)	Moorslede
5 Aug	Sopwith Camel (No. 70 Sqn RFC)	W. Staden
23 Aug	Sopwith Triplane (No. 70 Sqn RFC)	Boesinghe
1 Sep	Sopwith Camel (No. 70 Sqn RFC)	Houthem
3 Sep	Sopwith Pup (No. 46 Sqn RFC)	Brielen
9 Sep	Sopwith Camel (No. 70 Sqn RFC)	E.Langemarck
25 Nov	Sopwith 1½ Strutter	Pfefferrucken

1918

1 Jun	Breguet XIV(*Escadrille Br* 134)	Priez
4 Jun	Balloon (88 *Compagnie Aérostieres*)	Chateau-Thierry
5 Jun	Balloon (88 *Compagnie Aérostieres*)	Chateau-Thierry
7 Jun	Balloon (88 *Compagnie Aérostieres*)	Chateau-Thierry
14 Jun	SPAD XIII (*Escadrille Spa* 163)	N Villers Cotterets
28 Jun	SPAD VII (*Escadrille Spa* 48)	Missy-aux-Bois
8 Jul	SPAD VII (*Escadrille Spa* 15)	Fismes
15 Jul	Breguet XIV (*Escadrille Br* 29)	SW Pourcy
16 Jul	Balloon (29 *Compagnie Aérostieres*)	Villers Allerand
24 Jul	Balloon (67 *Cie d'Aérostieres*)	Aisne sector
1 Aug	SPAD (*Escadrille Spa* 96)	Le Charmel
4 Aug	Balloon (68 *Cie d'Aérostieres*)	Hartness
4 Aug	SPAD 2 (*Escadrille Spa* 63)	
7 Aug	Balloon (2nd Balloon Co. USBS)	S Fismes
11 Aug	SPAD XIII (*Escadrille Spa* 163)	E Arcy
12 Sep	Salmson 2A2 (1st Aero Sqn USAS)	Thiaucourt
13 Sep	SPAD XIII (*Escadrille Spa* 155)	Thiaucourt
14 Sep	SPAD (22nd Aero Sqn USAS)	N Lachaussee
14 Sep	SPAD (22nd Aero Sqn USAS)	Lachaussee
22 Sep	DH 4	Conflans

Total victories claimed: 26

CHAPTER FORTY-FIVE

Oberleutnant Eduard Ritter von Dostler (1892 – 1917)

Born on the 3 February, 1892, in Pottenstein, Bavaria, Eduard Dostler was the son of a former army officer so it was no surprise that on leaving school he joined the army. The 2nd Pioneer Battalion was his choice and he joining as a cadet and after graduating on the 28 October, 1912, he was commissioned to *Leutnant* and assigned to the 4th Pioneer Battalion. In 1913, during a military exercise which involved crossing the heavily flooded Danube River, Dostler showed his bravery and leadership qualities when he saved the life of two fellow officers after they had got in difficulties. For this extreme act of bravery, he was awarded the Bavarian Life Saving Medal. Dostler's engineering unit was sent to the Front at the outbreak of war in August 1914, and almost immediately was into the thick of the fighting for which he was awarded the Iron Cross 2nd Class. Involved in more bitter fighting over the next couple of months, Dostler led his men into numerous skirmished for which he was awarded the Iron Cross 1st Class and the Bavarian Military Service Order 4th Class with Swords in March 1915. He continued to fight with his battalion until November 1915, when he heard that his brother, a pilot, had been killed in action. Dostler then applied to be transferred to the German Army Air Service, bent on revenging his brother's death.

On 5 February, 1916, he was posted to *Schutzstaffel* 27 training school at Schleissheim. After graduating on the 15 June, 1915, Dostler was posted to *Kampfstaffel* 36 flying Roland C.IIs. There he joined up with observer *Leutnant* Boes, and the two of them carried out reconnaissance missions throughout 1916. On 2 October, after carrying out his fifth mission, Dostler was officially awarded his Bavarian Pilot's Badge. The on the 17 December, 1916, he scored his first victory, when he shot down a Nieuport Scout from *Escadrille N* 23, whilst carrying out reconnaissance over Verdun.

On the 27 December 1916 Dostler was posted to *Jagdstaffel* 13, as a fighter pilot and the following day was told that he had been awarded the Bavarian Military Merit Order, 4th Class with Crown and Swords. After settling down into his new *Jasta* Dostler increased his tally by shooting

Studio portrait of
Oberleutnant *Eduard*
Dostler.

down a Caudron whilst on patrol over Nixeville on the 22 January, 1917.
His experience as a leader came to the fore on 20 February 1917, when
he was appointed *Staffelführer* of *Jasta* 34. Four days later he stamped his
mark on his appointment by shooting down two French Caudrons from
Escadrille C 18. Dostler stayed with *Jasta* 34 until the beginning of June,
by which time his tally had risen to eight. It was around this time the
Manfred von Richthofen was looking for men to command the *Jastas* now
being placed under his command as leader of the first permanent
Jagdgeschwadern. One of these *Jastas* was *Jasta* 6 and Dostler's name kept

A smiling Dostler wearing Richtofen's Pour le Mérite after being awarded it but not having actually recieved it.

coming up as someone who was a born leader. Then on the 10 June, Dostler was given command of *Jasta* 6.

Eduard Dostler rose to the challenge and by the end of the following month his score had risen to twenty-one for which he was awarded the Knight's Cross with Swords of the Hohenzollern House Order. *Jasta* 6 attained the highest scores of the whole *Jagdgeschwader* during the month of July. It was no surprise when Germany's highest award, the *Orden Pour le Mérite* was bestowed on Eduard Dostler on 6 August, 1917. Dostler's tally continued to mount and by the 18 August had reached twenty-six. In appreciation of his *Jasta* 6 leader, Manfred von Richthofen, on hearing of Dostler's award came to visit him. This was even more poignant because Richthofen was still suffering from the head wound he had received in July. At a party given in honour of Dostler's award and the visit of Manfred von Richthofen, Richthofen placed his own *Pour le Mérite* around Dostler's neck in recognition of the high award. The reason for this was that it usually took some weeks before the insignia actually came through and Richthofen thought it would be a nice gesture to one of his *Jasta* leaders.

Then on the 21 August whilst on patrol during the Battle of Ypres that Eduard Dostler's luck ran out. His four aircraft patrol attacked a lone British RE 8 from No. 7 Squadron, RFC. on a reconnaissance / photographic mission. As he led his flight into attack the gunner/observer opened fire and Dostler's Albatros D.V was hit several times and burst into flames and plunged to the ground. As the remaining German fighters went into attack the lone RE 8 that had killed their leader, they in turn were attacked by SE 5s who unknown to Dostler were flying cover for the reconnaissance aircraft. The attack was watched by *Leutnant* Josef Jacobs, Commanding Officer of *Jasta* 7, who in his diary wrote:

21 August, 1917.

At 11:00 am, Kunst, Meyer and I took off towards Ypres thinking that the low cloud ceiling at 1,000 meters would make conditions ideal for a surprise balloon attack. As we were emerging from a cloud layer, and before being able to warm up our guns, we became involved in combat with Camels and RE 8s. A salvo from the Vickers gun of a Camel hit me engine and for self preservation, I ducked into a cloud bank. *Jagdstaffel* 6, commanded by *Oberleutnant* Dostler, was also in this fight, and I noted that they were about to be jumped by a squadron of SE 5s flying cover for the RE 8 reconnaissance aircraft. Just as I disappeared into the cloud mist, I observed an Albatros D.V explode and fall in flames.

It appears that *Oberleutnant* Eduard Dostler, the commander of *Jasta* 6, was the occupant of the plane that I saw explode and fall in flames.

The remains of Dostler and his aircraft lay close to the German front line in the Frezenberg area for some days because heavy shelling from the British prevented anyone from getting close to the wreckage. It was this uncertainty that kept the *Jasta's* hoped alive that he may have survived the crash, but it was not to be. His death was a sad loss to his *Jasta* as he was a very well liked and respected officer. He was posthumously awarded the Bavarian Military Max Joseph Order, making him a *Ritter* (Knight). The award was backdated to the 18 August.

Awards

Orden Pour le Mérite
Knight's Cross of the Military Max Joseph Order (Posthumously)
Bavarian Military Merit Order 4th Class with Swords
Bavarian Life Saving Medal
Knight's Cross with Swords of the Royal Hohenzollern House Order
Iron Cross 2nd Class
Iron Cross 1st Class
Bavarian Prinzregent Luitpold Medal in Bronze
Pilot's Badge – Bavarian

Victory log

1916

17 Dec	Nieuport Scout (*Escadrille* N 23)	Verdun

1917

22 Jan.	Caudron G 4 (*Escadrille* C 224)	Nixeville
24 Mar	Caudron G IV (*Escadrille* C 18)	Dupay-Ancemont
24 Mar	Caudron G IV (*Escadrille* C 18)	Les Mesnil
14 Apr	Nieuport Scout (*Escadrille* N 315)	St. Mihiel
24 Apr	Caudron G 4 (*Escadrille* C 46)	Foret d'Aulanville
24 May	Nieuport 17 (No.40 Sqn RFC)	Dieulouard
3 Jun	SPAD VII (*Escadrille* N 69)	SE Belrupt
16 Jun	FE 2b (No. 20 Sqn RFC)	Ypres
16 Jun	Sopwith 1½ Strutter (No.45 Sqn RFC)	Houthem-Korentje
17 Jun	FE 2d (No. 20 Sqn RFC)	St Eloi
20 Jun	Balloon (Balloon Company 4-6-2)	Bailleul
5 Jul	Balloon (Balloon Company 4-13-5)	Ypres
7 Jul	DH 4 (No. 55 Sqn RFC)	SW Warneton
12 Jul	Nieuport Scout (No. 29 Sqn RFC)	Houthem
12 Jul	Sopwith Triplane (No. 10 Sqn RNAS)	Zillebeke
13 Jul	Sopwith 1½ Strutter (No. 70 Sqn RFC)	S Becalere
13 Jul	Nieuport XXIII (No. 29 Sqn RFC)	N Zonnebeke
28 Jul	DH 4 (No. 57 Sqn RFC)	NE Courtrai
28 Jul	DH 4 (No. 57 Sqn RFC)	Oostroubeke

31 Jul	Nieuport Scout (No. 1 Sqn RFC)	W Bellewarde
9 Aug	Nieuport XXIII (No. 29 Sqn RFC)	Poelcapelle
12 Aug	SPAD (No. 23 Sqn RFC)	Gheluve
14 Aug	SE 5 (No. 56 Sqn RFC)	NE St. Julien
17 Aug	DH 4 (No. 57 Sqn RFC)	Menin
18 Aug	DH 4 (No. 57 Sqn RFC)	oulers

Total victories claimed: 26

CHAPTER FORTY-SIX

Leutnant Arthur Laumann
(1894 – 1970)

B orn in Essen on the 4 July, 1894, Arthur Laumann like most of his contemporaries had an uneventful childhood, but it was the outbreak of the First World War that unravelled events that would change his life for ever. Almost immediately the war started, Laumann volunteered and joined Field Artillery Regiment Nr. 83. For two years Laumann fought on the Western and Eastern Fronts, during which time he was awarded the Iron Cross 2nd Class and a commission to *Leutnant*. Tired of living in trenches filled with mud and dying men, Laumann wrote numerous

*Portrait of Arthur
Laumann*

requests for transfer to the German Army Air Service and in August 1917 *Leutnant Arthur*
they acceded to his request.   *Laumann (left of camera)*

    Laumann was sent for training to Schleissheim and on graduating in *at a Fokker demonstration.*
March 1918, was presented with his certificate and pilot's badge and
posted to *Flieger-Abteilung* (A)(Fl.Abt.) 265 as a reconnaissance pilot. It is
interesting to note that at that time (A)Fl.Abt. 265 was commanded by his
brother so no doubt his brother influenced the posting. At the beginning
of May, Laumann was posted to *Jasta* 66 as a fighter pilot, but unusually
had not been given any training. This may have come about because of
the dire need for fighter pilots and Laumann had already displayed his
skills. Under the tutelage of *Jasta* 66's commander Rudolf Windisch over
the next two weeks, it soon became apparent that he was a natural fighter
pilot and soon opened his account on 27 May, 1918, by shooting down a
SPAD.2 whilst over Couvrelles. It was both a happy day for Laumann, *Leutnant Arthur*
but a sad day for the *Jasta*, as its commander, Rudolf Windisch, was shot *Laumann with an*
down and killed.   *unknown companion in*

    In the following month Laumann added another three to his tally and *front of his LVG CV.*

Leutnant Arthur Laumann with Anthony Fokker.

in July a further eleven Allied aircraft fell to his guns, raising his tally to fifteen. Then out of the blue he was asked to take command of *Jasta* 66. Throughout August the *Jasta* was active and Laumann in his Fokker DVII with its distinctive monogrammed 'AL' on the side of the fuselage, added another thirteen victories to his rapidly increasing score, bringing his total to twenty-three.

His influence on *Jasta* 66 had not gone unnoticed by the German High Command and on the 14 August, 1918, Laumann was posted to *Jasta* 10 of JG.1 to replace another of Germany's top aces, Erich Lowenhardt who had been killed.

Leutnant Arthur Laumann in the cockpit of his Fokker DII. Note the AL insignia on the fuselage.

On the 29 September, 1918, Laumann was rewarded with the award of the Iron Cross 1st Class and the Knight's Cross of the Royal Hohenzollern House Order, this was the precursor to Prussia's highest award – the *Orden Pour le Mérite*. His tally had been raised to twenty-eight

at this point and was recognised by the High Command on 29 October when he was awarded Germany's highest honour. Arthur Laumann stayed as commander of *Jasta* 10 until the end of the war.

During the period between the wars Laumann worked as an instructor, but joined the newly formed Luftwaffe in 1935 and became the commander of the new JG *Richthofen* squadron. He survived the Second World War and became the German Air Attaché to Yugoslavia and Greece. He died of a stroke in Munster on the 18 November, 1970.

Awards

Orden Pour le Mérite
Knight's Cross with Swords of the Royal Hohenzollern House Order
Iron Cross 2nd Class
Iron Cross 1st Class
Pilot's Badge – German Army

1918

27 May	SPAD 2 (*Escadrille Spa* 62)	Couvrelles
25 Jun	SPAD VII (*Escadrille Spa* 85)	
25 Jun	SPAD VII (103rd USAS)	
28 Jun	SPAD (*Escadrile Spa* 48)	Villers-Hellon
1 Jul	Nieuport 28 (94th Aero Sqn USAS)	Charly
4 Jul	SPAD	Villers-Cotterets
15 Jul	Breguet XIV (*Escadrille Br* 234)	
17 Jul	Breguet XIV (*Escadrille Br* 132)	
18 Jul	SPAD 2 (*Escadrille Spa* 77)	Billy
18 Jul	SPAD XIII (*Escadrille Spa* 82)	Festigny
18 Jul	Breguet XIV (*Escadrille Br* 104)	Villers-Cotterets
19 Jul	SPAD XIII (*Escadrille Spa* 84)	Villers-Cotterets
21 Jul	Breguet XIV (*Escadrille Br* 279)	La Ferte Milon
29 Jul	Breguet XIV (*Escadrille Br* 216)	Villers-Cotterets
31 Jul	SPAD (94th Aero Sqn USAS)	
2 Aug	SPAD VII (*Escadrille Spa* 38)	
7 Aug	Balloon (*Cie Aérostieres* 54)	
9 Aug	SPAD XVI (*Escadrille Spa* 289)	Reims
9 Aug	SPAD XVI (*Escadrille Spa* 289)	Reims
9 Aug	SPAD XVI (*Escadrille Spa* 289)	Reims
10 Aug	DH 9 (No. 49 Sqn RAF)	Ablaincourt
10 Aug	DH 9 (No. 49 Sqn RAF)	Ablaincourt.
11 Aug	SPAD XIII (*Escadrille Spa* 95)	
19 Aug	SE 5a (No. 24 Sqn RAF)	Bapaume
22 Aug	SE 5a (No. 40 Sqn RAF)	Becourt
22 Aug	SE 5a (No. 64 Sqn RAF)	Bray-sur-Somme
30 Aug	Sopwith Camel (No. 46 Sqn RAF)	Estrees
4 Sep	Sopwith Camel (No. 80 Sqn RAF)	

Total victories claimed: 26

CHAPTER FORTY-SEVEN

Leutnant Oliver Freiherr von Beaulieu-Marconnay (1898 – 1918)

Oliver Beaulieu-Marconnay was born in Berlin-Charlottenburg on the 14 September, 1898. the son of an aristocratic Prussian Army Officer. He spent his early childhood being brought up at a military college which was the fashion of the day. It was no surprise when at seventeen he enlisted in his fathers old regiment, the 4th Prussian Dragoon Regiment, as a cadet one year after the beginning of the First World War. Almost immediately he and his regiment were in combat and within months he had been awarded the Iron Cross 2nd Class. By the end of July 1916, after battles in the Rokitno Swamps, he was awarded the Iron Cross 1st Class and was promoted to the rank of *Leutnant* all by the age of eighteen.

The young *Leutnant* Beaulieu-Marconnay had been fascinated by the rise of the German Air Service and saw that it offered him the chance of achieving every Teutonic Knight's ambition, one-to-one combat. At the beginning of 1917 he applied to be transferred to the air service. His application was accepted and in the early spring of 1917 he was sent to the flying training school at *Jastaschule* – Halberstadt. After graduating in the November he was posted on the 1 December, 1918, to *Jasta* 18 (Royal Prussian), then a few months later to *Jasta* 15 (Royal Prussian) under the command of *Leutnant* Josef Veltjens.

He progressed rapidly under Josef Veltjens tutelage and on the 28 May, 1918, 'Bauli' as he became known, opened his account by shooting down an AR.2 of the United States Air Service over Soissons. Two more 'kills' quickly followed on the 6 June, a DH 4 from 27 Squadron, RFC, and an SE 5a from 32 Squadron, RFC. A further five Allied fighters, three Sopwith Camels, an SE 5A and a DH 4, by the end of June had raised his tally to eight. The 9 August saw him increase his tally to ten in a space of fifteen minutes when he shot down a Sopwith Camel and a SPAD 2. Then on the 2 September, at the age of nineteen, he was given

Leutnant *Oliver Frieherr
von Beaulieu-Marconnay*

command of *Jasta* 19 (Royal Prussian) a remarkable achievement for one
so young. By the end of September he had raised his tally to twenty-one.

Continuing to fly combat missions in the first two weeks of October,
Oliver Beaulieu-Marconnay raised his tally to twenty-five. Then on 4
October, 1918, whilst attacking a French Salmson 2a2, he suffered a
slight wound, but he refused to be taken off flying duties – a decision he
was to regret. Fate caught up with him on the 18 October 1918, whilst
flying his favourite aircraft, a Fokker DVII with his personal insignia –
'4D' (The 4th Dragoons) – painted on the side of the blue fuselage.
During a combat mission, in which his *Jasta* was attacked by Allied
aircraft, his aircraft was caught in crossfire from a Fokker DVII from
Jasta 74 and he was badly wounded. Managing to land the aircraft he was
rushed to hospital. When the authorities were told that he would not
survive his injuries, he was informed that the Kaiser himself had

Leutnant *Oliver Freiherr von Beaulieu-Marconnay (second on left) with pilots from* Jasta *15.*

commanded that he be awarded the coveted *Orden Pour le Mérite*. The order was rushed through and *Leutnant* Oliver Freiherr von Beaulieu-Marconnay became the youngest recipient of the Blue Max, as it was colloquially known, in the First World War and at the age of only twenty years. He died on the 26 October, 1918.

Awards

Orden Pour le Mérite
Iron Cross 2nd Class
Iron Cross 1st Class
Pilot's Badge – German Army

Victory log

1918

28 May	AR 2 Dorand	Soissons
6 Jun	DH 4 (No. 27 Sqn RAF)	Assainvillers
6 Jun	SE 5 (No. 32 Sqn RAF)	SW. Montdidier
7 Jun	Sopwith Camel (No. 80 Sqn RAF)	S. Noyon
11 Jun	Sopwith Camel (No. 73 Sqn RAF)	Mery
12 Jun	Sopwith Camel (No. 43 Sqn RAF)	NE. Compiegne
16 Jun	DH 9 (No. 25 Sqn RAF)	Roye
18 Jun	SE 5a (No. 84 Sqn RAF)	SE Abancourt

9 Aug	SPAD XVI (*Escadrille Spa* 289)	NW Tricot
9 Aug	Sopwith Camel (No. 201 Sqn RAF)	N Beaucourt
10 Aug	SE 5a (No. 56 Sqn RAF)	Chaulnes
11 Aug	SE 5a (No. 56 Sqn RAF)	Gruny
16 Aug	SPAD XIII (*Escadrille Spa* 88)	Tracy le Val
21 Aug	Breguet XIV (*Escadrille Br* 131)	Chauny
7 Sep	Salmson 2A2 (*Escadrill Sal* 5)	NE Montsec
13 Sep	Breguet (96th Aero Sqn USAS)	Charney
13 Sep	Breguet (96th Aero Sqn USAS)	Charney
14 Sep	Breguet XIV (96th Aero Sqn USAS)	Jonville
15 Sep	SPAD XIII (*Escadrille Spa* 154)	Petry
16 Sep	Breguet XIV (96th Aero Sqn USAS)	SW Briey
16 Sep	Breguet XIV (96th Aero Sqn USAS)	Fleville
23 Sep	Breguet XIV (96th Aero Sqn USAS)	Pont-a-Mousson
28 Sep	DH 4 (9th Aero Sqn USAS)	Dannevaux
2 Oct	Breguet XIV (96th Aero Sqn USAS)	Brabant
3 Oct	SPAD XIII (95th Aero Sqn USAS)	Limey
9 Oct	SPAD XIII (95th Aero Sqn USAS)	Crepion
10 Oct	SPAD XIII (*Escadrille Spa* 77)	Landres

Total victories claimed: 25

CHAPTER FORTY-EIGHT

Leutnant Max Näther
(1899 – 1919)

Max Näther was born in Tepliwonda, East Prussia on 24 August, 1899. At the beginning of the war, at the young age of fifteen, Näther joined the infantry. Almost immediately he was thrust into the front line and into the war. Within one year he had been promoted twice, wounded once, awarded the Iron Cross 2nd Class and given a final promotion when on the 11 August, 1916 he was commissioned as an officer. After seeing the horrors of front line fighting, Näther applied for a transfer to the Air Service and was accepted.

He started his basic flight training at the *Fliegerschule* in Bucharest and then was sent to *Flieger-Ersatz-Abteilung* 7 at Brunswick to complete his training. His natural aptitude for flying was instantly recognized and he was sent to *Jastaschule* I at Valenciennes to be trained as a fighter pilot. On completion of his course on 31 March, 1918, he was posted to *Jasta* 62 and within two months had claimed his first victim – a SPAD XIII over Trignieres. This was followed by the shooting down of six balloons and on 1 July a Sopwith Dolphin from 23 Squadron, RFC, over Guerbigny. The last 'kill' resulted in Näther being promoted to commander of *Jasta* 62 at

Portrait shot Leutnant Max Näther.

the age of just eighteen and the award of the Iron Cross 1st Class.

By the end of September he had raised his tally to seventeen and had been awarded the Knight's Cross with Swords of the Royal Hohenzollern House Order. It was during the last encounter with the SPAD XIII that he was wounded and hospitalised for a short time.

Max Näther stayed as commander of *Jasta* 62 until the end of the war, by which time he had raised his score to twenty-six and on 29 October had been nominated for *Orden Pour Le Mérite* but never received the award because the end of the war prevented it from being approved.

At the beginning of 1919 whilst involved in Germany's border war with Poland, he was shot down by groundfire whilst over Kolmar in Schlesien and killed. He was just twenty years old.

Awards

Iron Cross 2nd Class
Iron Cross 1st Class
Knight's Cross with Swords of the Royal Hohenzollern House Order.

Victory log

1918

16 May	SPAD XIII (*Escadrille Spa* 85)	Trignieres
1 Jun	Balloon (*Cie Aérostieres* 54)	Cuvily
5 Jun	Balloon (*Cie Aérostieres* 54)	Cuvily
7 Jun	Balloon (*Cie Aérostieres* 45)	Montigny
16 Jun	Balloon (*Cie Aérostieres* 62)	Amienois
27 Jun	Balloon (*Cie Aérostieres* 75)	Ailly
28 Jun	Balloon (*Cie Aérostieres* 51)	Mesnil
1 Jul	Sopwith Dolphin (No. 23 Sqn RAF)	Guerbigny
15 Jul	SPAD XIII (*Escadrille Spa* 100)	Prosnes
16 Jul	SPAD XIII (*Escadrille Spa* 153)	Thuizy
22 Jul	SPAD VII (*Escadrille Spa* 100)	Courtagnon
6 Sep	Breguet (*Escadrille Br* 260)	Silléry
14 Sep	Balloon (French Balloon CIE 76)	Mailly
26 Sep	SPAD XIII (13th Aero Sqn USAS)	Bezonvaux
26 Sep	Balloon (9th Balloon Company USBS)	Thienville
27 Sep	SPAD XIII (*Escadrille Spa* 77)	Montzéville
9 Oct	Balloon (7th Balloon Company USBS)	Montfaucon
9 Oct	SPAD XIII (213th Aero Sqn USAS)	Montfaucon
10 Oct	Breguet XIV (*Escadrille Br* 281)	Haumont
10 Oct	SPAD XIII (*Escadrille Spa* 77)	Haumont
18 Oct	SPAD XIII (*Escadrille Spa* 84)	Gercourt
23 Oct	Balloon (7th Balloon Company USBS)	Cierges
29 Oct	SPAD XIII (94th Aero Sqn USAS)	Exermont
29 Oct	DH 9 (135th Aero Sqn USAS)	Sivry
29 Oct	DH 4 (135th Aero Sqn USAS)	Montfaucon

Total victories claimed: 26

CHAPTER FORTY-NINE

Leutnant Fritz Pütter
(1895 – 1918)

Fritz Pütter was born in Duelmen, Westphalia on the 14 January, 1895, and like most of his contemporaries his childhood was uneventful, but an incident of the 28 June, 1914, was to change not only his life but the lives of millions. The assassination of the Archduke Ferdinand was to send shock waves that were to have catastrophic ramifications world wide.

War was declared on the 4 August, 1914, and three weeks later Fritz Pütter joined the Westphalian Infantry Regiment. After the barest of training he was sent to the Eastern Front and almost immediately was involved in heavy fighting. In February 1915, Pütter was involved in a bitter battle in which he showed not only his courage but his leadership qualities. Through his actions the lives of many soldiers were saved, and this act of heroism not only earned him the Iron Cross 2nd Class, but a battlefield commission to *Leutnant*. He was transferred to the 370th Infantry Regiment on the 12 October, 1915, and it was whilst serving with them that he began to get interested in the newly formed German Army Air Service. So much so, that in the February of 1916 he applied

Leutnant *Fritz Pütter (third from left) with fellow pilots from* Jasta *68*

for a transfer. He was accepted and posted to *Flieger-Ersatz-Abteilung* (FEA). 8 at Graudenz on the 20 May, 1916, for training.

On the 9 December, 1916, after completing his flying training, he was posted to *Flieger-Abteilung* (Fl.Abt.) 251 as a reconnaissance pilot. For the next two months Fritz Pütter flew reconnaissance missions, and although these missions were vital to the war, he wanted to be more involved and so requested a transfer to fighter pilot duties. He was sent to *Jastaschule* 1 for advanced training and on 17 March, 1917, after graduating, was posted to *Jasta* 9.

On 14 April, he opened his tally when he shot down a French observation balloon whilst on patrol over E. Suippes. By the end of November he had increased his tally to five by destroying French observation balloons.

On the 12 January, 1918, Pütter scored his first victory over another aircraft when he shot down a SPAD XII from escadrille Spa 65, and then added another balloon to his tally. The end of the month saw another

Leutnant *Fritz Pütter*
with the Jasta *mascot.*

two aircraft and two balloons to his tally bringing the total to ten. For his
achievments Fritz Pütter was awarded the Iron Cross 1st Class in
February although the month itself was one of the quietest the *Jasta* had
known. On the 3 February, 1918, Pütter was posted to *Jasta* 68 as
Commandant and spent the next month familiarising himself with the
Jasta's aircraft and their pilots. At the beginning of March the quiet
period was over and things had changed. The *Jasta* was back in action
and by the end of the month Pütter had shot down another six aircraft
bringing his tally to fifteen. His work did not go unrecognised and he
was awarded the Knight's Cross with Swords of the Royal Hohenzollern
House Order.

He continued add victories to his list and by the end of May had raised
his tally to twenty-five. Then came the ultimate accolade, when, on the
31 May, he was awarded Germany's highest honour, the *Orden Pour le
Mérite*. Now leading by example, he continued to lead sorties against the
Allied fighters but tragedy was to strike on the 16 July when, whilst on
patrol he encountered some enemy aircraft and engaged them. During
the ensuing dogfight the tracer ammunition in his Fokker caught fire.
Although very badly burned he managed to limp back to his base, where
he was rushed to hospital. He was Later transferred to a burns hospital
in Bonn but died of his injuries on the 10 August.

Awards

Orden Pour le Mérite
Knight's Cross with Swords of the Royal Hohenzollern House Order
Iron Cross 2nd Class
Iron Cross 1st Class
Pilot's Badge – German Army

Victory log

1917

14 Apr	Balloon (*Compaigne d'Aerostieres* 48)	E Suippes
18 Aug	Balloon (*Compaigne d'Aerostieres* 48)	S Vauquois-Parois
19 Aug	Balloon (*Compaigne d'Aerostieres* 48)	Vraincourt-Brancourt
1 Nov	Balloon (*Compaigne d'Aerostieres* 65)	Massiges-St Jean
1 Nov	Balloon (*Copmaigne d'Aerostieres* 53)	Hans

1918

12 Jan	SPAD (*Escadrille Spa* 65)	Binarsville
12 Jan	Balloon (*Compagnie d'Aerostieres* 53)	Mourmelon le Petit
14 Jan	Balloon (*Compagnie d'Aerostieres* 36)	Vraincourt
19 Jan	Nieuport (*Escadrille* N 156)	Tahure
27 Jan	Nieuport (*Escadrille* N 151)	Dontrien
18 Mar	DH 4 (No. 5 Sqn RNAS)	Beaurevoir
21 Mar	SE 5a (No. 24 Sqn RFC)	Holnon Wood
24 Mar	Sopwith Camel (No. 53 Sqn RFC)	Assevillers
30 Mar	Balloon (*Compagnie d'Aerostieres* 64)	Assainvillers
31 Mar	Breguet XVII (*Escadrille Br* 111)	Guerbigny
3 Apr	SPAD XIII (*Escadrille Spa* 66)	Hergicourt
6 Apr	SPAD XIII (*Escadrille Spa* 154)	Moreuil
7 Apr	Caudron R 9 (*Escadrille* C 74)	Moreuil
7 Apr	SE 5a (No. 24 Sqn RAF)	Moreuil
11 Apr	Sopwith Camel (No. 73 Sqn RAF)	Villers-aux-Erables
12 Apr	SE 5a (No. 84 Sqn RAF)	Villers-aux-Erables
3 May	SPAD XIII	SE Mailly
19 May	SE 5a (No. 84 Sqn RAF)	Bois de Hangard
30 May	BF 2b (No. 48 Sqn RAF)	Castel-Montigny
30 May	SPAD (*Escadrille Spa* 37)	Lassigny

Total victories claimed: 25

CHAPTER FIFTY

Leutnant der Reserve
Erwin Böhme (1879 – 1917)

Erwin Böhme was born in Holzminden, on the Weser on 29 July, 1879. In 1895, and after finishing school, Böhme went to Dortmund to study engineering at the technical college. After qualifying in 1908, he was called up to serve his compulsory military service which he did in a Jaeger regiment. On completion of his service Böhme went back to engineering and worked in Elberfield, Germany and Zürich, Switzerland before taking up a post in East Africa. While in East Africa, whilst supervising the construction of a cable-car between Usambara rail and the New Hornow heights that Böhme learned to fly, a skill he was to put to use some years later.

Böhme had just returned to Germany when the First World War broke out and he immediately volunteered to rejoin the Jaeger Regiment in which he had served his compulsory military service. In the summer of 1914, the thirty-five year old Böhme volunteered for flying duties with the newly formed German Army Air Service and because of his experience as a pilot, was accepted and ordered to report to *Flieger-Ersatz-Abteilung* (FEA) I at Döberitz. Two weeks later he was transferred to the school at Leipzig-Lindenthal to begin his military flying training. He was promoted to *Unteroffizier* the following month and by December had been retained as an instructor. This was not what Böhme wanted, but typical of many Germans at that time, the defence of the Fatherland came above everything, and he realised that his role as an instructor was just as important as a fighter pilot.

After almost a year of being an instructor Böhme applied for a posting to a front line unit in June 1916, and because there was a sudden desperate need for experienced pilots on the front, he was posted at the end of July to *Kampstaffel* 10. This was a unit within *Kampfgeschwader* 2 commanded by *Hauptmann* Wilhelm Boelcke, older brother of the famous Oswald Boelcke. On 5 March, 1916, Oswald Boelcke visited his brother and was introduced to Erwin Böhme, the two quickly became friends.

On 3 May, 1916, whilst on leave with his brother Martin Böhme, an observer with a *Riesenflugzeug-Abteilung* (giant aircraft unit), Erwin

Böhme heard that he had been promoted to *Leutnant. Kaghol* 2 was suddenly moved to Kovel in the Ukraine, to help slow down the advance being made by the Russian Southwest Army Group commanded by General Aleksei Brusilov. Amongst the *Kaghol* 2 pilots with Böhme, was one Manfred Freiherr von Richthofen. Böhme opened his tally on 2 August by shooting down a Nieuport XII whilst on patrol over Rodzyse. He was later awarded the Iron Cross 2nd Class.

Later that month Böhme met up with Oswald Boelcke who was forming a new fighter unit *Jasta* 2. The two men had become friends when they had first met and Boelcke asked for Böhme, along with Manfred von Richthofen, to be assigned to his *Jasta* flying the new Albatros D.I. By the beginning of September 1916 the *Jasta* was ready for action. On 17 September Böhme scored his second victory whilst on patrol over Hervilly, a Sopwith 1½ Strutter from No.70 Squadron, RFC. He was awarded the Iron Cross 2nd Class. Meanwhile Boelcke notched up his twenty-seventh victim.

Erwin Bohme about to take off in his personalised Albatros D III.

On 28 October, 1916, tragedy struck for Böhme. With his tally now standing at five, he was on patrol with his friend Oswald Boelcke and Manfred von Richthofen, when they joined in a skirmish with DH 2s from No. 24 Squadron RFC. Böhme and Boelcke dived in tandem on one of the British fighters, then suddenly another British fighter, hotly pursued by Richthofen, cut across their path. Böhme banked sharply, as did Boelcke, but Böhme's undercarriage touched Boelcke's upper wing which was then seen to break-up. The speed at which they were travelling at the time, caused the wind to rip the fabric on the Boelcke's wing away. Böhme managed to keep control of his aircraft, but Boelcke's aircraft plunged to the ground killing him instantly. Böhme was devastated and blamed himself, but a board of enquiry cleared him of all blame. Böhme then dedicated himself to continuing the fight for his Fatherland.

By the end of the year Böhme had raised his tally to eight and the *Jasta* was now under the command of *Leutnant* Kirmaier. Within a month Kirmaier had been shot down and killed and his place had been taken by *Oberleutnant* Franz Josef Walz. On 7 January, 1917, Böhme opened the new year by shooting down a DH 2 from No. 32 Squadron, RFC, whilst on patrol over Beugny. Two more victories on 4 February, another DH 2

from No. 32 Squadron, RFC, and a BE 2c from No. 15 Squadron, RFC, brought his score to 11. Then on 11 February he was wounded in the head after being involved in a scrap with a Sopwith 1½ Strutter and although he managed to get away, he was hospitalised for a month. Whilst in hospital he was awarded the Iron Cross 1st Class, this was followed on 12 March by the award of the Knight's Cross with Swords of the Hohenzollern House Order. Meanwhile the *Jasta* had started to go into a decline as the more senior and experienced of the pilots were either shot down or given command of their own *Jastas*.

Leutnant *Erwin Bohme (third from left) with Manfred von Richthofen (far left) welcoming Oswald Boelke from a mission.*

On being released from hospital at the end of March, Böhme was assigned as an instructor to *Jastaschule* 1 at Valenciennes as an instructor as part of his recuperation. Then on 2 July he was posted to *Jasta* 29 as Commander, but only managed to claim one more victory before being posted back to *Jasta* 2 (*Jasta* Boelcke) as its Commander. On 10 August, 1917, he was wounded again when his aircraft was shot up by a Sopwith Camel whilst he was in the process of attacking a two-seater bomber. Wounded in the hand the injury kept him behind the desk at *Jasta* 2 for a month. On returning to active service he notched up two more 'kills' in the September and another six in October bringing his tally to twenty-one.

Böhme continued to increase his score when on 6 November, 1917, he shot down a Sopwith Camel from No. 65 Squadron RFC, followed by a Nieuport Scout from No. 1 Belgian *Escadrille*. Then on 24 November 1917, came the ultimate accolade, when he was awarded Germany's highest decoration, the *Orden Pour le Mérite*. But the fame was shortlived. A few days later, on 29 November, whilst on the patrol over Zonnebecke, his flight was attacked by a patrol from No. 10 Squadron, RFC. Settling on the tail of a Sopwith Camel Böhme raked the aircraft with machine-gun fire and shot it down, but failed to see an AWFK.8 slip in behind him. Seconds later his aircraft was similarly raked with machine-gun fire and burst into flames, crashing over the British lines. His body was recovered from the charred wreckage and two days later he was buried by the British with full military honours at Keerselaarhook. His remains were reinterred at Unter den Linden after the war.

Awards

Orden Pour le Mérite.
Iron Cross 2nd Class.
Iron Cross 1st Class.
Knight's Cross with Swords of the Royal House Order of Hohenzollern.
Brunswick War Merit Cross.
Austrian Military Merit Cross 3rd Class with War Decoration.
Pilot's Badge – Army, Germany.

Victory log

1916

2 Aug	Nieuport XII (No. 4 Wing RNAS)	Radzyse
17 Sep	Sopwith 1_ Strutter(No. 70 Sqn RFC)	NW Hervilly
23 Sep	Martinsyde G 100(No. 27 Sqn RFC)	Hervilly
10 Oct	DH 2 (No. 32 Sqn RFC)	E. Longueval
20 Oct	FE 2b (11 Sqn RFC)	Monchy
22 Oct	Sopwith 1½ Strutter (No. 45 Sqn RFC)	Les Boeufs
9 Nov	FE 8 (No. 40 Sqn RFC)	Areleux
22 Nov	Morane Parasol (No. 3 Sqn RFC)	Longueval
26 Dec	BE 2c (No. 5 Sqn RFC)	Courcelette

1917

7 Jan	DH 2 (No. 32 Sqn RFC)	Beugny
4 Feb	DH 2 (No. 32 Sqn RFC)	Sally-le-Transloy
4 Feb	BE 2c (15 Sqn RFC)	Hebuterne
10 Feb	FE 2b (No. 25 Sqn RFC)	Gommecourt
14 Jul	Nieuport XVII (No. 40 Sqn RFC)	Capelle
19 Sep	RE 8 (No. 9 Sqn RFC)	Boesinghem
21 Sep	RE 8 (No. 53 Sqn RFC)	Comines
5 Oct	BF 2b (No. 20 Sqn RFC)	N Dadizeele
10 Oct	SE 5a (No. 56 Sqn RFC)	Zillebeke

13 Oct	Sopwith Pup (No. 54 Sqn RFC)	SW Kokelare
14 Oct	Nieuport Scout (No. 29 Sqn RFC)	Wieltje
16 Oct	Nieuport Scout (No. 29 sqn RFC)	Magermeirie
31 Oct	SE 5a (No.84 Sqn RFC)	Zillebeke Lake
6 Nov	Sopwith Camel (No. 65 Sqn RFC)	Molen
20 Nov	Nieuport Scout (No. 1 Belgian Escadrille)	Osterke
29 Nov	Sopwith Camel (No. 10 Sqn RFC)	Zonnebeke

Total victories claimed: 24

CHAPTER FIFTY-ONE

Vizefeldwebel Karl Paul Schlegel (1893 – 1918)

Karl Paul Schlegel was born on 7 May, 1893, in Wechselburg, Saxony, the son of a former army officer. Immediately on leaving school he followed in the family tradition and joined the army and was assigned firstly to the Royal Sachsenburg Machine-gun Section Nr. 19 and then to Section 8 of the same regiment as an *Unteroffizier*. At the outbreak of war Section 8 were assigned to the 8th Cavalry Division on the Eastern Front where his leadership qualities quickly earned him the Iron Cross 2nd Class. He continued to fight both in Russia and France and after a series of extremely brave actions at the beginning of 1915, was awarded the Silver Military St Henry Medal. This was followed in July by the Iron Cross 1st Class, the first *Unteroffizier* in the German Army to be awarded the medal.

The mud, the cold, the hand-to-hand fighting and living in trenches, was slowly getting to Schlegel and, like many other of his contemporaries, he looked to find another avenue for his talents. At the beginning of 1917 he applied to be transferred to the German Army Air Service and was accepted. He was posted to *Flieger-Ersatz-Abteilung* (FEA) 1 at Altenburg for training and on graduating was posted to FEA 4 at Halle. After a month he was posted again, this time to FEA 6 at Grossenhaim where he was involved in test flying the latest aircraft.

After having spent some time in action on the Front, Schlegel yearned to get back and after some negotiations was sent to *Kampfeinsitzer-Staffel* 1 for a refresher course on single-seat aircraft and then posted to *Jasta* 45. It is interesting to note the *Jasta* 45 was commanded by *Leutnant* Hans Joachim Rolfe, who had the distinction of being the *Jasta's* commander from its inception on 23 December 1917 until the end of the war. Also newly arrived at the *Jasta* was another non-commissioned officer, *Offizierstellverterer* Gustav Doerr, with whom Schlegel became friends. The two NCOs rapidly started to score and their friendly rivalry with regard to scoring victories, boosted the morale of the *Jasta* to a large degree.

On 14 June, 1918, Schlegel scored the first of his victories, an observation balloon over Villers Cotterets. This was to be the first of twenty balloons he was to destroy in the coming year. Four more

balloons and six aircraft in July were rewarded with a promotion to *Vizefeldwebel*, but his friend Gustav Doerr was always that one 'kill' ahead.

Seven more 'kills' in August took his score to nineteen and this was followed by a well earned two weeks leave. On his return, Schlegel was greeted with the news that he had been awarded the Golden Military Merit Cross also known as the *Pour le Mérite für Unteroffiziere*. At the same time he was told that his name had been put forward for promotion to *Leutnant*. As if to celebrate Schlegel and Doerr went out on patrol on 27 October, 1918, and shot down another balloon and a SPAD XI. Then Gustav Doerr was forced to withdraw because of engine trouble, leaving Schlegel on his own. A few minutes later Schlegel's aircraft was seen to suddenly spin out of control and plunge headlong into the ground. Schlegel was killed instantly.

Again like a number of fighter pilots at the time the number of 'kills' bore no resemblance to the awards they received and Schlegel case was no different.

Awards

Silver St. Heinrich Medal
Iron Cross 2nd Class
Iron Cross 1st Class
Golden Military Merit Cross
Pilot's Badge

Victory log

1918

14 Jun	Balloon (85 *Cie d'Aerostiers*)	Villers Cotterets
4 Jul	Balloon (45 *Cie d'Aerostiers*)	Comblizy
6 Jul	Balloon (2nd US Balloon Company)	Bezu
15 Jul	SPAD XIII (Spa 87)	Comblizy
15 Jul	SPAD XIII (Spa 100)	Comblizy
19 Jul	Balloon (92 *Cie d'Aerostiers*)	Creuves
20 Jul	Balloon (25 *Cie d'Aerostiers*)	Neuilly
22 Jul	Breguet XIV	Gland
25 Jul	Breguet XIV (12th USAS)	Missy-aux-Bois
25 Jul	Balloon (1st US Balloon Company)	La Croix
29 Jul	Breguet XIV (*Escadrille Br* 216)	Armentieres
30 Jul	Breguet XIV (*Escadrille Br* 287)	Grisolles
4 Aug	SPAD XI (*Escadrille Spa* 63)	Braisne
6 Aug	Balloon (1st US Balloon Company)	Marcuilen-Dole
12 Aug	Balloon (89 *Cie d'Aerostiers*)	Drocy
12 Aug	Balloon (68 *Cie d'Aerostiers*)	Loupeigne
21 Aug	Balloon (33 *Cie D'Aerostiers*)	Brangex
21 Aug	Balloon (83 *Cie d'Aerostiers*)	Vic
29 Aug	SPAD XIII (*Escadrille Spa* 96)	Fismes

1 Sep	Balloon (29 *Cie d'Aerostiers*)	Ouilly
4 Sep	Balloon (26 *Cie d'Aerostiers*)	Sarcy
5 Sep	Balloon (47 *Cie d'Aerostiers*)	Fismes
27 Oct	Balloon (42 *Cie d'Aerostiers*)	La Malmaison
27 Oct	SPAD VII (*Escadrille Spa* 93)	La Malmaison

Total victories claimed: 24

CHAPTER FIFTY-TWO

Oberleutnant Hermann Wilhelm Göring (1893 – 1946)

Hermann Göring was probably the most famous, or infamous, German pilot to come out of the First World War. It was not for his actions during the First World War that brought him notoriety, but for his part in the Second World War.

Born on the 12 January, 1893, in Rosenheim, Upper Bavaria, Hermann Göring was the son of Heinrich Göring, a high ranking army officer who had also been a Governor of German South-West Africa. Hermann Göring was an unruly, rebellious and undisciplined boy, in his early school years so his parents sent him to a military academy in an attempt to instill some discipline in him. Using a great deal of his influence, Heinrich Göring and a family friend von Epstein, managed to get Hermann into one of the best military academies at Karlsruhe. From there he went to Lichterfelde, an army cadet college for future officers in the German army. College behaviour here was based on medieval codes and the cadet society in to which Hermann Göring was elected, was one that adhered strictly to them. In 1912 Hermann Göring graduated from Lichterfelde with brilliant results and was commissioned into the Prinz Wilhelm Regiment Nr. 112 and assigned to its headquarters at Mülhausen.

Within hours of the war starting Göring's regiment was in action albeit in a retreating manoeuvre. This was because of the location of the garrison town of Mülhausen. The town was situated in Alsace-Lorraine which had been annexed from the French after the war of 1870 and it was also on the wrong side of the Rhine. The moment war was declared, the Prinz Wilhelm Regiment retreated across the Rhine on to German territory. The regiment was moved to the Vosges region and it was while stationed here that Göring contracted rheumatic fever and was hospitalised.

One of Göring's visitors, whilst he was in hospital, was his friend Bruno Loerzer. Loerzer had served with Göring in the regiment, but had transferred to the German Army Air Service not long after the retreat and had become a pilot. Göring reflected on the cold, muddy trenches

Göring being suited up for a mission.

that awaited his return and wrote to his commanding officer requesting a transfer to the German Army Air Service. After waiting over two weeks and receiving no reply, Göring obtained the papers and signed them himself, including a transfer paper to the flying school. During this two week period he had been flying with Loerzer at every opportunity, getting in all the training he could. His transfer was refused and he was ordered to return to his unit, which was something Göring had no intention of doing. This situation posed a very serious problem for Hermann Göring, as he was open to a charge of desertion and forging papers. He immediately telegraphed his godfather, *Ritter* von Epstein, who moved in extremely high circles. Then suddenly the Crown Prince Friedrich Wilhelm intervened and asked that Göring be posted to the German Fifth Army field air detachment. The charges were suddenly reduced to one of lateness and he was given a medical certificate saying that he had contracted rheumatoid arthritis and was not fit for duty on the front line.

Göring completed his training with *Flieger-Ersatz-Abteilung* (FEA) in October 1914 and joined his friend Loerzer at *Feld-Flieger-Abteilung* (FFl.Abt.) 25 as a cameraman-observer. The two friends soon acquired a

(Above) Leutnant *Hermann Göring, seated extreme right, when OC of* Jagdstaffel 27 . *(Below) Holders of the* Pour le Mérite. *Seated: Göring, Loerzer, von Boenigk. Standing: Klein, Veltjens, Everbusch (designer of the Pfalz) Udet, Jacobs.*

name for carrying out the most dangerous of mission and in March, received the Iron Cross 2nd Class. Then in May 1915, Göring and Loerzer carried out one of their most dangerous missions. They were assigned to carry out a reconnaissance of the fortresses in the Verdun area that were held by the French and photograph them in detail. All attempts up to this point had failed. For three consecutive days Göring and Loerzer carried out flights over the Verdun area and came back with photographs so detailed that General Erich von Falkenhayn asked to see them personally. Crown Prince Wilhelm was so delighted with the results, as were the High Command, that he exercised his royal prerogative and invested both Göring and Loerzer with the Iron Cross

1st Class in the field.

Göring briefing pilots of JG 1 prior to mission.

Göring was bored with taking a backseat on all the missions so asked to be considered for pilot training. It was agreed and in June 1915 he was sent to *Jastaschule* 1 at Freiburg and graduated at the beginning of October 1915. He was then posted back to *Feldfleiger-Abteilung* (FFl.Abt.) 25 and on the 16 November, 1915, opened his tally by shooting down a Maurice Farman whilst on patrol over Tahure.

In 1916, he was posted first to *Kek* Stennay flying Fokker E.IIIs, then in the March to *Kek* Metz, where, on the 30 July, he shot down a Caudron whilst he was escorting bombers over Memang. He then returned to FFl.Abt. 25 on the 9 July, then back again to *Kek* Metz on the 7 September. From there he went to *Jasta* 7 and a few weeks later *Jasta* 5 on the 20 October. It was whilst on patrol on the 2 November, 1916, that he first encountered the British Handley-Page bomber. He dived to look at the huge aircraft and came under fire from the gunners. He returned the fire killing one of the gunners, but then from out of the clouds swooped a flight of Sopwith Camels who proceeded to rake his aircraft from nose to tail. Göring felt the bullets rip into his fuselage and in to his thigh and he passed out from the pain. He came to as his aircraft plunged out of control toward the ground. Struggling to control the aircraft, he steered it toward what looked like a cemetery just over the German lines. As good fortune would have it, it turned out to be an emergency hospital and within a very short time of crash landing, he was on the operating table being repaired.

His friend Bruno Loerzer had just taken command of *Jasta* 26 and requested that Hermann Göring be posted to his *Jasta* after he had recuperated from his imjuries. At the beginning of February 1917, Göring arrived at his new *Jasta* to be welcomed by his friend. A rejuvenated Göring had raised his tally to six by the end of April and was

Hermann Göring, with the leaders cane that belonged to Manfred von Richthofen, standing beside his all-white Fokker D VII.

attracting the attention of the High Command. He increased his tally on the 10 May, when he shot down a DH 4 of 55 Squadron, RFC. One week later he was given command of *Jasta* 27 and by the end of October had raised his tally to fifteen.

Hermann Göring was awarded the Military Karl-Friedrich Merit Order, the Knight's Cross with Swords of the Hohenzollern House Order and Knight's Cross 2nd Class with Swords of the Baden Order of the Zähringer Lion on 20 October, 1917. By the end of the year his tally had risen to sixteen.

He increased his tally steadily during the first half on 1918 and by the end of June had taken his tally to twenty-two. He was awarded Germany's highest award, the *Orden Pour le Mérite* at the beginning of June 1918, when his total number of victories stood at eighteen. The stringent requisite number required at the time was twenty and it was the subject of much speculation as to how he managed to get the prestigious award so early. It has to be remembered that Göring's earlier problems that almost caused him to be courtmartialed, but for the interception by friends in very high places, both in the government and diplomatic corps, led to the charges disappearing. One can only assume that it was the same friends who once again spoke on his behalf.

Then on the 9 July Göring was given command of *Jagdgeschwader* (JG).1 – the Richthofen Squadron and promotion to *Oberleutnant*. At this point

Hermann decided that his fighting days were over and did very little combat flying. At the end of the war, he was ordered to instruct his pilots to fly their aircraft to an Allied field. He knew that the Allies just wanted the latest Fokkers, so he ordered his pilots to do so, but to set fire to the aircraft the moment they were on the ground. After Munich *putsch* in 1923 war Hermann Göring fled to Denmark in a flight advisory capacity, but returned to Germany a few years later.

Hermann Göring joined the Nazi Party and became Adolf Hitler's right hand man. He progressed through the party as its strength grew and took over command of the newly formed Luftwaffe. Göring held a number of other posts throughout the Second World War, but the Luftwaffe was dearest to his heart. During the Second World War he received the Knight's Cross of the Iron Cross and the Grand Cross of the Iron Cross, the only person ever to receive it. He was promoted to *Feldmarschall* then later to *Reichsmarschall*, and heir apparent to Hitler. Captured by the Americans at the end of the war, Hermann Göring stood trial for war crimes and was convicted. He was sentenced to death by hanging, despite his pleas to be executed by firing squad. In the end he cheated everybody by committing suicide on the 15 October 1946, the day before his palnned execution, using poison he had been concealing on his person since his capture.

Awards

Orden Pour le Mérite
Knight's Cross with Swords of the Royal Hohenzollern House Order
Iron Cross 2nd Class
Iron Cross 1st Class
Knight's Cross of the Military Karl-Friedrich Merit Order
Knight 2nd Class with Swords of the Order of the Zähringer Lion
Wound Badge in Black
Pilot's Badge
Observer's Badge

Victory log

1915

16 Nov	Farman	Tahure

1916

14 Mar	Caudron (*Escadrille* C 6)	SE Haumont Wood
30 Jul	Caudron G4 (*Escadrille* C 10)	Mamang

1917

23 Apr	FE 2b (No. 22 Sqn RFC)	NE Arras
28 Apr	Sopwith 1½ Strutter (No. 43 Sqn RFC)	S St Quentin
29 Apr	Nieuport XVII (No. 6 Sqn RNAS)	Ramicourt
10 May	DH 4 (No. 55 Sqn RFC)	NE Le Peve
8 Jun	Nieuport Scout (No. 1 Sqn RFC)	Moorslede
16 Jul	SE 5 (No. 56 Sqn RFC)	NE Ypres
24 Jul	Sopwith Camel (No. 70 Sqn RFC)	Passchendaele
5 Aug	Sopwith Camel (No. 70 Sqn RFC)	NE Ypres
25 Aug	Sopwith Camel (No. 70 Sqn RFC)	SW Ypres
3 Sep	DH 4 (No. 57 Sqn RFC)	N Lampernisse
21 Sep	BF 2b (No. 48 Sqn RFC)	W Roulers
21 Oct	SE 5a (No. 84 Sqn RFC)	Linselles

| 7 Nov | DH 5 (No. 18 Sqn RFC) | Polecapelle |

1918

21 Feb	SE 5a (No. 60 Sqn RFC)	Ledeghem
7 Apr	RE 8 (No. 52 Sqn RFC)	SW Merville
5 Jun	AR 2 Dorand	N Villers Cotterets
9 Jun	SPAD (*Escadrille Spa* 54)	S Coroy
17 Jun	SPAD (*Escadrille Spa* 93)	Ambleny
18 Jul	SPAD XIII (*Escadrille Spa* 77)	St. Bandry

Total victories claimed: 22

CHAPTER FIFTY-THREE

Leutnant Rudolf Windisch
(1897 – ?)

Born in Dresden on the 27 January, 1897, Rudolf Windisch came from an ordinary working-class background. On leaving school he worked in a variety of jobs before he entered military service in 1912, joining the No.177th Infantry Regiment, Saxon 1st Army Corps. Within weeks of the war starting, Windisch's regiment was in the Front line and during one bitter engagement Windisch was wounded by a grenade though not seriously. Whilst on sick leave he applied to be transferred to the German Army Air Service and was accepted. He was assigned on the 22 January, 1915, to the Leipzig-Lindenthal Military Pilot's School.

Windisch was a very intelligent young man and excelled throughout the course and on graduating on the 10 June, was promoted to *Unteroffizier* and assigned to *Flieger-Ersatz-Abteilung* (FEA).6 as an instructor. Having already tasted action on the Front line and been wounded for his trouble, he soon became bored with teaching, although it was a responsible and safe post he wanted action. Windisch applied for a posting to a combat unit, and on the 1 May, 1916, was sent to *Feldflieger-Abteilung* (FFl.Abt.) 62 and it was here that he teamed up with his observer Maximillian von Cossel. One month later the whole unit was moved to the Russian Front and it wasn't long before they had made there mark with a number of daring reconnaissance flights over the fron. For this he was awarded the Iron Cross 2nd Class together with a promotion to *Vizefeldwebel*.

Windisch's first victory came on the 25 August, 1916, when he shot down an observation balloon over SE Brody. It was for this action, and previous missions he and his observer had carried out, that he was awarded the Iron Cross 1st Class. This was followed some weeks later by the award of the Prussian Crown Order 4th Class with Swords. This award rose out of a special mission carried out by Windisch and his observer *Oberleutnant* Maximillian von Cossel. The mission required Windisch to land his aircraft behind the Russian lines, drop off von Cossel, whose brief it was to blow up a strategic railway bridge near Rowno-Brody, this was to happen on the 2nd October. The following

day, the 3 October, Windisch was to return to pick up his observer. The mission was a complete success. Both men were presented to the Emperor on the 18 October and for this extremely daring mission, received the Honour Cross with Swords from the Principality of Waldeck and the St Henry Medal in Silver from Saxony. Von Cossel also received the Knight's Cross with Swords of the Royal Hohenzollern House Order for his part in the mission. *Vizefeldwebel* Rudolf Windisch was the only non-commissioned officer ever to receive the order and the award was without precedent.

Windisch was sent to *Kampfstaffel* 12 of *Kampfgeschwader* (KG)2 on the Western Front, on the 24 November after a brief leave. Then on the 5 December, he was promoted and commissioned to the rank of *Leutnant*. Windisch applied to be trained as a fighter pilot and while he waited for his application be processed, he continued reconnaissance patrols. Then on 20 February he was posted to *Jasta* 32 as a fighter pilot and after further training he started to make his mark on the Allied fighters. On

Vizefeldwebel *Windisch*
with his observer
Oberleutnant *von Cossel*.

the 18 September he shot down an AR.2 and this was followed by a SPAD VII on the 27th brought his tally to three. His fourth victim, a SPAD VII on the 1 November, 1917, brought him the Knight's Cross 1st Class with Swords of the Albert Order from Saxony.

Windisch's tally had risen to six by the end of November. Then on the 10 January, 1918, Windisch was posted to *Jasta* 50 for just two weeks, he was then posted to *Jasta* 66 as commanding officer. One of the reasons given for Windisch's removal from *Jasta* 32 was that the unit had been regarded as belonging to the Royal Bavarian Army and it was the policy only to have Bavarians in the *Jasta*. With all the in-fighting going on it is surprising that they weren't at war with each other, such was the bitterness between the different kingdoms and principalities.

Windisch continued to set by example and on 24 March he claimed three aircraft to add to his tally. By the end of May 1918, he had raised his tally to twenty-two during which time he was awarded the Knight's Cross with Swords of the Royal Hohenzollern House Order, the Austrian-Hungarian Bravery Medal in Silver 2nd Class and the Saxon St Henry Medal in Gold.

On the day of his twenty-second victory, Windisch took off on a routine patrol in his new Fokker DVII, 2035/18. His aircraft had a distinctive leaping white stag emblazoned on the fuselage, said to be a tribute to the clinic in Dresden that looked after him when he had been wounded. He attacked a SPAD over Couvrelles and shot it down and then he himself

came under attack and his fuel tank was hit forcing him to crash land his
aircraft. The wreckage of the SPAD and the almost intact remains of his
Fokker were found by a German patrol soon afterwards. The
undercarriage of his aircraft had been wiped out but the rest of the
aircraft survived. But of *Leutnant* Rudolph Windisch there was no sign.

Rudolf Windisch, wearinfg a belted raincoat, with felllow pilots of Jasta 32

Later a message was dropped over the German lines stating that
Leutnant Windisch had been captured and was a prisoner of the French
but this was never confirmed. It was assumed that he was a prisoner-of-
war, and the *Orden Pour le Mérite* was awarded to him but it was never
collected.

Efforts were made to locate *Leutnant* Windisch after the war and the
repatriation of prisoners commenced, but he was never seen again. The
story of his disappearance is shrouded in mystery. There were a number
of explanations given, including one that he was shot trying to steal a
French aeroplane, but this was never confirmed. Another was that after
crash-landing he chanced upon a French patrol and because of the
hostility felt by the ground troops toward airmen who carried out
strafing missions against them, was just shot out-of-hand and buried in
an unmarked grave.

Rudolf Windisch in the cockpit of his Fokker D VII with a leaping stag on the fuselage.

To this day it is still a mystery what happened to *Leutnant* Rudolf Windisch and one that may never be solved.

Awards

Orden Pour le Mérite
Knight's Cross with Swords of the Royal Hohenzollern House Order
Saxon Knight 2nd Class with Swords of the Albert Order
Saxon St Henry Medal in Silver
Prussian Crown Order 4th Class with Swords
Iron Cross 2nd Class
Iron Cross 1st Class
Waldeck Honour Cross with Swords

Austro-Hungarian 2nd Class Bravery Medal in Silver
Pilot's Badge
Victory log

1916

25 Aug	Balloon	SE Brody

1917

18 Sep	AR 2 Dorand (*Escadrille* F 41)	Fleury
27 Sep	SPAD VII	Belleville
1 Nov	SPAD VII (*Escadrille Nr* 112)	W Bray
7 Nov	SPAD VII	Brancourt
18 Nov.	SPAD VII (No. 19 Sqn RFC)	Laval

1918

3 Jan	Balloon (62 *Cie d'Aérostieres*)	Villers
4 Jan	SPAD VII	S Staubecken
15 Mar	SPAD VII (No. 23 Squadron RFC)	Vitry-Reims
17 Mar	SPAD VII (No. 23 Squadron RFC)	Vitry-Reims
23 Mar	Sopwith 2 *Escadrille Sop* 229)	Le Bruin Ferme
24 Mar	SPAD 2 (No. 23 Squadron RFC)	Bretigny
24 Mar	SPAD XIII (No. 23 Squadron RFC)	Tergnier
24 Mar	SPAD XIII (No. 23 Squadron RFC)	Tergnier
11 Apr	Breguet XIV (*Escadrille Br* 217)	S Noyon
21 Apr	SPAD VII (*Escadrille Spa* 12)	Guy
21 Apr	SPAD VII (*Escadrille Spa* 12)	Guy
3 May	Balloon (88 *Cie d'Aérostiers*)	Juvigny
4 May	SPAD XI (*Escadrille Spa* 54)	Carlepont
15 May	SPAD 2 (*Escadrille Spa* 265)	Trosly-Loire
16 May	SPAD XIII (*Escadrille Spa* 3)	Thiescourt
27 May	SPAD 2 (*Escadrille Spa* 62)	Couvrelles-Lesges

Total victories claimed: 22

CHAPTER FIFTY-FOUR

Leutnant Gerhard Fieseler
(1896 – 1987)

Gerhard Fieseler was born on 15 April, 1896, in Bonn. Like many other children of his day his childhood was uneventful but the advent of the First World War was soon to change that for almost everyone. With the start of the First World War, Fieseler applied to join but was deemed to be to young, but the following year he was accepted and in June 1915 he immediately applied to join the newly formed German Army Air Service. After being accepted he applied to train as a pilot and was sent to *Flieger-Ersatz-Abteilung* (FEA) 7 near Cologne for his initial training, and then on to *Jastaschule* II at Johannisthal for further flight training. Then during one of his instructional flight he crashed and suffered serious injuries. He was in hospital for three months before being able to continue his training and he graduated at the end of September 1915.

After leave he was assigned to *Flieger-Abteilung* (A)(FA(A)).243 and was immediately in action on the front line flying reconnaissance missions. Two weeks later he was transferred to FA.41 and then to *Armee-Flug-Park* 11, where he underwent single-seater conversion training before being posted, on 12 July 1917, to *Jasta* 25 in Macedonia flying Roland D.IIs. He was also promoted from *Unteroffizier* to *Vizefeldwebel*.

On 20 August, 1917, whilst on patrol south of Prilip he engaged a Nieuport XVII from No. 17 Squadron, RFC, and shot it down. He was jubilant and so was his *Jasta*, because unlike the air war on Western and Eastern Fronts, aerial victories in Macedonia were much harder to achieve. For this Fieseler was awarded the Iron Cross 2nd Class and a second on 9 September, a Nieuport Scout, brought the Iron Cross 1st Class. Then suddenly on 21 September, Fieseler contracted a serious illness which hospitalised him for the next two months, and he was not able to return to his *Jasta* until 5 November, 1917. By this time he had received the Bulgarian Soldier's Cross 3rd and 4th Class.

Gerhard Fieseler gradually got back into the routine of flying patrols, but it wasn't until 30 January that he 'notched' up his next victory, a Nieuport XVII over S. Moglia. It was to be two months before the next 'kill', another Nieuport of *Escadrille* N 407 over NW Caniste. By the end of August

Fieseler had raised his tally to thirteen and on the 3 September came the award of the Golden Military Merit Cross and the Austrian Merit Cross in Silver with Crown. As if to crown this achievement in September Fieseler scored another six victories for which he was awarded the Bulgarian Soldier's Cross 1st and 2nd Class and in October 1918 he was promoted to *Leutnant.*

After the war Fieseler went in to the aircraft industry as a designer but he still flew and was World Aerobatic Champion five times. During the war Fieseler had his own aircraft company and one of his creations was the renowned Fieseler Fi 156 'Storch', which had the shortest take-off and landing of any aircraft in the world, and even today there a number still flying, a real testament to the designer. Gerhard Fieseler died in

Group of pilots from Jagdgeschwader 25 in Macedonia with Gerhard Fieseler in the centre.

Kassel on 1 September 1987 at the age of ninety-one.

Awards

Iron Cross 2nd Class
Iron Cross 1st Class
Golden Military Merit Cross
Austrian Merit Cross in Silver with Crown
Bulgarian Soldier's Cross 1st Class
Bulgarian Soldier's Cross 2nd Class
Bulgarian Soldier's Cross 3rd Class
Bulgarian Soldier's Cross 4th Class

Victory log

1917

| 20 Aug | Nieuport XVII (No.17 Squadron RFC) | S Prilip |
| 9 Sep | Nieuport Scout (No.1 Squadron RFC) | Pogradec |

1918

30 Jan	Nieuport XVII	S Moglia
5 Apr	Nieuport XXIV (*Escadrille* N 508)	NW Caniste
20 Jun	SPAD VII (No. 23 Squadron RFC)	Makova
5 Jul	Nieuport XXIV (*Escadrille* N 506)	SE Prilip
24 Jul	Nieuport Scout (No. 29 Squadron RFC)	S Dobro-Polje

25 Jul	Nieuport Scout	Gradesnica
28 Jul	Breguet XIV	Kanatlarci
4 Aug	Nieuport Scout (*Escadrille* N 503)	E Vitole
5 Aug	Nieuport Scout (*Escadrille* N 95)	Gradesnica
11 Aug	Nieuport Scout (*Escadrille* N 524)	NE Vodena
16 Aug	AR2	N Negocani
23 Aug	SPAD 2 (*Escadrille* N 524)	E Vitole
4 Sep	Breguet (*Escadrille* N 524)	Budmirtsa
9 Sep	Nieuport	Orchida
13 Sep	Nieuport Scout (*Escadrille* N 508)	E Vitole
15 Sep	Nieuport Scout (*Escadrille* N 505)	Debedesa
18 Sep	SPAD XII (*Escadrille* N 154)	E Cerna-Rajks
19 Sep	Nieuport Scout (*Escadrille* N 506)	Monastir
20 Sep	Breguet (*Escadrile Br* 132)	Trojviarci

Total victories claimed: 19

CHAPTER FIFTY-FIVE

Leutnant Kurt Wintgens
(1894 – 1916)

Kurt Wintgens was born in Neustadt on 1 August, 1894, the son of a career army officer. On leaving college at the age of nineteen, he joined the Telegraphen-Battalion Nr. 2 in Frankfurt as a cadet and then was sent to the military academy to start his career. When war broke out he immediately rejoined his unit and within a matter days was in action against the Allied forces.

After a series of bitter engagements during the next few months Kurt Wintgens was awarded the Iron Cross 2nd Class. Even at this early stage the thought of spending the war in mud-filled trenches was not that appealing to the young soldier and so he thought about the new form of warfare – aviation. This was a new challenge amongst the young German officers and Kurt Wintgens was not slow to see the advantages and excitement it had to offer. At the end of November 1914, Kurt Wintgens applied to be transferred to the aviation section and was accepted as an observer, and after completing his training, because of his experience in telegraph, was attached to the AOK IX (Army Wireless Abteilung).

His first experiences of war in the air were initially on the Western Front then Poland, then in the March of 1915 he was accepted for pilot training. Within four months he had qualified as a pilot, exhibiting exceptional skills that had him immediately posted to a fighter squadron, *Feldflieger-Abteilung* (FFA).67 flying Fokkers then on to FFA.6b.

During a patrol close to Luneville on the 1st July, 1915, he encountered a Moranne Parasol and after a brief fight shot it down. Unfortunately there were no witnesses to confirm the 'kill' and the claim was not allowed. Had it been, it would have been the first 'kill' by a German fighter in history. Three days later a second claim of another Moranne Parasol on the 4 July was also unconfirmed.

Four days later he was posted to FFA.48 and given ostensibly a roving commission as he commented in a letter to a friend,

'I do not appear to belong to any *Abteilung* in particular'.

Then, whilst on patrol over Schlucht on the 15 July, 1915, Wintgens encountered another Moranne Parasol from *Escadrille* MS 48, and, after a brief fight, it fell in flames – this time it was confirmed. Kurt Wintgens had officially opened his score, but it was to be almost another month before he shot down his second aircraft. This was on the 9 August, 1915, when he shot down a Voisin whilst on patrol over Gondrexange. It was then that he fell ill with the influenza virus that swept across the Western Front, curtailing his flying. But on his return in the January of 1916 he resumed his scoring by shooting down a Caudron G.IV and the award on the Iron Cross 1st Class quickly

(Above) Leutnant *Kurt Wintgens with his Fokker Eindecker. (Below)* Leutnant *Kurt Wintgens in the cockpit of his Fokker Eindecker. Wintgens was one of three German pilots who wore glasses.*

followed.

On 17 June, 1916, he was awarded the Knight's Cross with Swords of the Hohenzollern House Order and by the end of the month had raised his tally to eight. On 1 July, 1916, Kurt Wintgens was awarded Germany's highest award, the *Orden Pour Le Mérite*, only the fourth German pilot to be honoured with it. Later that month he was posted to FA.23's Kek Vaux and then on to *Jasta* 4, when it was amalgamated. Another award came his was at this time, the Bavarian Military Merit Order 4th Class with Swords. By the end of September his tally had risen to nineteen and with it came the award of the Saxon Albert Order, Knight Second Class with Swords.

Then on the 25 September, 1916, whilst flying escort to a two-seat reconnaissance aircraft, they came under attack from aircraft of the French *Escadrille* N 3. As one of the French aircraft swept in to attack the reconnaissance aircraft, Wintgens placed himself between them and in doing so fell under the guns of the French ace Lieutenant Hurteaux and was shot down in flames. It is said that the observer in the German two-seat aircraft that Wintgens protected was Josef Veltjens who was later to become a pilot and an ace.

Kurt Wintgens was twenty-two years old when he died.

Awards

Orden Pour le Mérite
Saxon Albert Order, Knight 2nd Class with Swords
Bavarian Military Merit Order 4th Class with Swords
Knight's Cross with Swords of the Royal Hohenzollern House Order
Iron Cross 1st Class.
Iron Cross 2nd Class.

Victory log

1915

1 Jul	Morane Parasol (*Escadrille* MS 48)	E.Luneville
4 Jul	Morane Parasol (*Escadrille* MS 3)	
15 Jul	Morane Parasol	Schlucht
9 Aug	Voisin (*Escadrille* VB 112)	Gondrexange

1916

24 Jan	Caudron G.IV (*Escadrille* C 47)	
20 May	Nieuport XII (*Escadrille* N 68)	Chateau-Salins
21 May	Caudron G IV (*Escadrille* C 42)	Chateau-Salins
17 Jun	Farman (*Escadrille* MF 70)	S.Chateau-Salins
23 Jun	Nieuport XVI (*Escadrille* N 124)	Blamont
30 Jun	Farman (*Escadrille* C 106)	SW Chateau-Salins
19 Jul	Sopwith 1½ Strutter (No. 70 Squadron RFC)	Arras
21 Jul	Morane Scout (No. 60 Squadron RFC)	Combles
21 Jul	BE 2c (No. 12 Squadron RFC)	S.Douai
30 Jul	Martinsyde G 100 (No. 27 Squadron RFC)	E.Peronne
2 Aug	Morane Parasol (No. 60 Squadron RFC)	S.Peronne
14 Sep	Nieuport (*Escadrille* N 62)	Bussau
14 Sep	BE 2c (No. 4 Squadron RFC)	N.Rancourt
15 Sep	BE 12 (No. 19 Squadron RFC)	Manancourt
17 Sep	Martinsyde G 100 (No. 27 Squadron RFC)	Beaumetz
24 Sep	BE 12 (No. 19 Squadron RFC)	Flesquires
24 Sep	BE 12 (No. 19 Squadron RFC)	Flesquires

Total victories claimed: 19

CHAPTER FIFTY-SIX

Leutnant Wilhelm Frankl
(1893 – 1917)

Wilhelm Frankl was born on the 20 December, 1893, in Hamburg, the son of a Jewish furniture salesman. Resentment against the Jews even in this early time was plain to see in Germany and Wilhelm Frankl was to find that obtaining promotion was not going to be easy.

After finishing school Frankl joined his father as a salesman, but he had greater ambition and at the age of twenty, Frankl gained his pilot's licence after learning to fly at the local flying school. At the outbreak of war in August 1914, he immediately applied to join the German Army Air Service and was accepted. Despite being a qualified pilot, he was sent to observer training school and on qualifying was posted to the *Feldflieger-Abteilung* (FFl.Abt.) 40 in Flanders. During 1914 Frankl carried out numerous reconnaissance missions and was awarded the Iron Cross 2nd Class.

More reconnaissance missions followed during the early part of 1915 and then on the 10 May, 1915, he scored his first victory by shooting down a Voisin with a carbine. For this incident, he was awarded the Iron Cross 1st Class and later that year was promoted to *Vizefeldwebel*.

In his diary Wilhelm Frankl wrote about the reason he felt were behind him being awarded the Iron Cross 1st Class:

'I received my Iron Cross 1st Class for three feats:

Directing of the Langen Heinrich on Dunkirk together with others during which we flew over the town under fierce shellfiring whilst our observers took count of the hits made. The damage was colossal. On 10 May, 1915, I shot down an enemy aircraft armed with a machine gun, with a five-shot carbine. The French admitted this loss in their official daily report. Finally in May I had logged some 16,000 kilometres on reconnaissance flights, artillery directing, etc. It did not always go well; my machine can show about fifty bullet hits and not long ago a button on my coat was shot away. Add to that several emergency landings just behind our lines and a couple of crashes with other machines.

Tired of being just an observer Frankl applied for training as a fighter pilot in October 1915, and was sent to *Jastaschule* in the November of

Leutnant *Wilhelm Frankl wearing his newly awarded* Pour le Mérite.

1915. Because of his previous flying experience he was able to graduate in the December, and was posted to KEK Vaux at the beginning of January 1916, flying Fokker Eindeckers. On 10 January, 1916, he scored his second victory, another Voisin, whilst on patrol over Woumen. A third Voisin fell to his guns nine days later whilst over the same area and added that one to his tally.

On 30 May Frankl was promoted to *Leutnant* with his tally standing at six. Five days later came the award of the Knight's Cross with Swords of the Hohenzollern House Order and the Hanseatic Cross. June and July were lean months as far as 'kills' were concerned, but on the 9 August, Wilhelm Frankl took his score to eight and three days later, on 12 August, 1916, he was given Germany's highest award, the *Orden Pour le Mérite*.

On the 1 September Frankl was posted to *Jasta* 4 and by the end of the month had raised his tally to thirteen. Two more victories in October raised Frankl's total of victories to fifteen, the year ending on a quiet note. The beginning of 1917 started quietly, but then in the early hours of the morning of 6 April Frankl carried out one of the first nighttime missions where another aircraft was shot down. That same morning he shot down three more aircraft, all within a space of one hour bringing his total for the day to four. The nighttime victory might quite possibly be the first confirmed one ever scored by the German Air Service. On the 7 April, 1917, whilst on patrol over Fampoux he claimed his twentieth victory a Nieuport XVII.

Wilhelm Frankl and Oswald Boelke (far right) at a demonstration of Fokker's synchronised machine-gun.

Two days later, on the afternoon of the 8 April, 1917, Wilhelm Frankl took off on patrol over Vitry-en-Artois and flew into a patrol of British fighters from No. 48 Squadron, RFC. Despite being heavily outnumbered, Frankl dived to attack but then his Albatros took a succession of devastating hits and was seen to break up in the air. The flaming wreckage of his aircraft crashed to the ground over German lines near Vitry-Sailly. His body was recovered and sent back to Germany. *Leutnant* Wilhelm Frankl was buried with full military honours in Berlin-Charlottenburg.

Because Wilhelm Frankl was Jewish, the Nazi party in the 1930's removed his name from the list of air heroes of World War One. It wasn't until 1973, that his name was reinstated and Luftwaffe Squadron Nr. 74 was named after him.

Awards

Orden Pour le Mérite
Knight's Cross with Swords of the Royal Hohenzollern House Order
Iron Cross 2nd Class
Iron Cross 1st Class
Hamburg Hanseatic Cross
Pilots's Badge

Victory log

1915

10 May	Voisin LA (No. 4 Squadron RFC)	

1916

10 Jan	Voisin (*Escadrille* 36 CA)	Dixmude
19 Jan	Voisin (*Escadrille* VB.101)	Woumen
1 Feb	Voisin	Chaulnes
4 May	BE 2C (No. 7 Squadron RFC)	S Warneton
21 May	FE 2b (No. 20 Squadron RFC)	Houthem
2 Aug	Morane Parasol (No. 60 Squadron RFC)	Beaumetz
10 Aug	Voisin	
10 Aug	Voisin	
7 Sep	Nieuport XI (*Escadrille* N 73)	NE Combles
15 Sep	Nieuport (No.60 Squadron RFC)	Peronne
17 Sep	FE 2b (No.11 Squadron RFC)	Equancourt
26 Sep	Caudron G 4 (Escadrille C 6)	Rancourt
10 Oct	Nieuport XIV (*Escadrille* N 62)	Villers Carbonnel
22 Oct	Sopwith 1½ Strutter (No. 45 Squadron RFC)	Driencourt

1917

6 Apr	FE 2b (No. 100 Squadron RFC)	Quierry La Motte
6 Apr	FE 2b (No. 11 Squadron RFC)	Feuchy
6 Apr	FE 2b (No. 11 Squadron RFC)	Arras
6 Apr	BE 2c (No. 2 Squadron RFC)	Douai
7 Apr	Nieuport XVII (No. 60 Squadron RFC)	SE Fampoux

Total victories claimed: 19

CHAPTER FIFTY-SEVEN

Oberleutnant Otto Kissenberth
(1893 – 1919)

Sopwith F1 Camel from No. 3 Naval Squadron in German markings and flown by Otto Kissenberth who can be seen peering into the engine.

Otto Kissenberth was born on the 26 February, 1893, in Landshut, Bavaria, the son of a local businessman. It was obvious from the start that his interests were in engineering and after his initial schooling was sent to study engineering at Grenoble University in France, then on to technical college in Munich to complete his degree in mechanical engineering. After graduation Kissenberth went to work for the Gustav Otto Aircraft Works where he took a diploma in aircraft engineering.

At the outbreak of war, he volunteered for the newly formed German Army Air Service as a pilot. He was posted to *Flieger-Ersatz-Abteilung* (FEA).1 at Schliessheim for training, where, after graduating, he was awarded his pilots certificate and badge and posted to FA.8b as a reconnaissance pilot in October 1914. Early in March 1915, he was promoted to *Vizefeldwebel*, but on the 21 March whilst on a reconnaissance patrol over the Vosges Mountains, he was attacked by Allied fighters. Although seriously wounded he managed to get his aircraft back to base.

The injuries put him into hospital for over three months but, when he had recovered, he was posted on the 8 July to *Flieger-Abteilung* (Fl.Abt.)9b which was based Toblach in the Dolomite Alps.

His first mission with the squadron, was a long range bombing raid to Cortina on the 31st July, 1915. The raid was a complete success and Kissenberth's status amongst his fellow pilots rose dramatically. Not long afterwards the squadron was moved from Italy to the comparatively quiet Front on the Vosges Mountains. The lack off action soon inspired Otto Kissenberth to apply for fighter pilot training and in the early part of 1916 he was accepted and posted to *Jastschule*. A number of other

Otto Kissenberth standing in front of his 'acquired' Sopwith Camel.

pilots from *Flieger-Abteilung* (Fl.Abt.) 9b had also requested pilot training and on completion were posted to Kek Einsisheim which grew out of Fl.Abt. 9b

There followed a number of uneventful months, then on the 12 October, 1916, whilst on a bombing raid to Obendorf, a raid which was later to become famous, Kissenberth shot down three Allied aircraft, two Maurice Farmans from *Escadrille* F 123 and a Breguet V from No. 3 Naval Wing, RNAS. This was made even more remarkable considering

Kissenberth wore glasses, something virtually unheard of in fighter pilot circles. For his major part in the raid, Kissenberth was awarded the Iron Cross 2nd Class and commissioned to *Leutnant*.

The German air force was expanding and Kek Einsisheim formed part of a new *Jasta* 16. By the beginning of July, Kissenberth's tally had risen to six, then on the 4th August he was made commander of *Jasta* 23. He was awarded the Iron Cross 1st Class later the same month and continued to increase his tally steadily in his Albatros D.V with his personal insignia, a white and yellow Edelweiss on the fuselage. On the

2 October, 1917, Kissenberth scored eighteenth victory. He was awarded the Bavarian Military Merit Order 4th Class with Crown and Swords on the 5 December.

On the 29 May, 1918, with his tally standing at twenty, Kissenberth was flying a captured Sopwith Camel with which he had scored his last victory, when he crashed on landing and was severely injured. So bad were the injuries, that he was told that he would not be fit enough to fight again. Whilst in hospital, he was awarded the Knight's Cross of the Royal Hohenzollern House Order and on the 24 July, Germany's highest honour, the *Orden Pour le Mérite*. On the 19 August, just two days after being discharged from the hospital, Kissenberth was promoted to *Oberleutnant* and made commandant of the Schliessheim Flying School where he stayed until the end of the war. Otto Kissenberth died whilst mountaineering in the Bavarian Alps in 1919.

Awards

Orden Pour le Mérite
Knight's Cross with Swords of the Royal Hohenzoller House Order
Iron Cross 1st Class
Iron Cross 2nd Class
Bavarian Military Merit Order 4th Class with Crown and Swords
Bavarian Military Merit Order 4th Class with Swords
Bavarian Military Merit Cross 2nd Class with Swords
Knight's Cross with Swords of the Royal House Order of Hohenzollern
Saxon Albert Order Knight 2nd Class with Swords
Knight's Cross 2nd Class with Swords of the Friedrich Order
Knight's Cross 2nd Class with Swords of the Baden Zähringer Lion Order
Hamburg Hanseatic Cross
Wound Badge in Black
Pilot's badge
Austro-Hungarian Field Pilot's Badge (Franz-Joseph Patten)

Victory log

1916

12 Oct	Farman (*Escadrille* F 123)	Windensolen
12 Oct	Farman (*Escadrille* F 123)	Ihringen
12 Oct	Breguet V (No. 3 Wing RNAS)	Oberenzen

1917

26 May	SPAD (*Escadrille* N 37)	Somme
19 Jun	Balloon (Compaigne d'Aerostieres 38)	Aubreville
16 Jul	SPAD VII (*Escadrille Spa* 85)	Morte Homme
12 Aug	SPAD VII (No. 40 Squadron RFC)	Avecourt Wood
17 Aug	Nieuport XVII (*Escadrille* N 92)	Morte Homme
19 Aug	SPAD VII (*Escadrille* N 86)	Morte Homme

20 Aug	SPAD VII (No. 23 Squadron RFC)	Morte Homme
20 Aug	SPAD VII (*Escadrille Spa* 84)	Haumont
22 Aug	Paul Schmitt (*Escadrille Spa* 67)	Verdun
6 Sep	SPAD VII (*Escadrille* N 65)	Beaumont
19 Sep	SPAD VII (*Escadrille* N 80)	Montzeville
22 Sep	SPAD VII (*Escadrille* N 65)	Vaux
23 Sep	Sopwith 1½ Strutter (No. 3 Squadron RNAS)	Verdun
23 Sep	SPAD VII	Vaquois
2 Oct	Sopwith 1½ Strutter (*Escadrille* C 28)	Avecourt

1918

| 25 Jan | SPAD (*Escadrille Spa* 67) | Verdun |
| 16 May | SE 5a (No. 60 Squadron RAF) | Tilly-Neuvill |

Total victories claimed: 19

CHAPTER FIFTY-EIGHT

Leutnant Franz Hemer
(1894 – 1982)

Born in 1894 in Frankfurt, Franz Hemer's childhood was taken over by his love of music and the cello. In his early teens this gifted cellist played with a variety of orchestras and gave numerous recitals. Then at the outbreak of war he was called up and joined the German Army. After serving in the infantry for a period he quickly became dissatisfied with life in the trenches, a far cry from the concert platforms of the previous years, so he applied to join the German Army Air Service (*Fliegertruppe*). At the end of 1916 Hemer was assigned to flight training and after his initial course was posted to *Armee-Flug-Park* 14 on 29 April, 1917. On completing his course in July 1917, he was awarded his pilot's certificate (the pilot's badge was only awarded after the pilot had carried out a number of missions and had proved himself to be worthy of the badge) and was assigned to Fl.Abt.(A) 283.

During the next few months he carried out a number of reconnaissance missions and his success drew the attention of his superiors as in August 1917 he was posted to *Jastaschule* I for training as a fighter pilot. On 10 September he was assigned to *Jasta* 6 at Marckebeke, Flanders, one of the four *Jastas* that were at Marckebeke, of *Jagdgeschwader* I under the command of Manfred Freiherr von Richthofen – the Red Baron. The very afternoon that *Vizefeldwebel* Franz Hemer had arrived at the airfield, Werner Voss had scored his forty-third, forty-fourth and forty-fifth victories, two Sopwith Camels and one SPAD.

The battle around Flanders was at its height when Hemer arrived and in a matter of days he was in the air alongside some of Germany's premier fighter pilots, *Rittmeister* Manfred von Richthofen, *Leutnant* Hans Adam, *Leutnant* Werner Voss and *Leutnant* Kurt Wolff.

On 27 October whilst on patrol over Gheluvelt, Franz Hemer with three other members of *Jasta* 6, came upon an RE 8 from No. 52 Squadron, RFC, and attacked it. Hemer hammered the aircraft with his guns and watched it go down with smoke trailing from its engine. Assuming that it had crashed, on his return he claimed his first victory. Some time later it

*Leutnant Franz Hemer in
front of his Fokker Triplane*

was discovered that the RE 8, flown by Captain G C Rogers, had managed
to get back to his own lines despite being wounded. One month later a
similar situation arose and again Hemer claimed a victory and once again
the 'victim' managed to reach his own lines.

During the next four months aerial activity in the area became almost
non-existent, mainly because of the weather and because there was a lull
in the fighting on the ground. Then on 10 March, whilst on patrol at
high altitude (14,000 feet), Hemer encountered a Sopwith Camel and
after a brief fight forced it to land behind German lines. The pilot,
2/Lieutenant C H Flere was taken prisoner and Hemer had scored his
third victory and was awardedthe Iron Cross 2nd Class. Because Hemer
was very small in stature and weighed much less than his comrades, he
found that flying at heights did not bother him as much as it did some of
the other pilots. This enabled him to get above his adversaries and attack
them from this unexpected quarter.

His fourth victory on 13 March, 1918, an SE 5 on No. 24 Squadron,
RFC, shot down over Cambrai, was a shared claim. The dispute over the
claim came about after *Leutnant* Franz Piechuluk of *Jasta* 56 also claimed
to have a shot down an SE 5 in roughly the same area as Hemer's
aircraft. It was decided that both pilots had attacked the aircraft and
brought about the death of its pilot 2/Lieutenant E A Whitehead, so both
were given the credit. How both pilots could have attacked the same
aircraft without noticing each other is a mystery.

One more victory at the end of March 1918 brought his tally to five. This
was the start of the German spring offensive and sixty-two divisions, using
storm troop tactics, smashed their way through the beleaguered British 3rd
and 5th Army divisions. On the ground the attackers were aided by a
combination of fog and shell smoke from the massive five-hour
bombardment carried out by the German artillery. In the air the smoke and
fog hung about, hampering both sides from aiding those on the ground,
but when lifted intense aerial fighting took place. Things went well for a

couple of days as the German offensive continued, twenty-five enemy aircraft were claimed to have been shot down for a loss of twenty-one.

On 1 April, 1918, the Royal Air Force was born, incorporating the RFC and the RNAS, not that it made any difference to the fighter pilots already on the front line. Hemer claimed his next victim on that day shooting down a DH 4 from No. 57 Squadron, RAF, whilst on patrol over Achiet-le-Petit, a small town near Bapaume. Then on 21 April came the news no one wanted to hear, the invincible *Rittmeister* Manfred Freiherr von Richthofen had been shot down and killed. *Jagdgeschwader* I became *Jagdgeschwader* 'Freiherr von Richthofen' Nr.I, Richthofen's Flying Circus was still alive and fighting.

Hemer continued to increase his tally to twelve by the beginning of July and a new commander, *Oberleutnant* Hermann Göring, took over from *Hauptmann* Wilhelm Reinhard, who had been killed testing a new aircraft at Aldershof. On the 14 July the French artillery, supported by American ground troops, opened up and tore the German positions apart. In the air JG I's Fokker Triplanes had been replaced with the new Fokker DVII and on the 16 July Gustav Hemer accounted for two Sopwith Camels, but the writing was on the wall and the offensive created by the Allies gathered pace putting the entire German Army on the retreat. By the end of August 1918 the war in the air had all but finished, Hemer scoring his eighteenth and last victory when he shot down a DH 9 whilst on patrol over Nesle.

On 20 September, 1918, Franz Hemer's long overdue promotion to *Leutnant* came through followed on 8 November with the Knight's Cross with Swords of the Royal Hohenzollern House Order. With the war over *Leutnant* Franz Hemer returned to Frankfurt where he died in 1982.

Leutnant *Franz Hemer inspecting bullet holes in his wing after returning from a mission.*

Leutnant *Franz Hemer
with his three mechanics in
front of his Fokker Dr 1.*

Awards

Knight's Cross with Swords of the Royal Hohenzollern House Order
Hesse General Honour Decoration 'for Bravery'
Iron Cross 2nd Class
Iron Cross 1st Class
Pilot's Badge – German Army

Victory log

1917

27 Oct	RE 8 (No. 52 Squadron RFC)	N Gheluvelt
12 Nov	RE 8 (No. 6 Squadron RFC)	N Ypres

1918

10 Mar	Sopwith Camel (No. 80 Squadron RFC)	Montbrehain
13 Mar	SE 5a (No. 24 Squadron RFC)	S Cambrai
27 Mar	Sopwith Dolphin (No. 79 Squadron RFC)	SE Albert
1 Apr	DH 4 (No. 57 Squadron RAF)	Achiet-le-Petit
6 Apr	Sopwith Dolphin (No. 79 Squadron RAF)	Demuin
9 May	RE 8 (No. 3 Squadron AFC)	E Cachy
10 May	Sopwith Camel (No. 80 Squadron RAF)	Cherisy
19 May	SPAD VII (*Escadrille Spa* 91)	Harbonnieres
28 Jun	SPAD 2 (*Escadrille Spa* 62)	Silly-la-Potterie
3 Jul	SPAD (*Escadrille Spa* 65)	E Courtieux
16 Jul	Sopwith Camel (No. 54 Squadron RAF)	S Dormans
16 Jul	Sopwith Camel (No. 54 Squadron RAF)	S Dormans
18 Jul	Breguet XIV (*Escadrille Br* 132)	
22 Jul	SPAD VII (*Escadrille Spa* 100)	
1 Aug	Nieuport 28 (27th Aero Squadron USAS)	Fere-en-Tardenois
8 Aug	DH 9 (No.98 Squadron RAF)	Nesle

Total victories claimed: 18

CHAPTER FIFTY-NINE

Leutnant Albert Dossenbach
(1891 – 1917)

Albert Dossenbach was born in St Blasien in the southern part of the Black Forest, the son of a local innkeeper. As with most young men at the time it was intended that he would follow in his father's footsteps. But Albert Dossenbach was a very intelligent young man and had other ideas about his life and so applied to go to medical school and was starting his hospital internship when war was declared. Dossenbach immediately enlisted in the Grossherzoglich Mecklenburgisches Füsilier-Regiment Nr. 90 Kaiser Wilhelm and because of his background and training was promoted to *Unteroffizier* within weeks.

Within weeks his regiment was in the heat of battle on the Front Line and one of these missions concerned the fortress at Liege, which, after a heated battle surrendered, earning the two Generals involved the *Orden Pour le Mérite*, an award Dossenbach himself was to earn two years later. During the battle Dossenbach carried his commanding officer away from the front line to safety after he had been wounded and for this he was awarded the Iron Cross 2nd Class. During the next four months, Dossenbach was involved in a number of dangerous missions, for which he was awarded the Iron Cross 1st Class, the Military Merit Cross 2nd Class and had been promoted to *Vizefeldwebel*.

On 27 January, 1915, Dossenbach was commissioned to *Leutnant* and awarded the Baden Knight's Cross 2nd Class with Swords of the Zähringen Lion. By the end of the year the German advance had ground to a halt and both sides were dug in not giving an inch of ground. Dossenbach's thoughts soon turned to other things so he applied for transfer to the newly formed German Army Air Service.

In the November of 1915, Dossenbach was posted to *Flieger-Ersatz-Abteilung* (FEA) 3 at Gotha to train as an observer, but after arguing his case for being a pilot, he was posted to FEA 4 at Pozen to train as a pilot and graduated in June 1916. Posted to *Feldflieger-Abteilung* (FFl.Abt.). 22 at Bapaume, he joined up with his new observer *Oberleutnant* Hans Schilling and their Albatros C.II. Schilling had

joined the air service from 2 Thüringisches Infantrie Regiment Nr. 32 and, together with Dossenbach, created a most formidable team.

Almost immediately the pair were in the thick of the action and just three months after graduating, Dossenbach and Hans Schilling were credited with shooting down eight Allied aircraft. On the 27 September, 1916, whilst on patrol over Tourmignies, the last of the eight victims, an FE 2b from No. 25 Squadron, RFC, inflicted considerable damage to Dossenbach's aircraft before crashing himself. Dossenbach had to crash land and both he and his observer were slightly burned in the ensuing fire, but were soon in action again.

For his part in the action Dossenbach was awarded the Knight's Cross 2nd Class with Swords of the Order of the Zähringer Lion and both he and Schilling celebrated the awards by shooting down an FE 2b of 25 Squadron whilst on patrol over Mory. However in the fight the observer was badly wounded, which took the edge off the celebrations and end their association in the air. One month later on the 12 October, 1917, both men were awarded the Knight's Cross of the Hohenzollern House Order.

Leutnant *Dossenbach with his observer* Oberleutnant *Schilling.*

The ultimate accolade was paid to Albert Dossenbach on 11 November, 1916, when he was awarded Germany's highest honour, the *Orden Pour le Mérite*, the first two-seater pilot ever to receive this prestigious award. His friend Hans Schilling, who had been with him throughout was given nothing. A further award was made to Dossenbach on the 9 December, when he was given the Knight's Cross of the Karl Friedrich Military Merit Order. But this honour was overshadowed by the death of his friend Hans Schilling who was killed whilst on a bombing mission with another pilot, the nineteenth victim of the French ace Charles Nungesser.

The fact that Dossenbach had come from relatively humble beginnings prompted the powers that be to question whether or not he came from 'decent people' and a letter was sent to a senior official in St Blasien to confirm this. This only goes to highlight the class war that was going on in Germany at the same time as the Great War. The following is a translation of the letter that was sent:

> Kr (Karlsruhe) 11.12.16.
>
> To the Honourable Senior Administrator Gest in St Blasien
>
> Esteemed Sir,
>
> His Royal Highness, the Grand Duke, has learned that *Ltn.d.R.* Albert Dossenbach, FFA 22, who shot down a considerable number of enemy air ships was decorated by HM the Kaiser with the Hohenz.Hausorden and the order Pour le Mérite. Said person was born on 5 June, 1891, in St Blasien.
>
> I should like to request information about the personal circumstances.
>
> With my respects,
>
> Govt. Director B.

It was just after this that Dossenbach applied to go to *Jasta* 2 for single-seater training. After graduating he took command of *Jasta* 36 on the 22 February, 1917, after the commanding officer Böhme had been wounded. He set the standard by scoring the units first victory, a French Caudron from *Escadrille Spa* 12 on the 5 April. By the end of the month Dossenbach had raised his personal tally to ten.

Further victims fell to his guns over the next few months, then an attack by bombers on his airfield at Le Chatelet on the 2 May, left Dossenbach badly wounded from bomb splinters and put him in hospital for a month. On release from hospital on 21 June, he was given command of *Jasta* 10 and took up the post the same day. Six days later on 27 June, he opened his score by shooting down an observation balloon over Ypres.

On the 3 July, 1917, whilst leading his patrol over Frenzenberg, they were jumped by British fighters from No. 57 Squadron, RFC. Despite being heavily outnumbered, Dossenbach fought ferociously and, at one point, he himself was attacked by four fighters – such were the odds. During the ensuing mêlée his aircraft caught fire. It is not certain whether he jumped or fell from his blazing aircraft, but his body was

Dossenbach alongside his Albatros D II when with Fl Ablt 22.

seen to tumble from the blazing wreckage as it plunged towards the ground. His remains were returned to the Germans who buried him with full military honours at Freiburg.

Awards

Orden Pour le Mérite
Knight's Cross with Swords of the Royal Hohenzollern House Order
Iron Cross 2nd Class
Iron Cross 1st Class
Knight's Cross of the Baden Military Karl-Friedrich Merit Order
Knight 2nd Class with Swords of the Zähringen Lion
Mecklin-Schwerin Military Merit Cross 2nd Class
Pilot's Badge

Victory log

1916

The first four victories of Albert Dossenbach whilst with *Flieger-Abteilung* 22 were not recorded, if they were they have been lost, but it is accepted that he scored a total of fifteen victories during his time as a fighter pilot.

13 Aug	BE 12 (No. 19 Sqn RFC)	Bapaume
24 Sep	BE 12 (No. 19 Sqn RFC)	Morchies
27 Sep	FE 2b (No. 25 Sqn RFC)	Tourmignies
3 Nov	FE 2b (No. 22 Sqn RFC)	Mory

1917

5 Apr	Caudron G 4 (*Escadrille* C 39)	Sillery
11 Apr	Caudron G 4 (*Escadrille* F 215)	Berry-au-Bac
13 Apr	SPAD VII (*Escadrille* N 12)	Sapinguel
15 Apr	Nieuport XXIII (*Escadrille* N 83)	Bethany
15 Apr	SPAD VII (*Escadrille* N 15)	St Fergeux-Rethel
27 Jun	Balloon (Balloon Company 15-7-2)	Ypres

Total victories claimed: 15

CHAPTER SIXTY

Oberleutnant Max Immelmann
(1890 – 1916)

The son of a wealthy cardboard manufacturer in Dresden, Max Immelmann was born on the 21 September, 1890. Seven years later his father died of tuberculosis leaving Max to determine his own future. Being no academic, at the age of fifteen he was sent to the Dresden Cadet School. After completing the course, he joined the 2nd Railway Regiment in Berlin-Schöneberg with the rank of Fähnrich. After obtaining a commission, he entered the War Academy at the beginning of August, 1911, and returned to the railway regiment at the end of January 1912. The threat of war at the end of 1913, convinced Immelman that his military future did not lay with the Railway

Oberleutnant Max Immelmann standing by the wreckage of one of his victims.

Regiment. Since his youth his main interest had been in anything mechanical, so after seeing a notice from the Inspectorate of the Aviation Corps, looking for men to train as pilots, he applied for a transfer to the German Air Service.

On 18 August, 1914, his Railway Regiment was sent notice of mobilisation and Max Immelman suddenly realised that the days of waiting were over.

(Above) Max Immelmann's Fokker Eindecker in which he was killed. (Below) Wreckage of Max Immelmann's Fokker Eindecker

His transfer was approved and he was posted in the November of 1914 for basic ground training at the Aviation Replacement Section at Johannisthal. On completion of his initial course Immelmann was posted to Aldershof for advanced flying training before being qualified as a pilot. In February 1915 Max Immelmann passed his flying test and was posted to *Feld-Flieger-Abteilung* (FFl.Abt.) 62 (later to become Kek Douai) flying LVG Two-seaters on observation and escort patrols. With him on these patrols was another recently qualified pilot by the name of Oswald Boelcke and within a few months they had established themselves a reputation as top scouting pilots.

In the May of 1915, Immelmann was moved from the LVGs to the unit's single-seat fighter, the Fokker Eindecker. The 1 August brought him his first victory, a BE 2c of No. 2 Squadron, RFC. By the end of September his tally had risen to three confirmed – two possibles and the award of the Iron Cross 2nd Class. October and November brought another four victories and a promotion to *Oberleutnant*, the Iron Cross 1st Class and the Knight's Cross with Swords of the Hohenzollern House Order. On the 12 January, 1916, Max Immelmann or the 'Eagle of Lille' as he has become known, was awarded the coveted *Orden Pour le Mérite*. His tally rose to thirteen by the end of March and more awards were given to him: the Saxon Commander's Cross to the Military St Henry Order 2nd Class; the Knight's Cross to the Military St Henry Order; the Saxon Albert Order 2nd Class with Swords; the Saxon Friedrich-August Medal in Silver and the Bavarian Military Merit Order 4th Class with Swords.

On the 18 June, 1916, he was engaged in a fight with FE 2bs of 25 Squadron in his Fokker (246/16). Twisting and turning around in the packed skies, he suddenly came under fire from an FE 2b flown by Captain G R McGubbin together with his gunner Corporal J H Waller.

The coffin containing Max Immelmann's body lying in state.

Their report states that they shot the propeller away causing the engine to tear loose from its mountings and sending the Fokker plunging to the ground. The German High Command however, saddened by the loss of one of their most decorated and promising fighter pilots, announced that Immelmann had died because of a defective synchronised gear in the gun. This had caused Immelmann, when engaged by overwhelming enemy odds, to shoot off his own propeller, with the result that the engine torque caused it to be ripped from its mountings, plunging Max Immelmann to his death.

Awards

Orden Pour le Mérite
Knight's Cross with Swords of the Royal Hohenzollern House Order
Commander's Cross 2nd Class of the Saxon Military St Henry Order
Knight's Cross of the Saxon Military St Henry Order
Knight 2nd Class with Swords of the Saxon Albert Order
Saxon Friedrich-August Medal in Silver
Iron Cross 2nd Class
Iron Class 1st Class
Bavarian Military Merit Order 4th Class with Swords
Anhalt Friedrich Cross 2nd Class
Hamburg Hanseatic Cross
Ottoman Imtiaz Medal in Silver
Ottoman War Medal
Pilot's Badge – German Army

Victory log

1915

1 Aug	BE 2c (No. 2 Sqn RFC)	Douai
26 Aug	French biplane	Souchez
21 Sep	BE 2c (No. 10 Sqn RFC)	Willerval
10 Oct	BE 2c (No. 16 Sqn RFC)	nr Verlinghem
26 Oct	VFB 5 (No. 11 Sqn RFC)	Cambrai
7 Nov.	BE 2c (No. 10 Sqn RFC)	Lille
15 Dec	Morane Parasol (No. 3 Sqn RFC)	Valenciennes

1916

12 Jan	VFB 5 No. 11 Sqn RFC)	NE Turcoing
2 Mar	Morane Biplane (No. 3 Sqn RFC)	Souain
13 Mar	Bristol Scout (No. 4 Sqn RFC)	Serre
13 Mar	BE 2c (No. 8 Sqn RFC)	Pelves
29 Mar	FE 2b (No. 23 Sqn RFC)	Bethincourt
30 March	BE 2c (No. 15 Sqn RFC)	Arras
23 Apr	VFB 5 (No. 11 Sqn RFC)	Monchy
16 May	Bristol Scout (No. 11 Sqn RFC)	Izel

Total victories claimed: 15

The end of the First World war brought the end of the Knights of the Black Cross. There has always been a dispute regarding the so called chivalry shown by pilots during the war, some say that there were examples of it, but most agree it was more of a kill or be killed philosophy with very little time to be merciful and generous with other people lives.

APPENDIX I

The Jastas

Royal Prussian Jastas:

Jasta 1	Jasta 9	Jasta 18	Jasta 30	Jasta 42	Jasta 52	Jasta 61	Jasta 70
Jasta 2	Jasta 10	Jasta 19	Jasta 31	Jasta 43	Jasta 53	Jasta 62	Jasta 71
Jasta 3	Jasta 11	Jasta 20	Jasta 33	Jasta 45	Jasta 55	Jasta 63	Jasta 73
Jasta 4	Jasta 12	Jasta 23	Jasta 36	Jasta 46	Jasta 56	Jasta 65	Jasta 74
Jasta 5	Jasta 13	Jasta 25	Jasta 37	Jasta 48	Jasta 57	Jasta 66	Jasta 75
Jasta 6	Jasta 14	Jasta 26	Jasta 38	Jasta 49	Jasta 58	Jasta 67	Jasta 81
Jasta 7	Jasta 15	Jasta 27	Jasta 39	Jasta 50	Jasta 59	Jasta 68	Jasta 82
Jasta 8	Jasta 17	Jasta 29	Jasta 41	Jasta 51	Jasta 60	Jasta 69	Jasta 83

Royal Bavarian Jastas:

Jasta 16 Jasta 79
Jasta 32 Jasta 80
Jasta 34
Jasta 35
Jasta 76
Jasta 77
Jasta 78

Royal Saxon Jastas:

Jasta 21
Jasta 22
Jasta 24
Jasta 40
Jasta 44
Jasta 54
Jasta 72

Royal Württemburg Jastas:

Jasta 28
Jasta 47
Jasta 64

A total of eighty-three *Jastas* had been formed by the end of the First World War by the Germans, sixty-four of which were Royal Prussian Jastas. This did not include the five *Marine Feldjagdstaffels* of the German Navy that operated independently from the German Army Air Service.

The first of the *Jastas* was *Jasta* 1 a Royal Prussian unit which was formed at Bertincourt on the Somme on 22 August, 1916, and began operations in the 1 *Armee* area at Bertigny. The *Jasta's* first commanding officer was *Hauptmann* Martin Zander from KG 1. The first aircraft assigned to the *Jasta* were Fokker D.I and D.II fighters, which were replaced a year later by Halberstadt D.IIs. Throughout the war, like all the other *Jastas*, command was passed constantly between what was seemed to be younger and younger men.

Jasta 2 was formed on 10 August, 1916, at Bertincourt under the command of one of Germany's top fighter pilots, *Hauptmann* Oswald Boelcke. Within days the unit moved to Velu followed a few days later by the first of the aircraft two Fokker D.IIIs and an Albatros D.II. The first victory was scored on 2 September by Oswald Boelcke, the twentieth victim to fall to his guns. The following month Boelcke was killed in a collision with one of his own aircraft and was replaced by Stephen Kirmaier. The *Jasta* had a succession of top aces as leader and by the end of the war had been credited with 336 victories second only to *Jasta* 11.

Jasta 3, Royal Prussian, was formed on 10 August, 1916, at Flieger-Ersatz-Abteilung Nr 5 at Braunschweig. The first commanding officer was *Leutnant* Ewald von Mellenthin who moved the unit to Vraignes, near Peronne to support the 2nd *Armee*. They were equipped with Halberstadt IIIs and were in action almost immediately. Most of its duties appear to have been as a reconnaissance unit, but still managed to score eighty-three victories for the loss of sixteen pilots by the end of the war.

Jasta 4 – 15 were all Royal Prussian units the most famous of which was *Jasta* 11. The unit was commanded at one time by the legendary Manfred von Richthofen, and during its existence contained some of the more famous, or in the case of Hermann Göring, infamous, fighter pilots of the German Army Air Service.

The first of the Royal Bavarian *Jastas* was *Jasta* 16, created on 16 October, 1916, and commanded by *Oberleutnant* Otto Doosloch. The formation of this Jasta highlighted the divisions that existed between the various principalities and states, so much so in fact that once when a Bavarian was placed in command of a Prussian *Jasta*, such was the outcry amongst the old guard, that he was replaced almost immediately, not because he wasn't the best man for the job, but simply because he came from Bavaria.

Jastas 17, 18, 19 and 20 were all Royal Prussian but *Jastas* 21, 22 and 24 were the first of the Royal Saxon *Jastas*. All three Royal Saxon units were formed on 25 October, 1916, and operated throughout the war. The first of the Württemburg *Jastas*, *Jasta* 28, was commanded by *Oberleutnant* Rudolf Lang who had been transferred from *Jasta* 11. It is interesting to note that Lang, although from the Württemburg States,

flew initially with a Royal Prussian *Jasta*, but would never be allowed to command one although he was considered suitable to command the first Württemburg unit. *Jasta* 28 was followed by *Jastas* 47 & 48.

The remaining *Jastas* were predominantly Royal Prussian because they were the largest state and the most autocratic. The five navy *Jagdstaffels* fortunately did not suffer from the Army's problem with inter-state/principality rivalry manily because they were limited to what they could get in the shape of aviation personnel.

Throughout the war all the *Jastas* fought the ever increasing number of Allied fighters tooth and nail for every piece of air space and for most of the war controlled the skies. But as the ground troops were forced to retreat, so did the Army Air Service but only because their airfields were left unprotected. Even in the last throes of the war, with the German Army in full retreat and offering little if no resistance, the Air Service stubbornly continued to be the aggressor and it wasn't until Germany finally capitulated and surrendered, that they gave up.

The *Jastas* of the German Army Air Service left an indelible mark on the history of aviation warfare.

APPENDIX II

German Fighter Aces of World War One
Victory Logs

Rittmeister Manfred Frh. von Richthofen	80
Oberleutnant Ernst Udet	62
Oberleutnant Erich Löwenhardt	34
Leutnant Werner Voss	48
Leutnant Fritz Rumey	45
Hauptmann Rudolf Berthold	44
Leutnant Paul Baümer	43
Leutnant Josef Jacobs	41
Hauptmann Bruno Loerzer	41
Hauptmann Oswald Boelcke	40
Leutnant Franz Büchner	40
Oberleutnant Lothar Frh. von Richthofen	40
Leutnant Karl Menckoff	39
Leutnant Heinrich Gontermann	39
Leutnant Theo Osterkamp	38
Leutnant Max Müller	36
Leutnant Julius Buckler	35
Leutnant Gustav Dörr	35
Hauptmann Eduard Ritter von Schleich	35
Leutnant Emil Thuy	35
Leutnant Josef Veltjens	34
Leutnant Otto Könnecke	33

Leutnant Kurt Wolff	33
Leutnant Heinrich Kroll	33
Leutnant Heinrich Bongartz	33
Leutnant Hermann Frommherz	32
Leutnant Paul Billik	31
Rittmeister Karl Bolle	31
Oberleutnant Gotthard Sachsenberg	31
Leutnant Karl Allmenroder	30
Leutnant Karl Degelow	30
Leutnant Josef Mai	30
Leutnant Ulrich Neckel	30
Leutnant Karl Schäfer	30
Leutnant Walter von Bülow	28
Leutnant Walter Blume	28
Oberleutnant Fritz Ritter von Röth	28
Leutnant Hans Kirchestein	27
Oberleutnant Fritz Otto Bernert	27
Vizefeldwebel Otto Fruhner	27
Leutnant Karl Thom	27
Hauptmann Adolf Ritter von Tutschek	27
Leutnant Kurt Wüsthoff	27
Oberleutnant Oskar Freiherr von Boenigk	26
Oberleutnant Eduard Dostler	26
Leutnant Arthur Laumann	26
Leutnant Oliver Freiherr von Beaulieu-Marconnay	25
Leutnant Max Näther	25
Leutnant Fritz Pütter	25
Leutnant Erwin Böhme	24
Vizefeldwebel Karl Schlegel	24
Oberleutnant Hermann Göring	22
Leutnant Rudolf Windisch	22

Leutnant Gerhard Fieseler   19

Leutnant Kurt Wintgens   19

Leutnant Wilhelm Frankl   19

Leutnant Otto Kissenberth   19

Leutnant Franz Hemer   18

Leutnant Albert Dossenbach   15

Oberleutnant Max Immelmann   15

APPENDIX III

Glossary of Terms

Formations and Organizations

Abteilung – Detachment or unit (but often familiarly referred to as a 'squadron')

Abteilungsführer – Detachment or unit leader, or Commanding Officer

Abwehrkommando – Defense command or establishment

Armee-Flug-Park (AFP) – Army aviation supply depot

Armeekorps – Army Corps

Artillerie-Flieger-Abteilung – Artillery aviation detachment or unit

Artillerie-Regiment-Nr – Artillery Regiment No.

Bombengeschwader der Obersten Heeresleitung (Bogohl) (BG) – Bombardment squadron of the Army High Command

Bombenstaffel (Bosta) (BS) – Bombardment section or flight

Brieftauben-Abteilung – *Metz (Ostende)* – Carrier Pigeon Detachment or Unit Metz (Ostend)

Feldflieger-Abteilung – Field aviation detachment or unit

Flieger-Abteilung – Aviation detachment or unit

Flieger-Abteilung (A) – Aviation detachment or unit assigned für artillery cooperation duties

Flieger-Ersatz-Abteilung (FEA) – Aviation replacement detachment or unit

Fliegerschule – Aviation training school

Fliegertruppe – The Aviation Troops or the Air Service

Fokkerstaffel – Section or flight equipped with first Fokker monoplanes

Geschwader – Squadron

Geschwaderführer – Squadron leader or Commanding Officer

Gruppenführer der Flieger (Grufl) – Officer attached to Corps Headquarters responsible for the employment of aviation units assigned to the Corps

Infanterieflieger (Ifl) – Infantry cooperation aircraft

Infanterie-Regiment-Nr. – Infantry Regiment No.

Inspeckteur der Fliegertruppe – Inspector of the Aviation Troops or the Air Service

Inspecktion der Fliegertruppe (Idflieg) – Inspectorate of the Aviation Troops or the Air Service

Jagdgeschwader (JG) – Permanent grouping of four *Jagdstaffeln*

Jagdgruppe – Temporary tactical grouping of several *Jagdstaffeln*

Jagdstaffel (Jasta) (J.) – Fighter section or flight

Jastaschule – Fighter pilot training school

Kampfeinsitzer-Abteilung – Single-seater fighter detachment or unit

Kampfeinsitzer-Kommando (KEK) – Single-seater fighter command or establishment

Kampfeinsitzerstaffel (Kest) – Single-seater fighter home defense section or flight

Kampfgeschwader der Obersten Heeresleitung (Kagohl) (KG) – Fighting squadron of the Army High Command

Kampfstaffel (Kasta) (KS) – Fighting section or flight

Kommandeur der Flieger (Kofl) – Officer in charge of aviation units assigned to an Army

Kommandierenden General der Luftstreit-kräftke (Kogenluft) – Commanding General of the Army Air Force or Army Air Service

Landflieger-Abteilung – Land aviation detachment or unit of the Navy

Landwehr – Territorial Army

Lichtbild (Lb) – Photograph

Luftstreitkräfte – Air Force or Air Service

Luftwaffe – Air Weapon or Air Force

Marine – Navy

Matrosenartillerie - Naval artillery

Reich – Empire

Reihenbildner (Rb) – Aircraft equipped with serial film camera

Reihenbildzug – Section of (usually) three aircraft within a Flieger-Abteilung equipped with serial film cameras

Riesenflugzeug-Abteilung – Detachment or unit equipped with 'Giant' aircraft

Schlachtgeschwader – Permanent grouping of four to six Schlachtstaffeln

Schlachtgruppe – Temporary tactical grouping of several Schlachtstaffeln

Schlachtstaffel (Schlasta) – Attack section or flight

Schutzstaffel (Schusta) – Protection section or flight

Seeflieger-Abteilung – Sea (Navy) aviation detachment or unit

Stabsoffizier der Flieger (Stofl) – officer for aviation within an Army

Staffel – Section or flight

Staffelführer – Section or flight leader or Commanding Officer

Ulanen-Regiment-Nr. – Lancer Regiment No.

Aircraft Types

A – Single engine monoplane without armament

B – Single engine biplane without armament

C – Single engine biplane with armament

D – Single engine single-seater biplane with armament

E – Single engine single-seater monoplane with armament

F – Single engine single-seater triplane with armament

G – Multi-engine biplane with armament

R – Biplane with three to six engines ('Giant' aircraft)

Dr – Single engine single-seater triplane with armament

CL – Light C - Type two-seater with armament

GL – Light G - Type aircraft with armament

N – Single engine aircraft with armament for night operations

J – Two-seater armored biplane with armament, for infantry cooperation

L – Biplane with armament, multi-engined

S – Two-seater armored biplane with armament, single-engined

DJ – Single-seater armored aircraft with armament, single-engined

Ranks

Feldwebel – Sergeant Major

Feldwebelleutnant - Sergeant Major-Lieutenant (commissioned officer without the prestige the rank usually enjoyed)

Flieger – *Flier*, or Private in the air service

Flugmeister – Aviation Petty Officer (Navy)

Fregattenkapitän – Frigate Captain (equivalent of US naval Commander)

Gefreiter – Private 1st Class

General der Flieger (Artillerie, Kavallerie, Infanterie) – General of Aviation

Generalfeldmarschall – Field Marshal

Generalleutnant – Lieutenant General

Generalmajor – Major General

Generaloberst – Colonel General

Hauptleute – Captains (Army)

Hauptmann – Captain (Army)

Infantrist – Infantryman, or Private in the infantry

Kapitänleutnant – Lieutenant Captain

Korvettenkapiştän – Corvette Captain

Leutnant – Lieutenant

Leutnant zur See – Naval Lieutenant

Major – Major

Oberflugmeister – Senior Aviation Petty Officer (Navy)

Oberst – Colonel

Oberstleutnant – Lieutenant Colonel

Oberleutnant – Senior Lieutenant (equivalent of US 1st Lieutenant)

Oberleutnant zur See – Senior naval Lieutenant

Offizier-Stellvertreter – Acting Officer

Reichsmarschall – Marshal of the German Nation

Rittmeister – Cavalry Captain

Sergeant – Sergeant

Stabsarzt – Medical Corps Captain

Unteroffizier – Corporal

Vizefeldwebel – Vice Sergeant Major

Other Terms

ausser Dienst – Retired (literally, 'released from service')

blauer Max – Blue Max (nickname for the *Orden Pour le Merite*)

Blücherstern – Star of the 1813 Grand Cross of the Iron Cross awarded to Blücher

Ehrenbecher dem Sieger im Luftkampfe – Honor Goblet to the Victor in Air Battle

Ehrenpreis – Honor Prize (Navy Equivalent to the Army *Ehrenbecher*)

Eichenlaub – Oakleaf

Eindecker – Monoplane

Feldschnalle – Bar with small ribbons representing awards

Flugsport – Sport Flying (a German magazine for flight enthusiasts)

Freiherr – Baron

Graf – Count

Grosskomtur – Grand Commander

Grosskreuz – Grand Cross

Grossordensschnalle – Bar with full size ribbons to which awards were attached

Heeresbericht – Army Report

Hindenburgstern – Star to the 1914 Grand Cross of the Iron Cross awarded to Hindenburg

Kaiser – Emperor

Kanone – Ace (literally, cannon or big gun)

Kette – Chain

Klasse – Class

König – King

Komtur – Commander

Kriegsarchiv – archive

Kriegsband – War ribbon

Mit Brillanten – with Brilliants (real or paste gems embellishing insignia)

Mit Eichenlaub – with Oakleaf

Mit der Krone – with Crown

Mit Schwertern – with Swords

Mit Schwertern am Ringe – with Swords-on-Ring

Nachrichtenblatt – Intelligence Report

ohne Schwertern – without Swords

Ordenskissen – Orders cushion (for displaying awards at funerals)

Prinz – Prince

Ritter – Knight

Ritterkreuz – Knight's Cross

Schrechlichkeit – Frightfulness

Sträf – Punish

Stern – Star

Stufe – Degree

zur Disposition – At the disposal of (half-pay)

Prussian Awards and Their German Spelling

Iron Cross – *Eisernes Kreuz*

High Order of the Black Eagle – *Hoher Orden vom Schwarzen Adler*

Order of St John - *Johanniter-Orden*

Royal Hohenzollern House Order – *Königlicher Hausorden von Hohenzollern*

Member's Cross of the Royal Hohenzollern House Order – *Kreuz der Inhaber des könig licher Hausorden von Hohenzollern*

Crown Order – *Kronen-Orden*

Louise Order – *Luisen-Orden*

Military Honor Decoration – *Militär-Ehren-zeichen*

Golden Military Merit Cross – *Militär-Verdienstkreuz in Gold*

Order for Merit – *Orden Pour le Merite*

Red Eagle Order – *Roter Adler-Orden*

Merit Order of the Prussian Crown – *Verdienstorden der Preussischen Krone*

Order of Wilhelm – *Wilhelm-Orden*